Development in Asia

Development in Asia

Interdisciplinary, Post-neoliberal, and Transnational Perspectives

Edited by
Derrick M. Nault

BrownWalker Press
Boca Raton

Development in Asia:
Interdisciplinary, Post-neoliberal, and Transnational Perspectives

Copyright © 2009 Derrick M. Nault.
All rights reserved.
No part of this book may be reproduced or transmitted in any form or by any means, electronic or mechanical, including photocopying, recording, or by any information storage and retrieval system, without written permission from the publisher.

BrownWalker Press
Boca Raton, Florida • USA
2009

ISBN-10: 1-59942-488-6 *(paper)*
ISBN-13: 978-1-59942-488-0 *(paper)*

ISBN-10: 1-59942-489-4 *(ebook)*
ISBN-13: 978-1-59942-489-7 *(ebook)*

www.brownwalker.com

Library of Congress Cataloging-in-Publication Data

Development in Asia : interdisciplinary, post-neoliberal, and transnational perspectives / edited by Derrick M. Nault.
   p. cm.
 Includes bibliographical references and index.
 ISBN 978-1-59942-488-0 (pbk. : alk. paper)
 1. Economic development--Social aspects--Asia. 2. Asia--Economic conditions--21st century. 3. Asia--Social conditions--21st century. I. Nault, Derrick M. II. Title.

HC412.D455 2008
338.95--dc22

2008043695

Contents

Preface vii
List of contributors ix

1. Introduction: Contextualizing Development in Asia 1
   Derrick M. Nault

Part One: Managing Development

2. Human Development and Governance in Central Asian
   Transition Countries 19
   Bayarjargal Ariun-Erdene

3. The Role of Social Capital in Microfinance:
   Evidence from Rural Java, Indonesia 45
   Agus Eko Nugroho

Part Two: Gender and Development

4. Negotiating Space and Gender: Female Street
   Entrepreneurs and Tongdaemun Market in Seoul, Korea 75
   Ayami Noritake

5. On Identity and Development: Filipino Women
   Entertainers in Transition in Japan 107
   Ma. Ledda B. Docot

Part Three: Culture and Development

6. Imagining Others: A Study of the "Asia" Presented in Japanese Cinema 135
   Kinnia Shuk-ting Yau

7. Developing Extremists: *Madrasah* Education in Pakistan 165
   Riaz Ahmed Shaikh

Part Four: Globalization and Development

8. Globalization and Development in Sport: Perspectives from South East Asia 195
   Charles Little and *John Nauright*

9. Globalization, Tourism Development, and Japanese Lifestyle Migration to Australia 215
   Jun Nagatomo

10. Saffron-robed Monks and Digital Flash Cards: The Development and Challenges of Burmese Exile Media 237
    Richard Humphries

Index 259

Preface

This book is the product of a conference entitled *Developing Asia: Past, Present and Future* held at Kobe Gakuin University in Kobe, Japan, March 28-29, 2008. Convened by the Asia Association for Global Studies (AAGS), an academic organization based in Osaka, Japan, the conference gathered scholars from across Asia and other world regions to discuss development and its implications for Asia.

The event would not have happened at all were it not for the dedication and hard work of fellow organizers and AAGS board members Anthony Torbert, Hans Peter Liederbach, and Keiji Fujimura. I would like to sincerely thank them for their help in conceiving and carrying out the conference. I would also like to extend my gratitude to Kobe Gakuin University for hosting the event, and, of course, the many presenters who attended and made the conference a success. It was highly gratifying to see scholars come from so many nations, 23 in total, and show such a deep interest in the conference theme.

As for the original inspiration for the conference, I am highly indebted to Bob Shenton, my former Ph.D. thesis supervisor at Queen's University in Canada, who helped hone my knowledge of development issues in tandem with my studies in African history. After graduating from Queen's, I began acquiring an interest in Asia and its development experiences, which I hoped would provide me with useful contrasts for better understanding development in Africa and other world regions. As fate would have it, I ended up teaching and residing in South Korea and Japan for a full decade, providing me with the opportunity to further explore this interest firsthand. When the idea finally came to me to hold a conference in Japan on development in Asia, my colleagues at AAGS fortunately agreed to the idea. That a book with the best papers of the conference be compiled to share with others seemed only natural given the high quality proposals we received.

The papers that form the chapters of this volume were selected for their intellectual rigor, originality and geographic breadth. As readers will note, the authors have training in a wide array of fields and examine development in diverse yet complementary ways. The intention was to discuss development in Asia from as many angles and perspectives as possible rather than from one discipline or framework. It seems to me that this approach was effective in that it shows development to be a multi-dimensional and complex phenomenon, rather than something that can be understood through monocausal explanations or overarching theories. Also notable about this volume is that the authors are mostly scholars from Asia or have significant Asian experience. Such insider perspectives from Asia, which are not always easy to find in the English language, are vital if we are to truly understand development in Asian settings. I would like to thank all the authors in this volume for their contributions.

In addition to the individuals already mentioned, many other people and institutions directly and indirectly helped make this book possible and deserve special mention. I would like, first of all, to thank my mother and father, Martha and Gib Nault, for always supporting me, wherever my work and travels have taken me. I would also like to thank Doo-Sun Ryu of Seoul National University, for helping me stay on track with my research; Tim Scrase, of the Centre for Asia Pacific Social Transformation Studies (CAPSTRANS) and the University of Wollongong, for his insights on development in Asia; and John Nauright, of George Mason University and Aarhus University, whose friendship I have had the pleasure of knowing since my years as a doctoral student at Queen's University and advice I greatly appreciate. I am most grateful as well to Kwansei Gakuin University, for generously providing crucial research and travel funding during my three year stay in Japan, and the Faculty of Communication and Culture and the Department of History at the University Calgary, where I currently teach courses in development studies and history. Finally, I would like to thank my wife, Eunhee Seo, for her unending patience and kindness. It is to her that this book is dedicated.

Derrick M. Nault
Calgary, Alberta
August 2008

List of Contributors

Bayarjargal Ariun-Erdene, National University of Mongolia, Mongolia
Ma. Ledda B. Docot, University of Tokyo, Japan
Richard Humphries, Kansai Gaidai University, Japan
Charles Little, London Metropolitan University, UK
Jun Nagatomo, University of Queensland, Australia
Derrick M. Nault, University of Calgary, Canada
John Nauright, George Mason University, USA/Aarhus University, Denmark
Ayami Noritake, The Australian National University, Australia
Agus Eko Nugroho, Curtin University of Technology, Australia
Riaz Ahmed Shaikh, Institute of Business and Technology, Pakistan
Kinnia Shuk-ting Yau, The Chinese University of Hong Kong, Hong Kong

• CHAPTER ONE •

Introduction: Contextualizing Development in Asia

Derrick M. Nault
University of Calgary

Development is one of the most ubiquitous concepts of our age. It is something governments, non-governmental organizations and even corporations claim to be engaged in and is considered desirable by scholars, activists, policymakers, and laypeople alike. Yet it is also a highly contested term. For some, development is synonymous with globalization and export-oriented economic growth (Bhagwati, 2007, pp. 56-57; Wolf, 2004; World Bank, 1981). Others maintain that it must entail improving life expectancy, literacy, education levels, and access to resources (Haq, 1995; Sen, 2001; United Nations Development Program [UNDP], 1996). Others yet, disillusioned by the results of past development initiatives, have rejected development altogether, calling for new approaches and solutions to global problems (Alvares, 1994; Escobar, 1995; Norberg-Hodge, 1995; Sachs, 1992).

Despite various problems associated with development as a theory and practice, this book accepts that development remains a valid organizing principle for understanding societies and promoting positive change. One reason not to abandon development as yet is that, with nothing credible or concrete offered in its place, such an exercise risks promoting an "intellectual disengagement from increasingly brutal inequalities" (Edelman & Haugerud, 2006, p. 50). Another reason is that in cases where "post-development" theorists have actually claimed to offer new concepts to replace development, they have simply reproduced previous notions of rural community development in a different guise (Cowen & Shenton, 1996, p. 476).

If development cannot be wished out of existence it is also clearly not a neutral concept. When development is under discussion or being considered, questions need to be raised such as, What is meant by "development"? Who is doing the developing? Whom or what is being developed? Why is development being promoted? and Who gains from development? Development involves varying degrees of both destruction and creation (Cowen & Shenton, 1996, viii-ix) and, if not carefully planned, may result in social upheaval, injustices, and harm to human health and wellbeing (Chang & Grabel, 2004, pp. 19-23). To recommend development policies without considering their impact on the lives of real people is to risk creating new and possibly more serious problems in the process.

This volume explores the meaning and implications of development in Asia in two broad senses. First, it examines what Cowen and Shenton (1996) term "intentional development" (pp. 173-253), or development as thought and practice. Whereas Cowen and Shenton (1996) see intentional development as related to state policies, this book also considers intentional development within civil society. Second, it analyzes what Cowen and Shenton call "immanent development" (pp. 173-253). This form of development refers to the ongoing global expansion of capitalism and occurs in societies beyond the realm of subjective intentions. In this book, this aspect of development is analyzed in terms of how it has occurred or might be expected to occur in particular places or with regard to certain groups or social classes. Where possible, an attempt is also made to understand how intentional and immanent development have interacted and produced positive and/or negative outcomes, depending on the situation in question.

This is not the first book on development in Asia – nor will it be the last (e.g., Brooks & Evenett, 2006; Dowling, 2007; Dowling & Valenzuela, 2004; Roy & Chatterjee, 2006; Tang, 2000). However, it is unique in its interdisciplinary breadth, incorporating insights from sociology, economics, anthropology, cultural studies, history, and other fields. Also significant is the authors' human-centered approach to development. While development is often conceived in terms of national income accounting, the chapters in this volume devote special attention to social, political, as well as economic issues and examine both large scale and small scale contexts in their analyses. By providing studies on a wide array of nations and contexts and devoting attention to transnational processes associated with development, the book also allows readers to make comparisons of development experiences and discern how development takes place across borders or in culturally diverse contexts.

THE NEED FOR INTERDISCIPLINARY PERSPECTIVES

When development became a major concern for nations worldwide following the Second World War, American social scientists mainly concerned themselves with seeking ways to promote economic growth. Walt W. Rostow, the doyen of modernization theorists[1] in the 1960s, envisioned poor nations as progressing through various "stages of growth" until they had consumer-oriented economies like those found in the West. Imbued with a sense of urgency stemming from the exigencies of Cold War politics and lacking confidence that former colonial nations could develop on their own, Rostow suggested that massive flows of American aid could help "modernize" the Third World's "traditional societies" along Western lines, promote rapid economic growth, and cure "diseases of transition" such as communism (Rostow, 1960).[2]

One early critic of such growth-oriented theories of development was the British economist Dudley Seers (1969, 1972, 1977). According to Seers (1972), if such problems as poverty, inequality or unemployment were worsening when an economy was growing "it would be strange to call the result 'development,' even if per capita income had soared" (p. 24). Though an economist, Seers adopted an interdisciplinary outlook, maintaining that additional wealth in a society did not constitute development if people could not satisfy needs related to food and shelter, jobs, education, political participation, and citizenship in an independent nation. For Seers, development should not merely be associated with rising national incomes or increased commoditization. If it was to benefit humanity, development had to possess "the necessary conditions for a universally accepted aim, the realization of the potential of human personality" (p. 22).

In more recent years other authors have echoed and expanded on Seers' holistic and multidimensional viewpoints. While accepting that economic growth remains important for improving living standards, they have also incorporated quality of life indicators into their analyses related to access to healthcare and education, human rights, and political freedom. Among the more influential proponents in the past decade of what has come to be known as "human development" have been the economists Mahbub ul Haq and Amartya Sen. In his book *Reflections on Human Development* (1995), Haq argues that "The objective of development is to create an enabling environment for people to live long, healthy and creative lives" (p. 14). In *Development as Freedom* (2001), Sen similarly adopts a people-centered viewpoint in place of the traditional commodity-oriented one, suggesting that development should be about enhancing individuals' capabilities so they can lead lives of their own choosing. Both Haq and Sen's ideas have been highly influential, with the UNDP's Human Development Reports (HDRs) adopting many of their concepts and the United Nations' Millennium Development Goals (MDG) also bearing the influence of these two thinkers (Stewart, 2006, p. 18).

The chapters in this volume confirm that development, being complex in nature, is best understood from interdisciplinary perspectives. As should become evident, analytical frameworks that transcend traditional boundaries of knowledge help us better understand the impact of intentional and immanent development in more concrete terms, counteract the formulation of overly simplistic conclusions and theories, and more cautiously design appropriate policies for the future. By including social along with economic dimensions in assessing development, it becomes easier to see how the livelihoods or wellbeing of individuals or groups may be affected by particular development policies or initiatives. It also becomes possible to gather relevant information on the viewpoints, experiences and feelings of those being "developed" or who are "developing," thereby adding a crucial human dimension to development research.

POST-NEOLIBERAL CONCEPTIONS OF THE STATE

Another important issue raised by contributors to this volume concerns the role of the state in development. Following the rise of figures such as Margaret Thatcher and Ronald Reagan in the 1980s, the collapse of the Soviet Union in 1991, the further ascent of the US as a global hegemon, and the discrediting of socialist models of development linked to these events, neoliberal discourses have dominated discussions on world trade suggesting that a downscaling of the state's role in national economies is the key to global economic prosperity (Rapley, 2004). The so-called Washington Consensus holds that breaking down global trade barriers and promoting greater economic competition is essential to encourage more efficient commercial transactions and technology transfers across borders for the benefit of humanity worldwide. For those holding such opinions, state interventions introduce distortions into markets, involve wasteful social spending, and needlessly curtail corporate economic freedom (Stiglitz, 2003, p. 92).

Many chapters in this volume are also concerned with states and how they undermine freedom in society – but the focus is on people as opposed to corporations. As will become evident, governments throughout Asia have impeded democratization, stifled dissenting voices, caused conflicts and wars, and harmed human development in other ways. Importantly, however, what several authors in the following pages emphasize are threats to the dignity, wellbeing and quality of life of those adversely affected by states privileging certain forms of development while ignoring or undermining others. Such issues are generally overlooked by proponents of neoliberal economic solutions, who obfuscate or fail to discern how unbridled market forces may worsen inequality, lead to political instability, and prompt states to take away citizens' freedoms in a bid to maintain public order (Chang & Grabel, 2004, pp. 19-23).

This is not to suggest that the state does not have a positive role to play in ameliorating poverty and other social ills. The issue is not that the influence of the state should recede in all respects and that a Smithian "unseen hand" will solve the world's problems. Rather, it is a more a question of what role the state should play and to what degree it should work to promote change and manage the effects of immanent development. The state is not inherently oppressive. It can act in ways that are beneficial for disadvantaged social groups and average citizens. The key is for states to provide "good governance," or "sound development management," which requires "A public service that is efficient, a judicial system that is reliable, and an administration that is accountable to its public" (World Bank, 1992, p. 1). While some critics have dismissed "good governance" as a "vague" concept (Sandbrook, 2001, p. 13) or even portrayed it a "reconfiguration of neoliberalism" (Crawford, 2006, p. 115), they have in the process either wrongly implied that governance quality has no impact on development or that it is only relevant for pursuing neoliberal economic reforms.[3] Additionally, they have failed to acknowledge how new methods and tools are increasingly being developed to evaluate governance from a human-centered perspective that cover not only how well states manage economies but also the degree to which they allow for freedom of expression, respect human rights, promote tolerance, accept cultural diversity, and enable access to healthcare and education for citizens (Ariun-Erdene, this volume; Turner & Hulme, 1997, p. 231).

While good governance and development go hand in hand it is also clear that non-state actors have a crucial role to play in promoting positive social and economic change. Thus, researchers are now exploring ways in which people in civil society can interpret, participate in, and influence development efforts (Howell & Pierce, 2002). For example, researchers have examined ways NGOs in the form of advocacy groups, churches, charities, and social service providers have endeavored to improve individuals' and communities' wellbeing at the local, national and global levels (Bebbington & Hickey, 2006, pp. 417-422). Although NGOs offer no quick fix to development problems and are not immune to criticism (Scrase, 2007)[4], as revealed by successes with microfinance institutions such as the Grameen Bank in Bangladesh (Bornstein, 2005), they nonetheless do have the potential for helping people in ways governments may not. In this book as well the importance of civil society for development is accorded recognition. The perspectives provided on non-state actors and common people are valuable in that they do not portray individuals and communities as mere victims of larger forces beyond their control, according them a degree of agency and the potential to overcome social injustices or improve the quality of their lives.

TRANSNATIONAL DIMENSIONS OF DEVELOPMENT

The transnational character of contemporary development in Asia is a third major theme covered in this book. Over the past three decades immanent and intentional development have both been occurring within increasingly globalized contexts. In practical terms this means that the traditional emphasis on the nation-state as a unit of analysis for understanding political, economic and social change cannot capture the full essence of the forces affecting particular peoples and societies in Asia or elsewhere in the world. Human relations have taken on a more transnational and supraterritorial character, with ideas, technologies, and peoples flowing more freely across borders, often irrespective of the desires, knowledge or actions of state authorities (Scholte, 2005, p. 8).

The transnational interchanges associated with globalization are not entirely negative in their implications. For example, communication technologies such as the Internet now allow individuals and groups to publicize social causes to a worldwide audience or connect to others with similar interests in acts of solidarity (Humphries, this volume; Porta, Andretta, & Reiter, 2006, pp. 92-117). To a certain extent, globalization has given rise to a post-national, cosmopolitan consciousness that encourages individuals and groups to empathize with people from other regions of the globe and overcome myopia and parochialism. Some theorists even go as far as to suggest that globalization might be harnessed to establish a "cosmopolitan democracy," or an "extension of democracy to the international level to make up for the perceived failings of the nation-state in the face of globalization" (Hayden, 2005, p. 33).

Yet if the world is becoming "one" in ways that could never have been envisioned in earlier eras, this oneness carries risks along with opportunities. Caldwell and Williams (2006) note that just as charitable organizations such as Doctors without Borders (Médecins Sans Frontières) do great good by providing healthcare to the poor worldwide "malevolence in the form of disease, nihilistic ideologies, drugs, child prostitution, and many other problems spread across the globe with few obstacles" (p. 186). Commenting on contemporary poverty and its worldwide implications, the United Nations Development Program similarly observes: "Poverty is no longer contained within national boundaries. It has become globalized. It travels across borders, without a passport, in the form of drugs, diseases, pollution, migration, terrorism and political instability" (UNDP, 1996, p. 2).

The authors in this volume also recognize that an understanding of development often requires one to look beyond the nation-state and incorporate transnational flows and processes into analytical frameworks. On this note, one relevant theme that appears throughout the book is that of diasporic communities. Reasons for individuals migrating abroad, their experiences in foreign nations, and relations between diasporic communities and people from their place of origin are explored by Jun Nagatamo, Ma. Ledda B. Docot, and Richard Humphries. Other transnational themes include changing Japanese perceptions of Asians as "others" (Kinnia Shuk-ting Yau), the impact of globalization on local sport development in South East Asia (Charles Little and John Nauright), and the wider causes and implications of extremism and terrorism in Pakistan (Riaz Ahmed Shaik). As these authors' chapters imply, the nation-state continues to remain important for understanding development, but an exclusive focus on the nation-state can obscure how non-state actors and those occupying liminal social spaces shape or are affected by change in particular places. It can also cause one to overlook how distant forces may influence local developments. In other words, it should not be assumed that the nation-state "is the 'container' of social processes and that the national framework is still the best one suited to measure and analyze major social, economic and political changes" (Beck & Beck-Gernsheim, 2002, p. xx).

SUMMARY OF CHAPTERS

This book is organized into four parts. Part I addresses the issue of managing development. While some critics assert that intentional development is little more than a "hoax" (Norberg-Hodge, 1995) and thus deny it can be managed in any way, such viewpoints ignore obvious "success" stories such as South Korea, Taiwan, Hong Kong, Singapore, and Malaysia. Even if many development-related problems remain to be surmounted in these nations, few researchers will disagree today that state policies have played a role in rapidly transforming their economies and that these nations have attained higher levels of human development than others in Asia. At another level of analysis, the NGOs and government agencies involved in development work worldwide cannot be wished away by claiming they are part of a conspiracy hoisted upon the poor. Rather, managers in such contexts require practical information that allows them to better carry out their tasks. The chapters by Bayarjargal Ariun-Erdene and Agus Eko Nugroho provide such information as well as insights regarding development management at the national and local levels.

At the state level, Ariun-Erdene discusses how quality of governance has impacted upon human development in six Central Asian transition nations – Kazakhstan, Kyrgyz Republic, Mongolia, Tajikistan, Turkmenistan, and Uzbekistan – from 1997 to 2004. An important contribution of her chapter is its synthesis of 19 available governance indicators into three indices – the political, economic and civic – to assess their impact on human development. Ariun-Erdene's findings indicate that there exists an overall positive correlation between governance and economic performance during the period in question. However, Ariun-Erdene also notes declines in non-income-related dimensions of development such as educational enrollments and life expectancy rates during the same period. Foreseeing continuing social strains in the region, she nonetheless concludes that more efforts should be made to build democratic systems and respect human rights in Central Asia. She also calls for further research to assess the aggregate indices she provides and other indices of governance.

Nugroho's chapter looks at development management from the perspective of microfinance institutions (MFIs) in rural Javanese villages in Indonesia. He focuses in particular on the link between social capital and access of poor people to microfinance, an area that has not been adequately researched to date. He also examines how social networks can reduce the probability of poor farmers facing credit rationing from formal finance. Nugroho provides convincing empirical evidence that microfinance institutions should consider the importance of social capital when dispersing loans. Not only could incorporating social capital into lending decisions lower loan default rates for MFIs, argues Nugroho, but poor borrowers could also use social capital as a form of collateral to access loans. He suggests that experiences in rural Javanese villages reveal the potential of non-market institutions for alleviating rural poverty and offer lessons for other Asian nations where microfinance institutions operate.

Part II of this volume covers the theme of gender and development. Ester Boserup's seminal work *Woman's Role in Economic Development* (1970) was one of the first in-depth studies to show that men and women are affected differently by the development process. Using data from Africa, Asia, the Caribbean, and Latin America, Boserup argued that colonialism and "modernization" generally undermined the position of women within the sexual division of labor while men gained access to additional economic resources and new technologies. As men were drawn away from the realm of family labor to work elsewhere, women's burdens increased while their status in society decreased. Since Boserup's classic study, other researchers have examined additional gender and development issues related to globalization, health and disease, technology, the environment, and other themes (Pearson, 2006, pp. 189-195). Such works have added greatly to our awareness of the importance of gender roles in development and help us understand challenges faced by average men and women worldwide.

The first chapter on gender and development by Ayami Noritake consists of an interesting account on female street entrepreneurs at Tongdaemun Market in Seoul, Korea. Although South Korea is often seen as an economic model for developing nations, Noritake shows that its national development policies have had a contradictory impact on particular classes of women. Female street entrepreneurs at the market have been marginalized by development processes and often regarded by the state and society in a negative light, with many having had to face forced relocations and other hardships. Making use of oral interviews, Noritake analyzes how the women in multilayered and diverse ways have shaped their social and work spaces and negotiated their life courses under challenging circumstances brought about by economic development. In Noritake's view, a reconceptualization of urban development is needed that better takes into account such women's creativity, resilience and agency.

Ma. Ledda B. Docot's chapter explores the experiences of Filipino women in Japan and their participation in a Filipino-run support organization in Tokyo known as the Center for Japanese Filipino Families (CJFF). She discusses how, thirty years after first arriving, the women are trying to locate themselves as members of Japanese society and transition from jobs as entertainment workers to English teachers through the CJFF. Docot weaves a complex narrative that begins by tracing the Philippines' colonial and post-colonial history, showing how labor policies in the 1970s led to the women's migration to Japan. She then shows how the CJFF has "subverted" an aspect of American colonial education policy and neocolonial relations – the English language – to enable women to resist subordination and achieve upward mobility in new careers. She predicts that Filipino women's participation in such transnational social movements as the CJFF may eventually have wider ramifications for development issues in contexts of international migration.

Part III of this volume consists of two chapters that examine how development and culture are related. The term "culture" is difficult to define and can be interpreted in numerous ways. In this part of the book, however, culture will be taken to mean the general attitudes, beliefs, and perceptions held by members of a particular group, community or nation.

After Max Weber first suggested that the "Protestant work ethic" played a pivotal role in the expansion of capitalism in Europe and North America (Weber, 1930), modernization theorists in the 1960s adopted similar viewpoints in which they proposed that development would only occur in places where societies adopted "modern" in place of "traditional" values (e.g., Hoselitz, 1961). Similarly, in a repackaging of Weber's thesis during the 1990s, "Asian values" were praised by leaders such as former Singapore Prime Minister Lee Kuan Yew for the economic successes of East Asian nations (Berger, 2004, p. 183). More recently, a collection of papers called *Culture Matters* (2000), edited by Samuel Huntington and Lawrence Harrison, was published to show that "culture...affects the extent to which and the ways societies achieve or fail to achieve progress in economic development and political democratization" (Huntington, 2000, p. xv). However, the notion that culture alone can explain a nation's development is too simplistic in itself. This can be gleaned from Huntington's comment that South Korea was able to develop more rapidly than Ghana from the 1960s because "South Koreans valued thrift, investment, hard work, education, organization, and discipline. Ghanaians had different values. In short, cultures count" (p. xiii). Such a view ignores how historical and a wide array of other factors may shape a given culture and nation's development.

Kinnia Shuk-ting Yau's chapter on Japanese cinema provides a fascinating historical perspective in this respect, revealing how immanent development can affect cultural perceptions, in this case analyzing how Japanese have viewed themselves and other Asians in Japanese films. In the 1940s when Japan's power in Asia was at its peak, such films reflected Japan's sense of superiority toward other Asian nations and were characterized by Japanese men "rescuing" poor and helpless Asian women, lending the impression that the Japanese were liberators of "less civilized" Asian nations. It was not until the Heisei period (1989-), following the rapid development of Asian Newly Industrializing Economies (ANIEs) and occurrence of political and economic crises in Japan, that a marked shift occurred in Japanese attitudes, with other Asians now seen as fashionable, dynamic and resourceful peoples who could become friends and even spouses of Japanese. Although Japanese less frequently portray themselves as superior to other Asians in their films, Yau notes that Japan's relations with other nations remain strained and that efforts need to be made on all sides to promote understanding in the region and overcome historical grievances.

Pakistan's development experiences have differed drastically from Japan's and thus provide many illuminating contrasts from a cultural standpoint. Riaz Ahmed Shaikh examines how the number of *madrasahs* (Islamic schools) in Pakistan has expanded since the 1980s and the *madrasah* has been transformed from an institution that used to encourage basic religious learning to one where extremist ideas are promoted that threaten stability in Pakistan, surrounding areas, and the world at large. While the *madrasah* itself is often singled out for breeding a culture of fanaticism and terror, Shaik demonstrates that historical factors molding the character of *madrasahs* need to be given more consideration. A crucial event was the Soviet-Afghan War (1979-1989), which prompted the Pakistani state to see *madrasahs* as a means to train Afghan refugees and other recruits for the anti-Soviet war effort. Also of major significance were Islamization policies under Zia-ul-Haq and foreign funding for *ma-*

drasahs from other Muslim nations and the United States. If the culture of the *madrasah* has shaped patterns of development in Pakistan, Shaik's chapter is valuable in that it shows that the *madrasah* in turn has been shaped by a complex array of competing economic and political interests.

Part IV of this volume explores the theme of globalization and development. Globalization, like culture, is open to interpretation and has spawned a voluminous literature (See Scholte, 2005). For reasons of clarity and convenience, however, globalization here will be defined as "a stretching of social, political, and economic activities across frontiers such that events, decisions and activities in one region of the world can come to have significance for individuals and communities in distant regions of the globe" (Held, McGrew, Goldblatt, & Perraton, 1999, p. 15). As Held et al (1999) further note, globalization is not uniform in its impact but "is best understood as a multifaceted or differentiated phenomenon. It cannot be conceived as a singular condition but instead refers to patterns of growing global interconnectedness within all the key domains of social activity" (p. 27).

The "stretching" Held et al (1999) describe can be clearly seen in the case of sport in recent years, as discussed by Charles Little and John Nauright, who show how globalization has affected local sports development in South East Asia. One key example they cite is the English Premier League, which has gained in popularity in South East Asia and made major profits at the expense of local soccer leagues. Little and Nauright also describe how nations such as Malaysia are increasingly emphasizing "mega-events" in a bid to raise their international profile and attract foreign capital while other nations with fewer resources or less power are marginalized in the process. Although globalization has often been seen as a process that undermines the nation-state, Little and Nauright consider how various South East Asian states have used sport to strengthen national identity and acquire more influence on the world stage. They conclude nonetheless that the impact of globalization on sports development in South East Asia has often been detrimental in that mainly global, national and local elites benefit while "spectators, participants and communities are increasingly removed from the sporting product whether this is in Europe, North America or South East Asia."

Offering an interesting contrast with Little and Nauright's analysis, the next chapter by Jun Nagatomo on tourism development and Japanese residents in Australia is more positive in its assessment of globalization. Following Australian efforts in the 1980s and 1990s to encourage tourism and foreign investment and a boom in the overseas tourist industry in Japan, the numbers of Japanese tourists as well as Japanese choosing to live in Australia have swelled dramatically, with Japanese who have decided to permanently reside in Australia generally retaining

Japanese citizenship rather than "immigrating" in the usual sense. Interestingly, Nagatomo shows how many Japanese have become permanent residents following positive experiences as tourists. Providing evidence from interviews conducted in South East Queensland, he argues that such individuals represent a new type of migrant in our era of globalization – the "lifestyle migrant." Whereas migration is usually seen as resulting from economic pull factors, Nagatomo shows how a desire to escape the strains of urban life in Japan – not gravitation toward higher incomes or improved economic opportunities – has prompted many Japanese to choose Australia as a place to live, work and raise their families.

Differing from the previous two chapters, Richard Humphries' contribution on globalization focuses on the "stretching" of political activities across borders and concerns the development of an exiled Burmese media and its relation to democratization efforts in Burma. Following the brutal suppression of the pro-democracy movement in Burma in 1988, an alternative Burmese media began to form abroad, with its growth assisted greatly by the globalization of new media technologies in the 1990s. Humphries discusses government efforts to stifle freedom of the press from this time onward and how the exile media have worked to circumvent state censorship through using the Internet and other up-to-date technologies. He devotes particular attention to the challenges faced by exiled media groups during and after the Saffron Revolution, a series of monk-led demonstrations in 2007. While the exile media had some successes in disseminating news about events to Burmese citizens and people from other nations, Humphries observes that the military junta remains in power for now and important struggles lie ahead for the media to aid in Burma's transition to a democratic society.

Conclusion

The noted post-development thinker Wolfgang Sachs once suggested that "development was a misconceived enterprise from the beginning" that "did not work" and thus its "obituary" should be written as soon as possible (Sachs, 1992, pp. 1, 3). In Sachs' favor, it could be said that examples of development failures can be found throughout history and development policies cannot always be assumed to be benign or effective (Hodge, 2007). Nevertheless, as Rigg (2003) writes, views such as Sachs' are "nihilistic" and within the post-development camp "There is no recognition of difference, or of the possibility there might be a 'good' development and 'bad' development" (p. 326). That development is not merely an oppressive discourse and "good" development is possible, suggests Rigg, can be gathered from marked improvements in human wellbeing in many South East Asian nations over the past five decades (p. 328).

The discussions in this volume also do not suggest that it is possible or desirable to discard development as a means of understanding or inducing social change. As the following chapters reveal, examples of both "good" and "bad" development can be found throughout Asia. Whether a particular development outcome is construed as "good" or "bad," both immanent and intentional development remain relevant concepts. This is so first of all because immanent development will occur regardless of human intentions and thus cannot be wished out of existence. Second, in the case of intentional development, to imply that inaction is preferable to development ironically risks supporting neoliberal economic agendas by default, or to recommend a post-development intervention of some kind may involve the use of different terminology but it nonetheless replicates the same processes associated with development (Grischow & McKnight, 2003; Hodge, 2007, pp. 275-276). To suggest that intentional development may yield positive results, as is accepted in this book, is also not to support each and every type of intervention in the name of development. It is also not to suggest that development policies cannot fail or have unintended consequences. However, regardless of whether the word "development" is used or not, intentional development will continue to be practiced and individuals, communities, and nations will be affected in some way in the process. While a critical stance toward development is essential, the main issue is to hone development in theory and practice to maximize positive and minimize negative development outcomes. Simply calling for an "end to development" (Escobar, 1995, pp. vi-vii) in this regard is more counterproductive than helpful.

Development clearly is in Asia and elsewhere to stay, despite protestations to the contrary. A question that naturally arises from this, however, is: What vision of intentional development should be promoted? Readers of this book will find no simple answers to this question. The authors herein offer no theories or policies that can be uniformly applied. The following chapters all discuss different contexts, each with their own unique features and development problems and needs. But where the authors do agree is in their human-centered concerns. If this book has succeeded in putting people first in its analysis of development in Asia, then it has achieved its main purpose.

Notes

1   For an excellent summary and critique of modernization theory see Engerman, Gilman, & Haefele (2003)'s *Staging Growth*. Boston: University of Massachusetts Press.
2   Unlike most of his academic contemporaries, Rostow was able to put his ideas into

practice. He served as a national security advisor to two US Presidents – John F. Kennedy and Lyndon B. Johnston – and helped coin the phrases "The Development Decade" and "The New Frontier" for Kennedy's presidential campaign. He also played a key role in conceiving US foreign policy in Vietnam. In a memo he wrote in 1961 on the Decade of Development initiative, Rostow both confidently and naively predicted that: "It should be possible, if we all work hard, for Argentina, Brazil, Colombia, Venezuela, India, the Philippines, Taiwan, Turkey, Greece – and possibly Egypt, Pakistan, Iran, and Iraq – to have self-sustaining growth by 1970" (quoted in Haefele, 2003, p. 94).

3 In fairness to the critics, the notion of good governance was first proposed in a 1989 World Bank document entitled *Sub-Saharan Africa: From Crisis to Sustainable Growth*. At that time, the World Bank did link structural adjustment policies to good governance. However, over the past several years a wide range of organizations, groups and scholars have adopted the concept and broadened its definition to include non-neoliberal and non-economic forms of governance (Najem, 2003, pp. 1-28). As noted by Najem (2003), despite some shortcomings associated with it, "[T]here seems to be no workable alternative paradigm that offers better prospects for the people of the developing world" (p. 26).

4 Scrase (2007)'s research raises questions about volunteers, NGOs and the development process in Asia. He argues that "Volunteers, and NGOs, are not neutral and, even if well-meaning, can in fact act as the *de facto* agents of unequal development policies and outcomes" (p. 187). He also suggests that NGOs tend to reinforce neoliberal development policies. While his point that NGOs and their aims cannot be taken at face value is valid, he nevertheless overlooks cases where NGOs can positively influence development patterns and challenge neoliberal power structures and ideologies (See Docot, this volume).

References

Alvares, C. (1994). *Science, development and violence: The revolt against modernity.* Bombay: Oxford University Press.

Bebbington, A., & Hickey, S. (2006). NGOs and civil society. In D. A. Clark (Ed.), *The Elgar companion to development studies* (pp. 417-423). Manchester: Edgar Elgar Publishing.

Beck, U., & Beck-Gernsheim, E. (2002). *Individualization: Institutionalized individualism and its social and political consequences.* London: Sage Publications.

Berger, M. T. (2004). *The battle for Asia.* London and New York: Routledge.

Bhagwati, J. N. (2007). *In defense of globalization.* New York: Oxford University Press USA.

Bornstein, D. (2005). *The price of a dream: The story of the Grameen Bank.* Oxford: Oxford University Press.

Boserup, E. (1970). *Woman's role in economic development.* London: Allen and Unwin.

Brooks, D. H., & Evenett, S. (2006). *Competition policy and development in Asia.* New York: Palgrave Macmillan.

Caldwell, D., & Williams, R. E. (2006). *Seeking security in an insecure world.* Lanham, MD: Rowman & Littlefield.

Chang, H.-J., & Grabel, I. (2004). *Reclaiming development: An economic policy handbook for activists and policymakers.* London: Zed Books.

Cowen, M. P., & Shenton, R. W. (1996). *Doctrines of development.* London and New York: Routledge.

Crawford, G. (2006). The World Bank and good governance. In A. Paloni & M. Zanardi (Eds.), *The World Bank, IMF and policy reform.* (pp. 115-142). London and New York: Routledge.

Dowling, J. M. (2007). *Future perspectives on the economic development of Asia.* Singapore: World Scientific Publishing Company.

Dowling, J. M., & Valenzuela, M. R. (2004). *Economic development in Asia.* Singapore: Cengage Learning Asia.

Edelman, M., & Haugerud, A. (Eds.). (2006). *The anthropology of development and globalization. From classical political economy to contemporary neoliberalism.* Oxford: Oxford University Press.
Engerman, D. C., Gilman, N., & Haefele, M. H. (Eds.). (2003). *Staging growth.* Boston: University of Massachusetts Press.
Escobar, A. (1995). *Encountering development: The making and unmaking of the Third World.* Princeton, NJ: Princeton University Press.
Grischow, J., & McKnight, G. (2003). Rhyming development: Practicing post-development in colonial Ghana and Uganda. *Journal of Historical Sociology, 16*(4), 517-549.
Haefele, M. H. (2003). Walt Rostow's stages of economic growth: Ideas and action. In D. C. Engerman, N. Gilman, & M. H. Haefele (Eds.), *Staging growth* (pp. 81-106). Boston: University of Massachusetts Press.
Haq, M. U. (1995). *Reflections on human development.* New York and Oxford: Oxford University Press.
Hayden, P. (2005). Cosmopolitan global politics. London: Ashgate Publishing Ltd.
Held, D., McGrew, A. G., Goldblatt, D., & Perraton, J. (1999). *Global transformations.* Palo Alto, CA: Stanford University Press.
Hodge, J. (2007). *Triumph of the expert. Agrarian doctrines of development and the legacies of British colonialism.* Athens: Ohio University Press.
Hoselitz, B. F. (1961). Tradition and economic growth. In R. Braibanti & J. J. Spengler (Eds.), *Tradition, values and socioeconomic development* (pp. 83-113). Durham, NC: Duke University Press.
Huntington, S. P. (2000). Foreword: Cultures count. In L. E. Harrison & S. P. Huntington (Eds.), *Culture matters* (pp. xiii-xvi). New York: Basic Books.
Howell, J., & Pearce, J. (2002). *Civil society and development.* Boulder and London: Lynne Reinner Publishers.
Najem, T. P. (2003). Good governance: The definition and application of the concept. In T. P. Najem & M. Hetherington (Eds.), *Good governance in the Middle East oil monarchies* (pp. 1-28). London and New York: Routledge.
Norberg-Hodge, H. (1995). The development hoax. In Just World Trust, *Dominance of the West over the rest* (pp. 110-123). Penang: JUST.
Pearson, R. (2006). Gender and development. In D. A. Clark (Ed.), *The Elgar companion to development studies* (pp. 189-196). Manchester: Edgar Elgar Publishing.
Porta, D. P., Andretta, M., & Reiter, H. (2006). *Globalization from below: Transnational activists and protest networks.* Minneapolis and London: University of Minnesota Press.
Rapley, J. (2004). *Globalization and inequality.* Boulder and London: Lynne Reiner Publishers.
Rigg, J. (2003). *Southeast Asia.* London and New York: Routledge.
Rostow, W. W. (1960). *The stages of economic growth: A non-communist manifesto.* Cambridge: Cambridge University Press.
Roy, K. C., & Chatterjee, S. (Eds.). (2006). *Readings in world development: Growth and development in the Asia Pacific.* Hauppauge, NY: Nova Science Publishers.
Sachs, W. (1992). Introduction. In W. Sachs (Ed.), *The Development dictionary: A guide to knowledge as power* (pp. 1-5). London: Zed Books.
Sandbrook, R. (2001). *Closing the circle: Democratization and development in Africa.* Toronto: Between the Lines.
Scholte, J. A. (2005). *Globalization: A critical introduction* (2nd ed.). New York: Palgrave Macmillan
Scrase, T. (2007). Globalization, NGOs, international volunteers and the development process in Asia. In D. M. Nault (Ed.), *Human security in Asia: Emerging issues and challenges. Proceedings of the 2nd international conference of the Asia Association for Global Studies* (pp. 172-189). Osaka: Global Studies Press.
Seers, D. (1972). What are we trying to measure? In N. Baster (Ed.), *Measuring development* (pp. 21-36). London: Frank Cass.

Seers, D. (1969). The meaning of development. *International Development Review, 11*(4), 2-6.
Seers, D. (1977). The new meaning of development. *International Development Review, 19*(3), 2-7.
Sen, A. (2001). *Development as freedom.* Oxford: Oxford University Press.
Stiglitz, J. (2003). *Globalization and its discontents.* New York and London: W. W. Norton & Company.
Stewart, F. (2006). Basic needs approach. In D. A. Clark (Ed.), *The Elgar companion to development studies* (pp. 14-18). Manchester: Edgar Elgar Publishing.
Tang, K.-L. (2000). *Social development in Asia.* New York: Springer.
Turner, M., & Hulme, D. (1997). Governance, administration and development: Making the state work. Basingstoke, UK: Macmillan Press.
UNDP. (1996). *Human development report 1996.* New York: Oxford University Press.
Weber, M. (1930). The Protestant ethic and the spirit of capitalism. New York: HarperCollins.
Wolf, M. (2004). *Why globalization works.* New Haven, CT: Yale University Press.
World Bank. (1981). *Accelerated development in sub-Saharan Africa: An agenda for action.* Washington, DC: World Bank.
World Bank. (1992). *Governance and development.* Washington, DC: World Bank.

Part One:
Managing Development

• CHAPTER TWO •

Human Development and Governance in Central Asian Transition Countries

BAYARJARGAL ARIUN-ERDENE
National University of Mongolia

Central Asian transition countries[1] diverge in terms of speed of transition, implemented reforms, paths of change, and performance yields (i.e., GDP growth rates, human development, poverty, inequality, etc.). Recently, such diverse outcomes in the transition process have increasingly been linked to the quality and impact of governance, a term which can be defined as "the exercise of authority through formal and informal institutions in the management of the nation's resource endowment" (World Bank, 1992, p. 1). The transition process seems, to a large extent, to be about institutional transformation, with what is taking place in transitional countries presenting a unique opportunity for researchers to observe large-scale institutional change.

However, the mainstream literature on the effects of governance in transition countries has mostly focused on economic performance. A human development approach considering not only income growth, but also non-income dimensions of human development, such as health, life expectancy, and educational attainment, has been largely neglected in empirical studies of transition countries.

According to the United Nations Development Program (UNDP), human development is about people, about expanding their choices to live full, creative lives with freedom and dignity. Fundamental to enlarging human choices is building human capabilities. The most basic capabilities for human development are leading a long and healthy life, being educated, having access to resources needed for a decent standard of living and enjoying political and civil freedoms to participate in the life of one's community (UNDP, 2004, p. 28). Hence, human development allows for a broader view of a country's development and human wellbeing than focusing on income alone, and it represents a key issue for development worldwide.

By international standards, formerly socialist countries in Central Asia made many impressive advances in basic human development over much of the twentieth century. Access to basic education and healthcare expanded rapidly in these nations, particularly from after the Second World War to the end of the 1980s. However, the transition to democracy and away from highly centralized economies in more recent times has entailed costs in terms of human development. Notable setbacks in health and education have occurred during the transition period. The life expectancy of males in some Central Asian countries has decreased by as much as five years. Some nations face the unusual prospect of mass illiteracy, with their school enrolments today lower than those of 1989. Serious breakdowns in social services and social safety nets have left people without secure access to the services which they require (UNDP, 2000, p. 35).

Promoting and consolidating governance so that it efficiently supports human development is essential for Central Asian transition countries. An important subject of discussion relevant to countries in transition is how the quality and efficiency of governance contribute to decision making in vitally important human development areas. Recent studies on the links between democratic governance and human development, to be discussed below, do not provide clear-cut support for the idea that improvement in governance in the area of democracy and freedom necessarily contributes to human development; therefore, it is important to carefully clarify the relationship between these phenomena.

This chapter is organized as follows. In the first section, the concept of governance for human development is developed. The second section presents an analysis of the relationship between human development and governance in Central Asian transition countries in terms of three dimensions of governance developed in the previous section. Finally, some conclusions are offered based on the findings and analysis presented.

GOVERNANCE FOR HUMAN DEVELOPMENT

Recently, the role of governance for development performance outcomes among transition countries has been recognized and, therefore, a sizeable literature on the subject has emerged. Since the early 1990s, governance as an analytical framework has become widely endorsed by development economists, policymakers, and international organizations. Governance is being assessed in terms of both formal and informal institutional environments and the interactions of individuals, social groups and policymakers in the design, implementation, and enforcement of socio-economic policies.

Governance has many implications and represents a key indicator for national development performance. In this regard, previous studies have largely examined the effects of governance on economic growth and inequality, focusing in particular on the institutional dimensions of governance and on the relationship between various institutional measures of governance and economic performance. Few researchers have actually provided empirical analyses on governance and its effects on human development performance in Central Asian transition countries.

Among the studies related to economic development, Brunetti, Kisunko, and Weder (1997) argue that differences in building institutional frameworks for governance may explain the diverse economic performances of 20 transition countries they include in their analysis. Indicators the authors provide on institutional uncertainty, which may also be considered as measures of governance quality, include indicators on the predictability of political stability, security of property rights, reliability of the judiciary, and lack of corruption. The results suggest that predictability within the institutional framework of governance may help account for differences in foreign direct investment and in economic growth among transition economies. Brunetti et al's study represents the first attempt to explain relative economic performance vis-à-vis the institutional dimensions of governance in transition countries.

Another mainly economic study by Ahrens and Meurers (2000) successfully summarizes the development of governance as a concept, noting the existence of a confusing array of definitions. Agreeing with the position of the World Bank that "good governance is synonymous with sound development management" (World Bank, 1992, p. 1), their paper examines three distinct schools of thought regarding governance. The first conception sees effective governance as corresponding to a democratic order that minimizes the size of government and ensures that economics dominates over politics. A second conception views governance as an approach supporting abstract universal principles and rules with enforcement mechanisms, as well as stable and transparent mechanisms of conflict resolution. The third conception, which is not related to the previous ones, adds the dimension of informal institutions to the governance framework (Ahrens & Meurers, 2000, pp. 8-9). Ahrens and Meurers also look at policy reforms in 25 post-socialist countries and investigate the impact of governance on economic transformation processes. They draw on governance data from various sources such as Freedom House, Transparency International, the European Bank for Reconstruction and Development (EBRD), the World Bank, as well as data collected by Brunetti, Kisunko, and Weder (1997) and others. The four dimensions of accountability, participation, predictability, and transparency in governance are employed in their analysis. They conclude that the experiences of transition countries show how governance as well as design of the economic and political order is of utmost importance for successful policy reform.

De Melo, Denizer, Gelb, and Tenev (2001) examine performance among 28 transition economies in Central and Eastern Europe, the Former Soviet Union (FSU), and various East Asian countries. Their particular focus is on the role of initial conditions and political developments in national development. Their work is unique in its attempt to explain the transition performances of East Asian countries, including China, Vietnam and Mongolia, and the authors' emphasis on the importance of economic development in influencing decisions to expand political freedoms.

Finally, Dabrowski and Gortat (2002) analyze the following institutional pillars of democratic society and the market economy: constitutional regimes, political party systems, electoral systems, legal frameworks, and monetary institutions in transition countries. They conclude that several formerly socialist countries recently accepted as European Union (EU) members are relatively close to the final destination of their transition while Central Asian nations and Belarus cannot claim such achievements, since they continue to maintain authoritarian regimes and try to preserve command economy mechanisms. Furthermore, they conclude that fast and complex reforms yield, on average, better socio-economic outcomes than slower or gradual changes, suggesting that the ability of individual countries to follow effective reforms is determined by the scale of initial political changes and further developments in the sphere of institutional and political reform. Since Dabrowski and Gortat chronologically assess political and economic reforms by region and nation, it is possible to note gradual institutional changes in individual countries. Their study of institutional change in transition countries is especially comprehensive and valuable.

In contrast to the above economic-related studies, the literature on human development mainly relates to global, regional and national human development reports (HDRs) that are published on an annual and bi-annual basis. The main characteristics of HDRs are determined by the UNDP. Global HDRs are a reliable source on critical issues concerning human development worldwide. Presenting the HDI (Human Development Index), every report provides agenda-setting data and analysis and calls international attention to issues and policy options that put people at the center of those strategies being implemented to meet the challenges of economic, social, political, and cultural development.

HDR 2000 placed a greater emphasis on human rights and human development than previous reports. These two aspects of development share a common purpose – to secure the freedom, wellbeing and dignity of people in all nations. The report's main contribution was to unify human development and human rights in its analysis. The former is usually seen as the focus of economists, social scientists, and policymakers, while the latter is viewed as the domain of political activists, lawyers, and philosophers. Human development in HDR 2000, however, was now considered essential for realizing human rights, and conversely human rights was seen as essential for full human development (UNDP, 2000, p. 2). As argued in the report, human rights can secure freedom and human development by providing necessary legal tools and institutions. The report also draws attention to civil and political rights as integral parts of the development process. Human development, in turn, directs attention to the socio-economic context through which human rights can be realized.

The next critical issue raised by the UNDP in its global HDRs was the role of good governance for human development. HDR 2002 was concerned with the means by which political power and institutions shape human progress. The report is a significant source for understanding and discerning the relationship between democratic governance and human development as it provides a key conceptual framework. Good governance for human development, according to the report, not only fosters effective public institutions but also fair and accountable institutions that protect human rights and basic freedoms. It also promotes wider participation through the institutions and rules that affect people's lives. Finally, the report argues that political freedom and participation are capabilities as important as other basic capabilities:

> Political freedom and participation have become much more prominent in public policy debates. The political shifts of the 1990s built greater consensus on the value of political freedom and human rights.... Political freedom and the ability to participate in the life of one's community are capabilities that are as important for human development as being able to read and write and being in good health. People without political freedom...have far fewer choices in life. (UNDP, 2002, pp. 52-54)

Given that democracy is based on two core principles, participation and accountability, democratic institutions and processes can contribute to human development. Hence, democratic governance must be about strengthening democratic institutions and promoting democratic policies that make participation and public accountability possible.

The second source of literature on human development is regional HDRs. In accordance with the UNDP's definition, regional HDRs serve to measure human progress and generate actions for change. Their primary focus is on promoting regional partnerships for addressing region-specific human development approaches in terms of human rights, poverty, inequality, education, economic reforms, health issues, and globalization.

Central Asia HDR 2005 stresses how good governance and institutions are crucial for economic growth. It considers in particular political and economic corruption in government, a nation's presidential apparatus, state and semi-state enterprises, and private enterprises closely working with the state. Governance problems in these areas, the report suggests, have reduced the effectiveness and efficiency of state policy, threatened the formulation of rational states, and increased uncertainty in business environments. The report concludes, moreover, that "key elements of democracy and good governance are not present in Central Asia more than a decade after independence" (UNDP, 2005, p. 195). It goes on to say that most Central Asian countries have minimized or eliminated accountability and transparency mechanisms through post-Soviet super-presidential systems, creating major problems for good governance, the securing of human rights, and the further promotion of human development.

The UNDP states that national HDRs can serve as a tool for national policy debates. The main objective of national HDRs is to place human development at the forefront of the national political agenda. As such, national HDRs are a valuable resource for developing socio-economic policies that affect human development. Moreover, the HDR is an instrument for policy analysis reflecting people's priorities, in addition to strengthening national capacities, identifying inequalities, and measuring progress. As a rule, countries prepare national HDRs in collaboration with the UNDP. Each national team addresses specific themes tied to the country's most urgent development issues such as governance, poverty, economic growth, gender, peace and security, education, and the environment. As of 2006, there were over 30 national HDRs prepared in Central Asian transition countries, out of which 7 national HDRs raised the issue of governance on behalf of human development.

Beyond the concept of governance for socio-economic development, several governance concepts have been presented to promote sustainable human development. The UNDP in particular, as will be discussed below, has played a significant role in this area.

The UNDP focuses more on those aspects of governance that support human development. Governance is considered a basic precondition for sustainable human development. Since sustainable human development is about expanding people's choices and opportunities, governance for human development should shape society to make this expansion possible. Expansion is empowered when it increases people's ability to lead full and satisfying lives that are free from hunger, want and deprivation. In 1998, the UNDP defined governance in three settings – economic, political and social. The economic setting includes the processes that affect a country's economic activities and the relationships with the economies of other states. Governance in the political setting is the process of decision making to formulate policies and laws. Administrative governance which has resulting consequences for the social setting is a system of policy implementation carried out through public services (UNDP, 1998, p. 15).

Governance has to be not just pro-people or people centered, but it also has to be owned by the people. Subsequently, in 1999 the Mahbub ul Haq Human Development Center provided a humane governance concept that requires effective participation of the people in state, civil society, and private sector activities. According to the Center, humane governance can "ensure that human development is sustainable" (Mahbub ul Haq Human Development Center, 1999, p. 28). All institutions – the state, government, market, and society – ultimately have only one purpose: to improve human wellbeing in terms of income and also capabilities. Humane governance is conceptualized according to three broad dimensions: good political governance, good economic governance, and good civic governance. Good political governance includes decentralization of power, accountability and transparency, full access of all citizens to justice, the elimination of all forms of discrimination, and the maintenance of peace and social cohesion. Economic governance is assessed by measures of fiscal policy, monetary policy, trade openness, social priority spending, and liberalization of the economy. Good civic governance has several components that are intended to protect the basic human rights and freedoms of people so they can improve their capacities. While the humane governance concept still has political and economic dimensions similar to the notion of governance developed by the UNDP in 1998, the main difference is the inclusion of a social domain within the economic dimension of governance, with the civic dimension conceptualized as an essential aspect of governance.

In 2002 the UNDP further improved upon the governance concept by including democratic issues. Governance for human development is about protecting fundamental human rights, promoting wider participation in decision making processes that affect people's lives, and achieving more equitable economic and social outcomes. From a human development perspective, good governance is democratic governance.[2]

Democratic governance can advance human development in three ways. First, democracy is the only political system that guarantees basic human rights, such as political and civil freedoms and the right to participate in decision making processes. Second, democracy helps to protect people from economic and political catastrophes. Democracies also contribute to political stability by allowing for political opposition and the handover of power. Third, democratic governance can trigger a virtuous cycle of development: political freedom empowers people to press for policies that expand social and economic opportunities, and open debates help communities shape their priorities (UNDP, 2002, p. 5).

However, these reasons for advancing human development as set out by the UNDP were already conceptualized in the humane governance concept, especially the civic dimension of governance just mentioned. To move the discussion forward, therefore, the present chapter will next summarize the development of governance concepts to date, synthesize them and then conceptualize governance for human development according to the following three dimensions: economic governance, political governance, and civic governance (see Figure 1).

All the governance concepts in question explicitly or implicitly involve the economic dimension of governance. From a human development perspective, good economic governance has to provide an economic environment in which people can expand their choices and opportunities. The macroeconomic environment is, therefore, comprised of business, fiscal, monetary, financial, investment and trade environments that affect a country's economic performance and relationships with other economies. It affects as well human wellbeing. In addition, policy implementation that makes these environments attainable is rendered effective through clear and efficient rules and regulations. With regard to transition economies, a reform component might also be added. This component would assess the outcomes of macroeconomic and institutional reforms that favor a more market-oriented economy, such as those related to privatization, liberalization, restructuring, and competition policy.

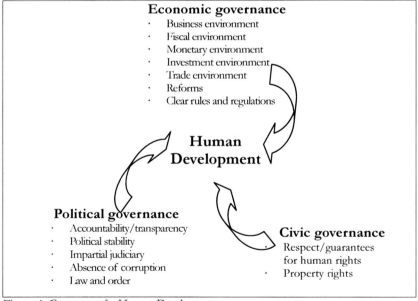

Figure 1 *Governance for Human Development*
Source: Author.

It can be seen that all of the governance concepts also maintain the political dimension as a substantial component of governance. Since the political setting involves the decision making process in formulating policies and laws and also has to provide a secure environment that expands political participation of the people in that process, this component should include accountability and transparency, political stability, absence of violence and corruption, and the supremacy of the rule of law.

Finally, one of the main characteristics of governance for human development is to provide an environment that allows people to experience basic human rights and fundamental freedoms. Civic governance contains components that allow for the expression of political rights and civil rights and guarantee people can enjoy those rights. The latter component of governance or civic governance must be represented by a democratic government, given that democracy is the only political system that ensures basic human rights. Property rights as well must be an inherent component of human rights, allowing people to accumulate private property, which in turn expands their economic opportunities.

As mentioned earlier, the relationship between governance and human development has been largely neglected in the economic literature, especially in the case of transition countries. Nonetheless, two exceptions, studies by Campos (1999) and Tridico (2005), deserve mention.

Campos' (1999) paper is an important source on the relationship between governance and human development in transition countries. He provides a mapping of institutional change during the transition from centrally planned to market economies using the concept of governance and five institutional dimensions (accountability of the executive, quality of the bureaucracy, rule of law, character of the policymaking process, and nature of civil society). In order to evaluate the effectiveness of governance, he assesses development performance as indicated by real per capita income, life expectancy and school enrolment across countries over time. According to his estimations, the rule of law (a component of political governance) is the most important institutional dimension of governance in terms of its effects on per capita income and school enrolment rates. As for life expectancy, however, the quality of bureaucracy plays a crucial role. The quality of bureaucracy is similar to the regulatory quality variable within the economic dimension of governance. Campos' research is unlike previous studies in the sense that it evaluates the impact of institutional dimensions of governance on non-income dimensions of human development.

Tridico (2005) points out that transition toward new political and economic systems entail high social costs. He suggests that human development, promoted by good governance, is a sufficient condition for economic growth. In order to achieve significant human development, Tridico argues that three conditions, together with GDP growth, are essential: the effective management of social conflicts, reduction of inequality, and provision of economic opportunities. While he emphasizes the importance of governance structure in human development, his work does not examine and estimate quantitatively the effect of governance on human development.

Despite the fact that the above empirical studies analyze the relationship between governance and human development by using different governance indicators, the results all suggest that good governance is essential for human development. Such studies tell us that governance should uphold institutions that assure people's freedom and empowerment, distribute benefits equitably, and foster social cohesion and cooperation.

HUMAN DEVELOPMENT AND GOVERNANCE IN CENTRAL ASIAN TRANSITION COUNTRIES

The following section now presents a descriptive analysis of data sets and the current situation of Central Asian transition countries in terms of human development and governance. Available data covers the period from 1997 to 2004.

Human Development: Descriptive Analysis

Human Development Reports published by the UNDP between 1999 and 2006 are a key source for global human development data. Since the HDR was launched in 1990, each report has provided a Human Development Index as a summary measure of human development for each country. However, because the index involves two-year lags, a complete series of HDI for selected countries is limited to the years 1997 to 2004.[3]

The HDI measures the average achievement of a country in three basic dimensions of human development: (1) living a long and healthy life, as measured by life expectancy at birth; (2) being educated, as measured by a combination of the adult literacy rate and the combined gross enrolment ratio at the primary, secondary and tertiary education levels; and (3) having a decent standard of living, as measured by the Gross Domestic Product (GDP) per capita and purchasing power parity (PPP) in US dollars. The HDI is calculated as a simple average of three dimensional indices. The scale of the HDI is within 0 and 1; a higher score represents a higher level of human development. Those countries more than 0.800, 0.500 to 0.799, and less than 0.500 are considered as high human development, medium human development, and low human development nations, respectively.

Table 1 *HDI and its Components*

	Central Asian transition countries				World				Developing countries			
	HDI	Education Index	Life Expectancy Index	GDP Index	HDI	Education Index	Life Expectancy Index	GDP Index	HDI	Education Index	Life Expectancy Index	GDP Index
1997	0.693	0.880	0.697	0.500	0.706	0.73	0.69	0.69	0.637	0.67	0.66	0.58
1998	0.690	0.860	0.705	0.508	0.712	0.74	0.70	0.70	0.642	0.68	0.66	0.58
1999	0.685	0.840	0.687	0.527	0.716	0.74	0.70	0.71	0.647	0.69	0.66	0.59
2000	0.710	0.890	0.688	0.543	0.722	0.75	0.70	0.72	0.654	0.69	0.66	0.61
2001	0.720	0.905	0.698	0.552	0.722	0.75	0.70	0.72	0.655	0.7	0.66	0.61
2002	0.712	0.917	0.705	0.517	0.729	0.76	0.70	0.73	0.663	0.71	0.66	0.62
2003	0.703	0.922	0.657	0.538	0.750	0.77	0.70	0.75	0.700	0.72	0.67	0.7
2004	0.707	0.920	0.662	0.542	0.741	0.77	0.71	0.75	0.679	0.72	0.67	0.65
Average value	0.703	0.892	0.687	0.528	0.725	0.751	0.700	0.721	0.660	0.698	0.663	0.618
Standard deviation	0.012	0.030	0.019	0.018	0.015	0.015	0.005	0.022	0.021	0.018	0.005	0.041

Source: UNDP, HDR, 1999–2006, Table 1.

In general, Central Asian transition countries are assessed to be at a medium level of human development in comparison to the average value of the HDI (0.703) across countries and over time. The HDI for Central Asian transition nations is lower than the world average of 0.725, but higher than the average value of developing countries by 1.1 times. The average value of the HDI in Central Asian transition countries increased from 0.693 to 0.707 over the eight-year period in question, even though these values were lower than the world average by 0.013 in 1997 and 0.034 percentage points in 2004, respectively (See Table 1).

Figure 2 shows the percentage changes in the HDI of Central Asian transition countries between 1997 and 2004. It can be seen that the country with the highest level of improvement in human development was Mongolia, where the HDI increased by 11.3 percent. On the other hand, Tajikistan and Uzbekistan encountered reverse human development between 1997 and 2004. Tajikistan experienced the greatest decrease in its HDI (3.0 percent) during the eight-year period.

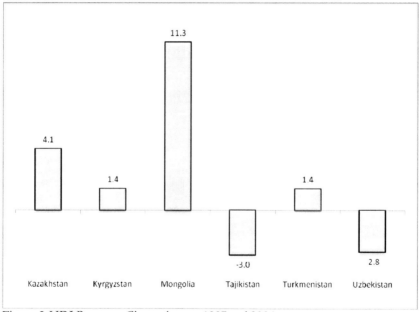

Figure 2 *HDI Percentage Changes between 1997 and 2004*
Source: Author's calculations.

Figure 3 shows the percentage changes in sub-indices of Central Asian transition countries between 1997 and 2004. Table 2 provides a more specific breakdown for each nation and its sub-indices.

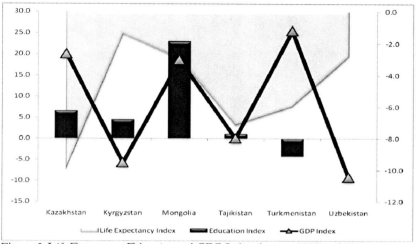

Figure 3 *Life Expectancy, Education and GDP Indices between 1997 and 2004*
Source: Author's calculations.

As mentioned earlier, the HDI is calculated using three sub-indices, which are the life expectancy, education, and GDP per capita PPP indices. By international standards, Central Asian countries achieved many impressive advances in basic human development over much of the twentieth century as access to basic education and healthcare expanded rapidly during the socialist period, particularly from the end of the Second World War to the start of the transition from centrally-planned to market-based economies in the beginning of 1990s. In Table 2 it can be seen that the average value within the education index of Central Asian transition countries over the eight-year period (0.892) is higher than the world average (0.751) and the average of developing countries (0.698). The education index across all countries was 0.880 in 1997. It increased over the years and peaked at 0.922 in 2003. On the other hand, a notable setback in life expectancy became evident during the period. In 1997, the average value of the life expectancy index of Central Asian transition countries (0.697) was almost similar to the world average (0.69). However, in 2004 the average value decreased to 0.662, which was lower than in 1997, while the world average rose slightly to 0.71. This means that life expectancy in Central Asian nations decreased during the period under study. The highest decline was recorded for Kazakhstan, where life expectancy decreased by 4.2 years between 1997 and 2004.

For Kazakhstan, Mongolia, and Turkmenistan, the GDP index improved, implying that the average per capita GDP (PPP) in those countries increased. The highest improvement in the GDP index occurred in Turkmenistan, where per capita GDP (PPP) increased over two times during

Table 2 Sub-Indices of the HDI of Central Asian Transition Countries

	Life expectancy at birth (years)			Education						GDP per capita ($US PPP adjusted)		
				ALR (%)			CGER (%)					
	1997	2004	CH	1997	2004	CH	1997	2004	CH	1997	2004	CH
Kazakhstan	67.6	63.4	-4.2	99	99.5	0.5	76	91	15	3,560	7,440	3,880
Kyrgyz Rep.	67.6	67.1	-0.5	97	98.7	1.7	69	78	9	2,250	1,935	-315
Mongolia	65.8	64.5	-1.3	84	97.8	13.8	55	77	22	1,310	2,056	746
Tajikistan	67.2	63.7	-3.5	98.9	99.5	0.6	69	71	2	1,126	1,102	-24
Turkmenistan	65.4	62.5	-2.9	98	98.8	0.8	90	81	-9	2,109	4,584	2,475
Uzbekistan	67.5	66.6	-0.9	99	99.3	0.3	76	74	-2	2,529	1,869	-660
Average	66.9	64.6	-2.2	96.0	98.9	3.0	72.5	78.7	6.2	2,147.3	3,164.3	1,017.0
Standard dev.	1.0	1.8	0.9	5.9	0.7	-5.3	11.5	6.9	-4.6	882.9	2,406.9	1,524.1
World average	66.7	67.3	0.6	78	78.4	0.4	63	67	4	6,332	8,833	2,501

ALR = Adult literacy rate / CGER = Combined general (primary, secondary and tertiary) enrolment ratio / CH = Change.
Source: Author's calculations.

the eight-year period. However, Kyrgyzstan and Uzbekistan experienced a drop in the GDP index due to a decline in per capita GDP (PPP). The highest decline in the GDP index occurred in Uzbekistan, where the decline in per capita GDP (PPP) was also the highest (Figure 3; Table 2).

As for the education sub-index, the adult literacy rate, a component of the education index, increased for all the countries. However, as indicated in Figure 3 and Table 2, the education sub-index declined in Turkmenistan. As shown in Table 2 the decrease was due to a significant drop in the combined gross enrollment ratio.

Governance: Descriptive Analysis

Many different agencies, both public and private, produce rankings and ratings of countries on some aspect of governance. The most comprehensive and easily accessible indicators for transition countries have been compiled by the EBRD since 1994, by the Heritage Foundation (HF) since 1995, by the World Bank since 1996, by Freedom House since 1997, and by the Polity IV Project since 1997.

The Heritage Foundation in collaboration with the *Wall Street Journal* provides an overall index of economic freedom as well as sub-indices based on evaluations provided annually by outside experts using ten specific indicators. The indicators are business freedom, trade freedom, monetary freedom, fiscal freedom, property rights, investment freedom, financial freedom, freedom from corruption, labor freedom, and freedom from government. Indices are scaled from 0 to 100, where 100 represent the maximum degree of freedom. Included in the analysis in this chapter are data from 1997 to 2004. Sub-indices rather than the overall index are used to assess governance dimensions.

As mentioned earlier, governance for human development should generate basic conditions that expand people's choices and opportunities. Thus, the components of governance should be interpreted through indicators that can engender these conditions. Accordingly, the indices of business freedom, trade freedom, monetary freedom, investment freedom, fiscal freedom, and financial freedom and freedom from government can be considered as representative components of economic governance.

I use the index of freedom from corruption to assess political governance. Corruption is defined as a failure in the integrity of the system. Political corruption in particular is considered to be most harmful to a country's development and its democracy and to the people's wellbeing, since it influences the formulation or content of laws, regulations, and policies. High-level corruption destroys individuals' ability to participate in decision making processes that significantly affect their lives.

Finally, the index of property rights is used to assess civic governance. The ability to accumulate private property can be considered one of the most important and basic human rights. The index of labor freedom is not used herein because it is a new indicator developed in 2007 and has been available only since 2005.

Since 1972, Freedom House has published *Freedom in the World*, which contains an annual comparative assessment of the state of freedom as experienced by individuals in 192 countries and 14 disputed or related territories. Freedom is assessed in two broad categories: political rights and civil liberties. Political rights enable people to participate freely in the political process, by voting freely in legitimate elections, competing for public office, joining political parties and organizations, and electing representatives who have a decisive impact on public policies and are accountable to the electorate. Civil liberties allow for freedom of expression, associational and organizational rights, the rule of law, and personal autonomy without interference from the state. The categories of political rights and civil liberties contain numerical ratings between 1 and 7, with 1 representing the highest and 7 the lowest level of freedom. I converted this data into a scale of 0 to 100. While the data for former socialist countries starts from 1991, along with the availability of other data sets the available data for this study covers the years 1997 to 2004. These two indicators are used to assess civic governance.

The next source for governance indicators used herein is from the Polity IV Project. This data contains coded regime and authority characteristics for all independent territories with total populations greater than 500,000. Although the data has been provided since 1800, full series for transition countries are only available for the years 1997 to 2004. From the indicators developed under the project, the Polity score will be used and analyzed in this chapter. The Polity indicator represents the political regime of a country, with the scale ranging from +10 to -10, where the highest value indicates a strongly democratic system and the lowest value indicates a strongly autocratic regime. The Polity variable is converted into a scale of 0 to 100 in which 100 represents a fully democratic regime. Since basic human rights are promoted under democratic governments, or in other words democracy can be a guarantee for basic human rights, the Polity variable is used to assess civic governance.

The fourth governance indicator source used herein is the EBRD's transition reports. This source has provided 14 structural and institutional reform indices for 26 transition countries since 1989. However, as mentioned previously, due to limitations in data availability only the data over the period 1997 and 2004 will be used in the present analysis. The scores are scaled between 1 and 4, with "+" and "-" (e.g., 4+). The "+" and "-" ratings are treated by adding 0.33 and subtracting 0.33

from the full values. From the indicators provided by EBRD, eight indicators were selected in order to express the macroeconomic reforms in a country. The eight indicators are classified into three categories: privatization, liberalization, and structural reforms. Privatization is a simple average of small scale privatization and large scale privatization. Liberalization is an average of price liberalization, the trade and foreign exchange system, and banking reform and interest rate liberalization indicators. Structural Reform contains the indicators of enterprise restructuring, competition policy, and overall infrastructure reform. Finally, the reform indicator is computed as a simple average of these three categories. This methodology was used in Beck and Laeven (2005) and Davron (2005). The variable is also rescaled into a range of 0 to 100, where the highest value represents the best performance regarding macroeconomic reform.

Besides developing the concept of governance, the World Bank has succeeded in measuring it. Six dimensions of governance – voice and accountability, political stability, government effectiveness, control of corruption, regulatory quality, and the rule of law – have been developed and widely used in empirical studies. Voice and accountability involves government's preparedness to be externally accountable through citizen feedback, democratic institutions, and a competitive press, thus including elements of restraint on the sovereign. Political stability measures the lack of violence, crime, and terrorism. Government effectiveness includes the quality of policymaking, bureaucracy, public service delivery, and the degree of its independence from political pressure. Rule of law is an assessment of protection of property rights as well as judiciary independence, and thus includes the elements of law and order. Control of corruption is a measure of which public power is exercised for private gain, including both petty and grand forms of corruption. These five measures are used to assess political governance. The last dimension, regulatory quality, is used to evaluate economic governance in as much as it represents the enforcement of rules and regulations that promote private sector development. Kaufman, Kraay, and Mastruzzi (2005) report the aggregate indicators of the six dimensions of governance between 1996 and 2005 for 213 countries. The indicators are measured in units ranging from about -2.5 to 2.5, with higher values corresponding to better governance outcomes. All indicators were converted in the present chapter into a scale of 0 to 100, in which a higher score represents better performance.

Just as governance itself is a broad concept, the indicators purporting to measure it are also varied. Developing such quantitative indicators has become a veritable growth industry (Malik, 2002, p. 3). Though no single index can represent the diverse indicators that have been created, there are some useful aggregations with regard to governance indicators. In order to develop aggregate indicators, researchers and scholars arrange individual indicators into clusters, and then produce aggregate indicators using different methods. As there has been remarkable growth in the governance indicators available relative to transition countries, a total of 19 indicators were examined to measure the quality of governance. All 19 indicators were segregated into three dimensions of governance as explained above. Hence, the economic dimension of governance encompasses nine variables: Business Freedom, Trade Freedom, Monetary Freedom, Investment Freedom, Fiscal Freedom, Regulatory Quality, Financial Freedom, Reform, and Freedom from Government. The political dimension of governance comprises six variables: Freedom from Corruption, Voice and Accountability, Political Stability, Government Effectiveness, Rule of Law, and Control of Corruption. The civic dimension of governance involves four variables: Political Rights, Civil Liberties, Property Rights, and Polity Type.

Through a simple average of variables subsumed under the economic dimension of governance and a subsequent division by 100, which is the highest potential value, the Economic Governance Index (EGI) is defined.[4] A similar calculation results in the Political Governance Index (PGI) and Civic Governance Index (CGI), using other respective components. There exists a strong correlation among the EGI, the PGI and the CGI (See Table 3).

Table 3 *Correlations between Governance Indices across Countries*

	EGI	PGI	CGI
EGI	1		
PGI	0.8013		
CGI	0.7865	0.9252	

Source: Author's calculations.

Therefore, I decided to construct an overall governance index (OGI) using these three dimension indices. For this OGI, the three dimension indices are simply averaged to obtain the following composite governance index:

$$OGI = \frac{1}{3} \cdot EGI + \frac{1}{3} \cdot PGI + \frac{1}{3} \cdot CGI$$

Tables 4 and 5 present average governance indices across countries and over time, respectively.

It can be seen that Central Asian transition countries have a lower ranking of governance in comparison to the average OGI, which is 36.54 out of a possible 100. Among dimension indices, the average value of the economic governance index is the highest with a lowest standard deviation of 10.27. The EGI varies from 35.51 in Uzbekistan to 59.11 in Mongolia. There is no significant divergence among countries.

Table 4 *Average Governance Indices*

	EGI	PGI	CGI	OGI
Kazakhstan	54.40	32.25	26.56	37.74
Kyrgyzstan	56.74	34.89	32.91	41.52
Mongolia	59.11	52.87	76.04	62.67
Tajikistan	43.86	19.99	25.84	29.90
Turkmenistan	37.34	22.82	8.75	22.97
Uzbekistan	35.51	24.96	12.93	24.47
Mean	47.83	31.30	30.51	36.54
Standard deviation	10.27	11.99	24.08	14.72

Source: Author's calculations.

Table 5 *Average Governance Indices over Time*

	EGI	PGI	CGI	OGI
1997	42.53	31.23	29.86	34.54
1998	43.81	32.09	32.09	35.99
1999	45.54	32.09	30.70	36.11
2000	48.53	32.03	30.70	37.08
2001	49.30	32.03	30.00	37.11
2002	49.63	30.96	30.97	37.19
2003	51.37	30.51	29.17	37.02
2004	51.89	29.45	30.55	37.30

Source: Author's calculations.

On the other hand, the civic dimension of governance is less developed in these countries at 30.51, with a standard deviation of 24.08. Amongst all the countries, Mongolia's scores on governance dimension indices are the highest, particularly for the civic governance index. The CGI varies between 8.75 in Turkmenistan to 76.04 in Mongolia. The average value of the CGI for Mongolia is 2.3 to 8.7 times greater than that of other countries. In accordance with ratings from the Polity IV Project, Mongolia is a country with a strongly democratic system (10, when the rating is scaled from -10 to 10, where the highest value indicates a strongly democratic government and the lowest value represents a strongly autocratic regime) that respects human rights (scores of political rights and civil liberties are 2 and 3 respectively, when the range is between 1 and 7, where the highest score represents the lowest amount of freedom). In contrast, Turkmenistan's CGI score is the worst of the countries in question. According to its scores of political rights (7) and civil liberties (7), which are two components of CGI from Freedom House, Turkmenistan is a country where political rights are absent or virtually nonexistent as a result of the extremely oppressive nature of the regime, and the nation also has virtually no civil freedom. Moreover, this country has an autocratic political regime, according to ratings from the Polity IV Project (-9); in addition, the score on property rights from the Heritage Foundation is relatively low (30, or the lowest score in the region, when the range is between 0 and 100).

Governance for Human Development

Promoting and consolidating good governance so that it efficiently supports human development is of great value to countries in transition. While all Central Asian transition countries face difficulties in developing good governance that respects human dignity and freedom, the process, speed and success rates have varied greatly across countries. In the next section, I will explore the relationship between governance and human development. Table 6 shows the correlation between governance dimension indices and the human development index among countries.

Table 6 *Correlation between Governance Dimension Indices and HDI*

	Human Dev't Index	Education Index	Life Expectancy Index	GDP Index
EGI	0.706	0.811	-0.625	0.774
PGI	-0.203	-0.699	0.695	-0.128
CGI	-0.291	-0.475	0.570	-0.364
OGI	0.703	0.608	-0.353	0.790

Source: Author's calculations.

From the table it can be seen that governance is positively related to human development in Central Asian transition countries in which the correlation between the OGI and the HDI is 0.703. However, correlations between sub-indices of the HDI and the OGI diverge greatly. Consistent with the concept that is developed above, governance is positively related to the GDP index. Economic governance has strong correlations with the education index (EI) and GDP index (GDPI), but a negative relationship with the Life Expectancy Index (LEI). On the other hand, political and civic governance in Central Asian transition countries positively correlates with the LEI. This result is due to a significant decline in life expectancy during the period in question while governance dimension indices have improved over time. Though political and civic governance are negatively correlated with the EI and GDPI, the correlation coefficients are weak.

The panel data estimation method was used to explore the relationship between governance and human development in Central Asian transition countries. A summary of estimation results is presented in Table 7.

Table 7 *Panel Data Estimation Results*

		Dependent variables		
		Education Index	Life Expectancy Index	GDP Index
Explanatory variables	Constant	1.64 (8.99)	0.863 (12.9)	-0.08 (-0.49)
	EGI	-0.006 (-2.56)	-0.003 (-2.36)	0.003 (1.76)*
	PGI		-0.003 (-2.28)	0.003 (1.72)*
	CGI		0.002 (1.83)*	
	Urbanization	-1.01 (-2.42)		0.811 (2.25)
R^2		0.764	0.817	0.939
AIC		-3.658	-5.022	-4.038

Note: *Indicates significance level is 10 percent.
Source: Author's estimations.

The results indicate that economic governance has negatively and significantly impacted on education in Central Asian transition countries. This result might be a product of improved economic governance in the sense that greater economic opportunities may act as a deterrent for individuals to acquire additional education. It also can be seen that economic and political governance have negatively affected the life expectancy index while civic governance is positively associated with it, with a 10 percent significance. These results may be related to the fragile development of political governance in Central Asian countries. On the other hand, it can be concluded that building the economic and political governance vital for transitioning to a market economy has had costs for non-income related dimensions of human development.

As for the GDP index, estimation results indicate that there are positive relationships between the GDP index and economic and political governance dimensions. These findings are in line with the results of previous studies suggesting that there exists a positive relationship between economic performance and governance quality. While several indicators such as contemporary inflation, growth rate and urbanization are included in the estimations as control variables, only the urbanization rate has a significant impact. No significant relationship between the income dimension of human development and civic governance was found.

CONCLUDING REMARKS

It is generally agreed that governance is positively related to development performance. However, the relationship between governance and human development has been largely neglected in the literature, particularly in the case of Central Asian transition countries. The objective of this chapter was to examine the relationship between governance and human development in these nations. For this purpose, I used the concept of humane governance to construct aggregate governance indexes. All 19 governance indicators available for the countries discussed were clustered into three aggregate dimension indices – the economic, political, and civic indices. The effects of governance on human development and on its dimensions were then analyzed.

Most Central Asian transition countries are governed by political regimes that restrict basic human rights. The main factors damaging political and civil freedoms in these countries are civil war, heavy military involvement in politics, unfair elections, and one-party dominance (Freedom House, 2006b). From this, it can be concluded that countries can make notable improvements with civic governance in relation to human development only after they establish democratic systems that respect people's freedoms and fundamental human rights.

Consistent with this theory, governance positively relates to human development in Central Asian transition countries, particularly to the GDP index, implying that growth and governance have a positive relationship. However, correlations between the political and civic dimensions of governance and human development are weak. During the transition period, establishing democratic institutions that respect the human rights essential for human development is a difficult and fragile process. Moreover, a negative relationship between economic governance and education was found. An improvement in economic governance that provides people with more opportunities and choices to engage in economic activities may result in people pursuing such opportunities at the expense of education. Building the economic and political governance that is vital for transitioning to a market economy has impacted negatively on the education and life expectancy indices, both of which are non-income dimensions of human development. In contrast, the economic and political dimensions of governance have positively influenced the income dimension of human development. No significant relationship between the income dimension of human development and civic governance was found.

Since this is the first attempt to calculate governance for human development in Central Asian transition countries in terms of three dimensions of governance, the findings presented should be viewed as somewhat tentative in nature. The present research is limited in scope due to a lack of complete time-series data; indicators related to private finance and provision of education and healthcare, development of social cohesion, the role of NGOs, international aid for human development and so on that have crucial effects on human development have not been included in the analysis. Moreover, with an eight-year sample, the analysis was not able to capture the long-term effects of governance.

Most studies analyzing the relationship between human development and governance use individual indicators of governance, such as those related to corruption, economic freedom, the rule of law, the accountability of the executive, and so on. This study attempted to construct aggregate indicators of governance. However, further refinement of the concepts used to assess governance is necessary. The three dimension indexes covered in this study should also be tested by other researchers to provide an independent assessment of their validity and applicability.

Notes

1   Central Asian transition countries include Kazakhstan, Kyrgyzstan, Tajikistan, Turkmenistan, Uzbekistan, and Mongolia.
2   In the global HDR 2002, democratic governance means the following:
    · People's human rights and freedoms are respected.
    · People have a say in decisions that affect their lives.
    · People can hold decision makers accountable.
    · Inclusive and fair rules, institutions and practices govern social interactions.
    · Women are equal partners with men in the private and public spheres.
    · People do not encounter discrimination based on race, ethnicity, class, or gender.
    · The needs of future generations are reflected in current policies.
    · Economic and social policies are responsive to people's needs and aspirations.
    · Economic and social policies aim at eradicating poverty and expanding life choices (UNDP, 2002, p. 51).
3   While the HDR publishes the HDI with a two-year lag, the HDR of 1998 provides the HDI for 1995.
4   This method was used to calculate dimensions of the Humane Governance Index (Mahbub ul Haq Human Development Center, 1999, p. 157).

References

Ahrens, J., & Meurers, M. (2000, June). *Institutions, governance, and economic performance in post-socialist countries: A conceptual and empirical approach.* Paper presented at the annual conference "Institutions in Transition" at Portorož, Slovenia.

Annan, K. A. (1998). Cooperating for development: Supporting good governance. Chap. 2 in *Partnerships for global community: Annual report on the work of the organization*. Retrieved November 15, 2007, from http://www.un.org/Docs/SG/Report98/con98.htm

Beck, T., & Laeven, L. (2005, April). *Institution building and growth in transition economies*. (Policy research working paper 365). Washington, DC: World Bank.

Brunetti, A., Kisunko, G., & Weder, B. (1997, August). *Institutions in transition: Reliability of rules and economic performance in former socialist countries*. (Policy research working paper 1809). Washington, DC: World Bank.

Campos, N. F. (1999, October). *Context is everything: Measuring institutional change in transition economies*. (Policy research working paper 2269). Washington, DC: World Bank.

Dabrowski, M., & Gortat, R. (2002). *Political and economic institutions, growth and poverty: Experience of transition countries*. (Background paper for HDR 2002). New York: UNDP.

De Melo, M., Denizer, C., & Gelb, A. (1996). Patterns of transition from plan to market. *World Bank Economic Review*, 10, 397-424.

De Melo, M., Denizer, C., Gelb, A., & Tenev, S. (2001). Circumstances and choice: The Role of initial conditions and policies in transition economies. *The World Bank Economic Review*, 15, 1-31.

EBRD. (2006). Economic statistics and forecasts. *Transition Report*. Retrieved December 1, 2007, from http://www.ebrd.org/country/sector/econo/stats/index.htm

Freedom House. (2006a). *Nations in transit*. Retrieved July 23, 2007, from http://freedomhouse.org/ template.cfm?page=17&year=2006

Freedom House. (2006b). *Freedom in the world*. Retrieved June 15, 2007, from http://freedomhouse.org/template.cfm? page=363&year=2006

Grubel, H. (1998). Economic freedom and human welfare: Some empirical findings. *Cato Journal, 18*(2), 287-304.

Heritage Foundation. (2006). *2006 Index of Economic Freedom*. Retrieved May 15, 2007, from http://www.heritage.org/research/features/index/

Heritage Foundation. (2007). *2007 Index of Economic Freedom*. Retrieved June 10, 2007, from http://www.heritage.org/research/features/index/

Huther, J., & Shah. A. (2003). A simple measure of good governance. In A. Shah (Ed.), *Measuring government performance in the delivery of public services* (pp. 1-30). Washington, DC: World Bank.

Kaufman, D., Kraay, A., & Mastruzzi, M. (2006). *Governance matters V: Aggregate and individual governance indicators for 1996-2005*. Retrieved April 12, 2007, from http://ssrn.com/abstract= 929549

Kaufman, D., Kraay, A., & Zoido-Lobaton, P. (1999). *Aggregating governance indicators and governance matters*. (Policy research working paper 2195). Washington, DC: World Bank.

Malik, A. (2002). *State of the art in governance indicators. A background paper for HDR 2002*. New York: UNDP.

Mahbub ul Haq Human Development Center. (1999). *Human development in South Asia 1999: The crisis of governance*. Oxford: Oxford University Press.

Marshall, M. G., & Jaggers, K. (2005). *Polity IV Project: Dataset users' manual*. Arlington, VA: George Mason University, Center for Global Policy.

North, D. (1997). *The contribution of the new institutional economics to the understanding of the transition problem. WIDER (World Institute for Development Economics Research) Annual Lectures 1*, Helsinki: UNU (United Nations University)/WIDER.

SADC (South African Development Community) & UNDP. (1998). *SADC regional human development 1998*. Belgravia: SAPES Books.

Tridico, P. (2005, November). *Institutional change and human development in transition economies*. Paper presented at the European Association for Evolutionary Political Economy (EAEPE) conference in Bremen, Germany.

United Nations. (2006). Governance, institutions and growth divergence. In *World economic and social survey 2006* (pp. 125-147). New York: UN, Department of Economic and Social Affairs.

UNDP. (1996). *Human development report: Economic growth and human development.* New York: Oxford University Press.

UNDP. (1997a). *Human development report: Human development to eradicate poverty.* New York: Oxford University Press.

UNDP. (1997b). *Governance for sustainable human development. A UNDP policy document.* Retrieved March, 23, 2007, from http://mirror.undp.org/magnet/policy/default.htm

UNDP. (1997c). *Reconceptualizing governance.* (Discussion Paper 2). New York: Management Development and Governance Division of UNDP.

UNDP. (1999). *Human development report: Globalization with a human face.* New York: Oxford University Press.

UNDP. (2000). *Human development report: Human rights and human development.* New York: Oxford University Press.

UNDP. (2002). *Human development report: Deepening democracy in a fragmented world.* New York: Oxford University Press.

UNDP. (2003). *Human development report: Millennium development goals: A compact among nations to end poverty.* New York: Oxford University Press.

UNDP. (2004). *Human development report: Cultural liberty in today's diverse world.* New York: Oxford University Press.

UNDP. (2005a). *Human development report: International cooperation at a crossroads: Aid, trade, and security in an unequal world.* New York: Oxford University Press.

UNDP. (2005b). *Central Asia human development report: Bringing down barriers: Regional cooperation for human development and human security.* Bratislava: UNDP.

UNDP. (2006). *Human development report: Beyond scarcity: Power, poverty and the global water crisis.* New York: Oxford University Press.

World Bank. (1992). *Governance and development.* Washington, DC: World Bank.

• CHAPTER THREE •

The Role of Social Capital in Microfinance: Evidence from Rural Java, Indonesia

AGUS EKO NUGROHO
Curtin University of Technology

The United Nations declared 2005 as the International Year of Microcredit, suggesting that improvement in the area of global access to microfinance can lead to the achievement of the Millennium Development Goals (MDGs) by 2015. Further support for employing microfinance strategies to alleviate poverty was provided by Dr. Muhammad Yunus, the founder of the Grameen Bank, who received the Nobel Peace Prize for his work on microfinance in 2006 (Hermes & Lensink, 2007). Meanwhile, economists over the past decade have examined the extent to which social capital affects group lending performance, such as in the case of the Grameen Bank model. Social capital is seen as enhancing loan repayment rates of group lending through generating social collateral, peer monitoring and informal sanctions (e.g., Armendariz de Aghion & Gollier, 2000; Ghatak & Guinnane, 1999; Karlan 2004, 2005; Wydick, 2001). The blueprint for the functioning of social capital in group lending stems from rotating saving and credit associations (ROSCAs) and moneylenders. These informal micro-finance institutions (MFIs) can minimize loan defaults by linking loans with the social networks of poor borrowers (Besley, Coate, & Loury, 1993; Hoff & Stiglitz, 1997; Stiglitz 1990, 1993; Zeller 2003). Representing grassroots institutions, ROSCAs and moneylenders utilize informal approaches to serve the poor. Mutual trust also underpins the performance of these MFIs, through reducing the uncertainty of lending to poor borrowers (Bebbington & Gomez, 2006). However, how social capital may enhance access of the poor to microfinance has not been deeply explored by many scholars. Hence, this chapter's aim is to examine the extent to which social networks and trust can enable poor people to utilize microfinance. The chapter also scrutinizes the relationship between social capital and the financial performance of MFIs.

Research data used in the study were obtained through questionnaire-based interviews conducted with respondents in rural areas of the Boyolali District in the Central Java province of Indonesia. The interviews were undertaken from June to December in 2006. A total of 231 people were surveyed, with respondents falling into the following categories: the very poor, the poor, the moderately poor and the non-poor.

The chapter is organized as follows. Section one begins by reviewing past research on how social networks and mutual trust can improve access of the poor to microfinance. Section two then analyzes the socioeconomic determinants of borrowing among the poor, emphasizing the way social networks affect poor people's demand for commercial and non-commercial loans. Section three investigates how social networks can reduce the likelihood of the poor facing credit rationing from formal MFIs, while section four examines the impact of social capital on loan repayment rates involving MFIs. Conclusions are then offered in section five.

TRUST, NETWORKS, AND ACCESS TO FINANCE

The central issue of credit contracts is trust between lender and borrower. Trust depends upon two factors: information and sanctions (Edgcomb & Barton 1998; Guinnane 2005). Lenders will trust borrowers for credits, if they can gather information about their creditworthiness and impose sanctions on defaulters. Here, collateral can provide information on the repayment capacities of borrowers (Edgcomb & Barton, 1998). It can also reinforce sanctions, as lenders will seize the collateral of loan defaulters (Guinnane, 2005). This conception of trust in credit is individualistic in scope and indicates the failure of banks to serve poor people. Banks distrust poor borrowers because they lack information on their creditworthiness and believe they cannot enforce sanctions due to the absence of collateral.

However, trust as a social behavior often goes beyond individualistic motives. Bebbington and Gomez (2006) define trust using the Mexican term *"confianza,"* referring not only to the notion of trust but also kindness, generosity, and personal interest as perceived among group members (p. 116). According to Fukuyama (1999), norms of tolerance and reciprocity provide the basis for social trust to exist. Uslaner (2002) puts forward the notion that societal-based trust is the core element of civic engagement and sociality. Unfortunately, however, economists often pay little attention to the concept of social trust. Indicative of this outlook, Guinnane (2005) argues that "trust is not an interesting concept in situations where a person I trust views my welfare as important to her own.

[Hence], treating her well cannot be distinguished from treating myself well" (p. 4). The author assumes that the utility (satisfaction) of borrowers should not be correlated with the utility of lenders. In economic theory this assumption is known as the independent utility function. Yet this assumption is not always relevant, as social trust underpins loan contracts among relatives, neighbors and friends. Socially close lenders do not maximize individual self-interest (e.g., profit), as loans carry no interest charged. In contrast, they seek to fulfill norms of reciprocity and solidarity. For instance, people provide loans to relatives because they expect to receive similar loans in the future (La Ferrara, 2003, p. 2). They consider norms of solidarity and engage in mutual insurance against financial difficulties (Dercon 2002; Reinke 1998). Borrowers are unlikely to violate loan contracts secured in this manner, as they are aware that social sanctions can have severe repercussions for them.

Table 1 presents cross-tabulation analyses between lending and borrowing among relatives, neighbors and friends. It shows that 20.34 percent of respondents who borrow money from relatives also often provide loans to them. This figure is greater than the number of borrowing respondents never providing loans to their relatives, who accounted for 11.26 percent of respondents. Turning to the second row of Table 1, the 23.81 percent of respondents who often (11.26 percent) and very often (12.55 percent) lend money to neighbors and friends also borrow money from them. Another 20.78 percent irregularly provide loans to their neighbors and friends. In contrast, the percentage of respondents who borrow money from neighbors and friends but never provide loans to them is 5.63 percent. As such loans are collateral and interest free, societal trust and reciprocity clearly underpin loan contracts among relatives, neighbors and friends.

Table 1 *Borrowing and Lending of Relatives, Neighbors and Friends in the Boyolali District*

Borrowing from relatives	Lending to relatives				
	Never	Not so Often	Often	Very often	Total percentage
No	3.03	12.55	4.33	1.30	21.21
Yes	11.26	38.10	20.34	9.09	78.79
Borrowing from neighbors and friends	Lending to neighbors and friends				
	Never	Not so often	Often	Very often	Total percentage
No	6.49	29.44	6.06	7.79	49.78
Yes	5.63	20.78	11.26	12.55	50.22

Source: Author's field survey research, 2006.

Willingness to Repay and Provide Loans to Others

Loans from socially close lenders are said to have low rates of default. La

Ferrara (2003) calculates the default rate of kinship loans in rural Ghana, finding they amount to 6 percent. For the present study, respondents were asked how often they make in-time repayments of loans from relatives, neighbors and friends. Respondents were allowed to select from four possible answers: (1) never, (2) not so often, (3) often, and (4) very often. The survey found that the majority of respondents (55.8 percent) often make in-time repayments of loans to people in their social networks. In contrast, only 5.6 percent of respondents never meet in-time repayments of such loans. The survey also asked to what extent poor people were willing to make in-time repayments of loans to socially close lenders. It was found that respondents make in-time repayments of such loans to avoid feeling disgraced as defaulters. They also seek to avoid financial exclusion. This indicates that poor borrowers recognize the negative effects of social sanctions on loan defaulters. For instance, social sanctions can lead to financial exclusion as unpaid lenders can inform others of defaulters' actions, harming their reputations. Defaulters seldom avoid such punishments by migrating to other regions. Permanent migration is not likely to occur because poor people are closely attached to their farmland, relatives and community. Low levels of education and skills also inhibit poor people from permanently migrating to the city.

Chi-square and correlation analyses can be used to investigate whether willingness to make in-time repayments of loans from relatives, neighbors, and friends varies with respect to the specific characteristics of borrowers. On this issue, income, gender, occupation, levels of education, and age of borrowers may be considered. If societal trust and reciprocity are examined, the willingness to repay such loans should not be affected by the specific characteristics of borrowers. Correlation analysis can recognize the degree of interaction between the specific characteristics of borrowers and their willingness to make in-time repayments of loans to socially close lenders. Here, I propose the *null* hypothesis (Ho) that the willingness to make in-time repayments of loans to relatives, neighbors and friends is not affected by certain specific characteristics of borrowers. The *alternative* hypothesis (Ha) is that the willingness to make in-time repayments of such loans is affected by certain specific characteristics of borrowers. If we can reject the null hypothesis and accept the alternative hypothesis, the relationship between the variables considered holds for the entire population.

Table 2 (column 1) presents the result of chi-square and correlation analyses between specific characteristics of borrowers and the willingness to make in-time repayments of loans to relatives, neighbors and friends. Regarding the probability value (p-value) of chi-square coefficients (χ^2), it shows that the variables of gender, age and occupation result in p-values greater than 0.05. This means that we cannot reject the *null* hypothesis

Table 2 Chi-square and Correlation Analyses on in the Boyolali District

Variable	Willingness to make in-time repayment to socially close lenders (1)		Willingness to provide loans to neighbors and friends (2)	
	χ^2	[p-value]	χ^2	[p-value]
1. Income	54.17	[0.00]	62.56	[0.00]
(r)	(0.27)	[0.00]	(0.24)	[0.00]
2. Gender	4.77	[0.19]	4.16	[0.24]
(r)	(-0.14)	[0.03]	(-0.06)	[0.41]
3. Occupation	6.12	[0.74]	22.44	[0.01]
(r)	(-0.09)	[0.15]	(-0.07)	[0.32]
4. Education	25.49	[0.01]	23.47	[0.02]
(r)	(0.15)	[0.02]	(-0.001)	[0.98]
5. Age	17.17	[0.31]	21.19	[0.38]
(r)	(-0.34)	[0.61]	(0.03)	[0.66]

Note: (r) is the coefficient of correlation.
Source: Author's field survey research, 2006.

(Ho). Hence, the willingness to make in-time repayments of loans to relatives, neighbors and friends is not significantly affected by the gender status, age and occupation of borrowers. The willingness to make in-time repayment of loans is not associated with the gender status of borrowers probably because a greater participation of women in wage laborer increases their capability to repay loans. In contrast, the chi-square tests for the variables of income and education levels of borrowers result in the p-value being smaller than 0.05. This means that the *null* hypothesis (Ho) can be rejected, in that the willingness to make in-time repayments of loans to socially close lenders is affected by the income and education levels of borrowers. However, the correlation test does not indicate a strong relationship between income and in-time repayments of loans to relatives, neighbors and friends. The computation results in the correlation coefficient of 0.27. The coefficient of correlation between the level of education and in-time repayments of such loans is 0.15. This indicates that higher levels of income and education significantly are not the major reasons for the willingness of borrowers to make in-time repayments of loans to relatives, neighbors and friends. This supports the hypothesis that the willingness to make in-time repayment of loans to socially close lenders is more likely associated with the norms of social trust and reciprocity than with any specific characteristics of borrowers.

Table 2 (column 2) presents the chi-square and correlation analyses between the gender, income, occupation, education and age of respondents and their willingness to provide loans to neighbors and friends. The chi-square tests for the variables of gender status and age of lenders result in p-values greater than 0.05. This indicates that the willingness to provide loans to neighbors and friends is not affected by the gender and age of the lenders. In contrast, the chi-square tests for the variables of income, occupation and education compute the p-values as being smaller than 0.05. This leads to a rejection of the *null* hypothesis (Ho) and acceptance of the alternative hypothesis that willingness to provide loans to neighbors and friends is affected by different levels of income and education as well as the occupation of lenders. However, the correlation coefficients of these variables are statistically insignificant at 5 percent. A notable exception is the variable of income. The correlation coefficient of 0.24 implies that income level significantly is not a major determinant of willingness to provide loans to neighbors and friends. As will be discussed more below, people in the survey area are willing to provide loans to relatives, neighbors and friends because they generally consider societal trust and reciprocity as important, rather than being influenced by individual characteristics such as gender, education, occupation, and age. Gender does not statistically affect such lending behavior probably because the patriarchal nature of the Javanese family has deteriorated in the survey area. As the husband is no longer the sole wage earner, the wife has a greater capacity to influence family decisions to provide loans to others. Such lending behavior is also not correlated with levels of education because the majority of respondents in the survey area have low levels of education. Higher incomes only slightly affect the willingness of people to provide loans to relatives, neighbors and friends.

Social Networks and Access of Poor People to Microfinance

Poor people undertake various strategies to cope with a lack of financial capital. In response to financial exclusion from banks, the poor establish informal arrangements, such as ROSCAs. Dercon (2002) observes that these financial arrangements often perform well within extended families, neighbors, and local business networks (e.g., farmer associations). Hence, maintaining relationships with relatives, neighbors and others is vital for the poor to participate in such arrangements. It also facilitates information gathering on banking procedures through communication and interaction with others. Table 3 presents a cross-tabulation analysis between frequent visits to relatives and gaining assistance from relatives to access loans from formal MFIs (e.g., microbanks). It shows that 28 percent of respondents who frequently visit relatives gain help from them to obtain formal loans. This figure is greater than respondents who never obtain assistance from relatives to access formal loans (19 percent). This implies that poor people who consistently maintain kinship relationships are more likely to obtain formal loans. According to respondents, relatives play facilitative roles in obtaining bank loans. Such roles include relatives acting as loan co-signers or witnesses, intermediaries with banking officers and providers of assistance for document preparation. Acting as loan co-signers and witnesses, relatives provide social collateral, which serves as a substitute for the poor's lack of physical collateral.

Table 3 *Percentage of Respondents by Visits to Relatives and the Obtaining of Help from Relatives to Access Formal Loans, Boyolali District*

Frequent visits to relatives	Relatives do not help to obtain loans	Relatives help to obtain loans
1. Never	0.87	0.43
2. Not-so often	11.26	7.36
3. Often	19.05	28.14
4. Very often	15.15	17.75
Total percentage	46.32	54.78

Source: Author's field research survey, 2006.

However, the capacity of individuals to utilize familial social capital diverges across social classes (O'Hara, 2007). In the survey, lower income groups were less likely to obtain help from relatives to access formal loans. For instance, the majority of respondents with monthly incomes less than Rp 500,000 (US$52.60) state that they never obtain help from relatives to access formal loans (e.g., microbank loans). On the other hand, respondents with income levels above Rp 1,500,000 (US$157.90) frequently obtain assistance from relatives to acquire formal loans. This implies that respondents with higher incomes are more likely to obtain help from relatives to access loans from formal MFIs. This also suggests that non-poor people gain more advantages from close relationships with relatives than poor people. Higher levels of education and better communication skills enable non-poor people to extract more benefits from interactions with their relatives. Conversely, poor people fail to maximize the benefits associated with kinship relationships, due to the lower quality of human capital, communication constraints and so on.

Being involved in social and business associations, individuals can enhance their networks to gain economic benefits from social interaction and communication (Collier, 2002; Streeten, 2002). By participating in borrowing associations, for example, poor people can develop networks to access formal credit (Rankin, 2006). Figure 1 presents perceptions of respondents on the benefits of membership in social and business associations. The majority of respondents recognize that social and business associations facilitate access to formal MFIs. In this regard, social and business networks enhance access to loans from formal MFIs in two ways. First, they enhance access through community leaders who play a facilitative role in accessing bank loans. These leaders are capable of linking social and business associations with banks. Banks recognize the role of community leaders to enforce loan repayments on the part of poor borrowers. Bank Rakyat Indonesia (BRI) microbanks known as BRI-units, for instance, utilize community leaders to encourage loan repayments among borrowers in Indonesia. Second, as members of social and business associations, poor people can develop networks and reputations through communication and interactions with others. This can enhance access to bank loans, as the poor can gather information and knowledge of banking procedures from their business associates. However, respondents with higher income levels tend to possess greater advantages when involved in social and business associations. For instance, the survey found that 44.4 percent of respondents with monthly incomes less than Rp 500,000 state that memberships in social and business associations do not help them access formal loans. In contrast, 75 percent of respondents with monthly incomes in the range of Rp 500,000 to Rp 749,900 gain benefits from being involved in

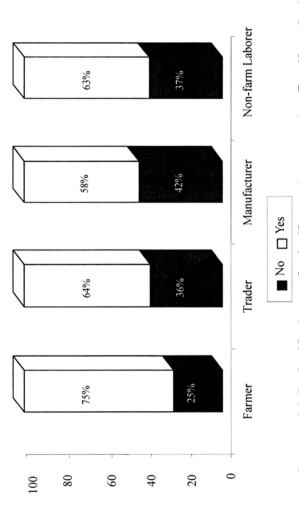

Figure 1 *Perceptions of the Benefits of Involvement in Social and Business Associations to Access Formal Loans, Boyolali District*
Source: Author's field survey, 2006.

such associations and can access formal loans. Similarly, the majority of respondents with monthly incomes above Rp 1,500,000 state that memberships in social and business associations do not help them access formal loans.

In contrast, 75 percent of respondents with monthly incomes in the range of Rp 500,000 to Rp 749,900 gain benefits from being involved in such associations and can access formal loans. Similarly, the majority of respondents with monthly incomes above Rp 1,500,000 state that memberships in social and business associations help them access loans from formal MFIs. This implies that capabilities to extract benefits from engaging in social and business associations diverge across different income level groups. The lower social classes, particularly the very poor, fail to maximize the benefits of being involved in social and business associations due to their low income levels, lack of education and inadequate communication skills. On the other hand, by having better educational backgrounds and communication skills, the non-poor can extract greater benefits from being involved in social and business associations. Hence, they can gain greater access to formal loans, usually through gathering knowledge of banking procedures from other members.

DETERMINANTS OF BORROWING AMONG POOR PEOPLE

It is evident that poor people utilize loans from different sources. Apart from microbanks, farmers in rural Vietnam utilize loans from relatives, moneylenders and ROSCAs (Duong & Izumida, 2002). According to Johar and Rommohan (2006), loans from ROSCAs and moneylenders contribute to 31 percent of household borrowings in Indonesia (p. 28). La Ferrara (2003) estimates that loans from relatives and private non-moneylenders comprise 67 percent of household borrowings in Ghana (p. 17). This section uses econometric analysis to examine the demand of poor people for loans from different sources: (1) relatives, (2) neighbors, (3) friends, (4) moneylenders, (5) cooperatives, and (6) banks. These variables are binary, as they have a value of one (1) if respondents borrow money from considered lenders (e.g., banks), and zero (0) if otherwise.

Various methods have been developed to estimate models with a binary dependent variable, such as the linear probability method (LPM), as well as probit, logit and tobit models, etc. The LPM method is methodologically weak, as it can result in the predicted values of dependent variables as being negative or greater than one (1). This does not make sense as probability is assumed to fall in the range of 0 and 1 (Greene, 2003 p. 666). Tobit estimations are commonly used when data are partly omitted or censored. However, the disadvantage of censoring the data is that it can reduce the quality of the data. Greene (2003) warns that "if data are always censored, the [estimate] result will usually not be useful" (p. 764). As the data are not censored, this econometric analysis does not utilize the tobit estimation. Probit and logit estimations follow the same procedure of computation, and often produce very similar results. The only difference is that the probit model is based on the standard normal distribution of probability, while the logit model utilizes logistic probability distributions. These probability distributions have the same bell shape, but the logistic distribution tends to be heavier in the tails than the normal probability distribution. The current analysis employs the logit estimation.

Table 4 reports the estimated results of poor people borrowing from relatives, neighbors and friends. The logit estimation results in 78.8 percent of correct predictions on the probability of borrowing from relatives. The probability of poor people borrowing from neighbors and friends is correctly predicted at the level of 72.7 percent and 76.6 percent, respectively. This indicates that the logit estimations fit relatively well with the distribution of data. The coefficient of the Breusch-Pagan LM test for each estimated regression is significantly large. Hence, we statistically reject heteroskedasticty problems in the regression estimations. Considering the t-statistic, the variable of child education statistically affects the demand of poor people for loans from neighbors, but it has no effect on borrowing from relatives and friends. The negative sign of the coefficient indicates that an increase in the level of child education reduces the likelihood of borrowing from neighbors. This is likely the case as improvement in child education levels benefits the poor through income transfers from children to parents in the long-term. The income transfers can, then, fulfill the needs of the poor for cash, reducing the demand for loans from neighbors.

As expected, an increase in monthly income reduces the demand of poor people for loans from relatives and neighbors. As loans from relatives and neighbors are mainly for consumptive purposes, a rise in income enables the poor to secure greater consumption on their own, thereby reducing their willingness to borrow from relatives and neighbors. Furthermore, the ownership of liquid assets does not statistically affect the likelihood of borrowing from relatives and neighbors. However, one cannot conclude that an increase in the ownership of liquid assets reduces the willingness of the poor to borrow money from relatives and neighbors. Loans from relatives and neighbors remain important to finance immediate consumption, while liquid assets are accumulated by the poor for emergency expenditures (e.g., medications). Nevertheless, an increase in liquid assets gives rise to demands among poor people for loans from friends. This takes place as poor people utilize loans from friends to finance production. Here, the ownership of liquid assets enhances the repayment capacity of the poor, giving rise to the demand for loans from friends.

Table 4 Logit Estimates of Borrowing from Relatives, Neighbors and Friends, Boyolali District

Explanatory variable	Relatives		Neighbors		Friends	
	Co-efficient	t-Statistic	Co-efficient	t-Statistic	Co-efficient	t-Statistic
Childedu	-0.157	-1.00	-0.374	-2.50[a]	0.163	1.15
Lincome	-0.425	-1.48[c]	-0.823	-3.00[a]	0.233	0.82
Laset	0.001	0.03	-0.024	-0.62	0.049	1.52[c]
Visit	0.231	1.06	-0.302	-1.42[c]	0.296	1.34[c]
Rosca	0.264	0.37	0.320	0.49	0.011	0.02
Basoc	0.378	1.04	0.995	2.81[a]	-0.594	-1.75[b]
Flend2R	0.307	1.40[c]				
Flend2NF			0.364	1.99[b]	0.423	2.20[a]
Constant	6.185	1.62	13.865	3.67	-5.081	-1.3

Log-Likelihood = -115.05
Correct Prediction = 78.80%
Breusch-Pagan LM test with 7 DF = 180.831

Log-Likelihood = -122.83
Correct Prediction = 72.7%
Breusch-Pagan LM test with 7 DF = 607.942

Log-Likelihood = -117.03
Correct Prediction = 76.6%
Breusch-Pagan LM test with 7 DF = 312.922

Note:

[a], [b] and [c] indicate statistically significant at 1%, 5% and 10% level, respectively.
t-table for 1% level of significance with N = ∞ is 2.32; 5% is 1.64 and 10% is 1.28.
Capital letter "L" in explanatory variables indicates computation of logarithm value.
Childedu is child education level (1 = primary school or below, 2 = junior high school, 3 = senior high school and 4 = university and diploma).
Lincome is monthly income in rupiah (Rp).
Laset is the amount of asset ownership in rupiah (Rp).
Visit is frequent visit to relatives (1 = never, 2 = not so often, 3 = often and 4 = very often).
Rosca is membership of rotating and saving association (1 = yes and 0 otherwise).
Basoc is membership of business association (1 = yes and 0 otherwise).
Flend2R is frequency of providing loans to relatives (1 = never, 2 = not so often, 3 = often and 4 = very often).
Flend2NF is frequency of providing loans to neighbor and friend (1 = never, 2 = not so often, 3 = often and 4 = very often).

Frequent visits to relatives increase the demand of poor people for loans from relatives, but reduce their willingness to borrow money from neighbors. This implies that frequent visits to relatives provide more opportunities for the poor to obtain loans from relatives. As a result, access to kinship loans reduces the demand for loans from neighbors. This indicates that loans from relatives have substitute effects on the demand for loans from neighbors. Moreover, frequent visits to relatives statistically increase the likelihood of borrowing from friends. This occurs as frequent visits to relatives improve the social networks of poor people. By visiting relatives who live in different places, for instance, poor people can make new friends and expand social networks, leading to more opportunities to obtain loans from friends.

Memberships in ROSCAs do not affect the borrowing of poor people from relatives, neighbors and friends. The estimated coefficients are statistically insignificant at 5 percent. This implies that access to loans from ROSCAs do not act as a substitute for the demand on loans from relatives, neighbors and friends. As loans from ROSCAs are small, they may complement loans provided by relatives, neighbors and friends. However, memberships in business associations significantly affect the probability of borrowing from neighbors and friends. The positive sign of the coefficient implies that business association membership increases the demand for loans from neighbors. Most likely this happens because membership within business associations, such as farmer associations, is among neighbors. Thus, by being involved in business associations, the poor can maintain friendships with neighbors to access loans from them. Loans provided by business associations are not a substitute for loans from neighbors, as they are used for different purposes. Loans from business associations are used to support production, while loans from neighbors are for consumption. However, membership in business associations reduces the demand for loans from friends. This indicates that access to loans from business associations has substitution effects on the demand for loans from friends. This is because the utilization of loans from friends and business associations has the same purpose: to finance production. Hence, an increase in access to loans from business associations potentially reduces the demand for loans from friends. Instead they imply reciprocal obligations for borrowers (e.g., La Ferrara, 2003; Zeller 2003). Hence, the more frequently poor people provide loans to relatives, neighbors and friends, the greater the possibility they will also obtain loans from them. Interestingly, providing loans to relatives increases the probability of borrowing from them. Similarly, frequently providing loans to neighbors and friends also increases the likelihood of borrowing from neighbors and friends. This indicates that the reciprocity obligation characterizes lending and borrowing among relatives, neighbors and friends, confirming that lending provisions for socially close lenders do not aim to maximize profits.

Table 5 presents the logit estimates of borrowing from such commercial financial sources as banks, cooperatives and moneylenders. The estimate model results in a 79 percent correct prediction for the probability of borrowing from banks. The probabilities of borrowing from cooperatives and moneylenders are correctly predicted at 69.7 percent and 77 percent, respectively. The coefficients of the Breusch-Pagan LM test are large for the estimates of borrowing from banks and moneylenders. This indicates that the estimated models do not face heteroskedasticity problems. However, the estimate of borrowing from cooperatives indicates heteroskedasticity issues. Regarding the t-statistic of the estimated coefficients, the variable of child education statistically affects the likelihood of borrowing from banks at a 10 percent level. This indicates that an increase in the level of child education enhances the access of poor people to bank loans, also implying that having children with higher levels of education can provide the poor with information about banking procedures, facilitating access to bank loans. On the other hand, an improvement in child education has no impact on borrowing from cooperatives and moneylenders. This indicates that poor people can access loans from these MFIs regardless of the education levels of their children.

Experience in undertaking enterprising activities does not statistically affect the likelihood of poor people borrowing from banks, cooperatives and moneylenders. This is evident largely because the business activity of the poor people under study has not significantly progressed over the years. For instance, 46 out of 87 farmer respondents have the same size of farmland since they first began farming. An increase in incomes for poor people enhances their borrowing from banks and cooperatives, but it reduces their demands for loans from moneylenders. This implies that the demand of poor people for bank and cooperative loans arises from a need to support production. Hence, an increase in incomes from business activities enhances the repayment capability of the poor, encouraging the utilization of loans from banks and cooperatives. On the other hand, rising incomes reduce the willingness of the poor to utilize loans from moneylenders.

An improvement in the ownership of liquid assets (e.g., jewelry and savings) is positively correlated with the likelihood of borrowing from banks, cooperatives and moneylenders. The ownership of liquid assets enhances the repayment capacity of poor people, thereby increasing their demand for commercial loans. Similarly, the level of housing ownership has a positive impact on the likelihood of poor people borrowing from banks. This is not surprising as lending provisions of banks require borrowers to provide collateral for loans. Thus, an increase in housing property value enables poor people to provide collateral to apply for bank

Table 5 *Logit Estimates of Borrowing from Bank, Cooperative and Moneylender in the Boyolali District*

Variable	Bank		Cooperative		Moneylender	
	Coefficient	t-Statistic	Coefficient	t-Statistic	Coefficient	t-Statistic
Childedu	0.245	1.44c	0.045	0.30	-0.022	-0.16
Lyear	-0.490	-1.19	-0.411	-1.13	0.078	0.24
Lincome	0.573	1.74b	0.185	0.71	-0.466	-1.90b
Laset	0.044	1.28	0.090	2.62a	0.026	0.82
Lhouse	1.233	4.20a	-0.069	-0.28	-0.020	-0.09
Visit	0.552	2.28b	0.093	0.46	-0.360	-1.88b
Rosca	0.835	1.15	-1.093	-1.34c	0.829	1.20
Basoc	0.710	1.86b	1.638	4.57a	-0.486	-1.62c
Constant	-16.448	-3.49	-1.544	-0.43	6.418	1.87
Log-Likelihood = -104.093			Log-Likelihood = -132.02		Log-Likelihood = -107.37	
Likelihood Ratio = 58.44			Likelihood Ratio = 36.62		Likelihood Ratio = 24.07	
Correct Prediction = 79.2 %			Correct Prediction = 69.7%		Correct Prediction = 77.1%	
Breusch-Pagan LM test with 8 DF = 456.913			Breusch-Pagan LM test with 7 DF = 8.114		Breusch-Pagan LM test with 5 DF = 686.96	

Note:

a, b and c indicate statistically significant at 1%, 5% and 10% level, respectively.

t-table for 1% level of significance with N = ∞ is 2.32; 5% is 1.64 and 10% is 1.28.

Capital letter "L" in explanatory variables indicates computation of logarithm value.

Childedu is child education level (1 = primary school or bellow, 2 = junior high school, 3 = senior high school and 4 = university and diploma).

Lyear is years of business establishment; Lincome is monthly income in rupiah (Rp); Laset is the amount of asset ownership in rupiah (Rp); Lhouse is the size of house in M2; Visit is frequent visit to relatives (1 = never, 2 = not so often, 3 = often and 4 = very often); Rosca is membership of rotating and saving association (1 = yes and 0 otherwise); and Basoc is membership of business association (1 = yes and 0 otherwise).

loans. In contrast, the size of houses does not statistically affect borrowing from cooperatives and moneylenders, as access to loans from these MFIs does not require collateral.

Frequent visits to relatives contribute to the likelihood of borrowing from banks. This implies that poor people utilize kinship networks to access bank loans. Frequent visits to relatives enable the poor to gather information about banking procedures from their relatives. Maintaining kinship relationships also enhances access to bank loans through relatives acting as loan co-signers and witnesses. However, frequent visits to relatives reduce borrowing from moneylenders while they have no impact on loan demand from cooperatives, as maintaining relationships with relatives enhances access of the poor to kinship loans, reducing their need to borrow money from moneylenders. Poor people prefer to utilize kinship loans over loans from moneylenders due to the high interest rates charged by the latter.

Memberships in ROSCAs do not statistically affect the likelihood of borrowing from banks and moneylenders, but they negatively affect the borrowing of poor people from cooperatives. This indicates that access to loans from ROSCAs has a substitution effect on the demand for loans from cooperatives. Poor people prefer to borrow money from ROSCAs, owing to their simple borrowing procedures. On the other hand, membership in business associations has a positive impact on the borrowing of poor people from banks. This is probably because the poor can gather knowledge on banking procedures from their business associates, enhancing their networking access to bank loans. In contrast, membership in business associations has a negative impact on demand for loans from moneylenders. Here, business associations expand networking access to more varied sources of funds, reducing the demand of poor people for loans from moneylenders.

SOCIAL NETWORKS AND CREDIT RATIONING

One can apply to banks in order to access loans. Based on information provided, banks will make a decision to approve or decline the loan application. Potential borrowers who apply for loans from banks but fail to get loan approval are said to face credit rationing. In the microfinance literature the term credit rationing refers to a condition when unsatisfied financial demand exists because banks are unwilling to serve poor borrowers at a given rate of loan interest (Izumida, 2004, p. 9). The cause of credit rationing arises from banks being unable to gather information about the quality of borrowers (Izumida, 2004). However, credit rationing can also arise because poor people lack information and knowledge of banking procedures. According to Aleem (1993), an absence of advertising often inhibits access of the poor to bank loans. Low levels of education and unfamiliarity with banking procedures as well constrain the ability of the poor to utilize bank loans (Baydas, Graham, & Valenzuela, 1997). In this case, the cause of credit rationing stems from borrowers' lack of incentive to borrow due to incomplete knowledge of banking procedures, with the result that poor people tend to rely on loans from informal sources, such as relatives and moneylenders. I focus here on poor borrowers' inadequate knowledge of banking procedures as a factor in constraining their access to bank loans.

The data indicate that poor people face credit rationing if they only have access to loans from informal MFIs (e.g., relatives, neighbors, friends and moneylenders). Conversely, respondents who can access loans from banks and cooperatives do not face credit rationing. In the logit estimation, then, respondents who have access to loans from banks and cooperatives take the value of one (1) and zero (0) otherwise. From this definition, 47.6 percent out of 231 respondents face credit rationing in the sense that they only have access to informal loans. The other 53.4 percent do not face credit rationing from formal MFIs. The logit model is employed to estimate the probability of poor people facing credit rationing (Ration). The logit (Ration) is, therefore, a function of the following explanatory variables: level of education (Edu), monthly income (Income), ownership of liquid assets (Aset), the size of house (House), discussions with family members before borrowing (Discus), frequent visits to relatives (Visit), memberships in ROSCAs (Rosca) and business associations (Basoc). In a functional form,

Logit (Ration) = F (Edu, Income, Aset, House, Discus, Visit, Rosca, Basoc)...(1)

Table 6 reports the estimated regression of the probability of poor people facing credit rationing from formal MFIs. The probability of facing credit rationing is correctly predicted at 66.7 percent. This means that the estimate regression fits satisfactorily with the data. The coefficient of the Breusch-Pagan LM test is 60.95, meaning that the regression does not suffer any heteroskedasticity problems. Except for memberships in ROSCAs, all estimated coefficients of the explanatory variables have the expected signs. This means that an improvement in human, physical and social capital enables poor people to reduce the probability of facing credit rationing from formal MFIs. Concerning the t-statistics, however, variable education is not statistically significant at 5 percent. This implies that low levels of education constrain the poor from gathering knowledge of banking procedures. Similarly, an increase in income also does not statistically reduce the likelihood of the poor facing credit rationing from formal MFIs. However, the ownership of liquid assets and housing property significantly decrease the probability of poor people facing credit rationing. Having more liquid assets, the poor become more capable of repaying loans from formal MFIs. An increase in the value of housing ownership enables the poor to provide collateral to support formal loans. The marginal effect indicates that a 10 percent increase in the size of housing property will be accompanied by a 2.8 percent decline in the likelihood of facing credit rationing. This result is consistent with a study by Duong and Izumida (2002), which suggested that an increase in the ownership of assets reduces the likelihood of poor people facing credit rationing from formal MFIs in Vietnam.

Table 6 *Logit Estimate of Credit Rationing in the Boyolali District*

Explanatory variable	Coefficient	*t*-Statistic	Marginal effect (dP/dX)*
Edu	-0.121	-0.83	-0.05
Lincome	-0.240	-0.90	-0.09
Laset	-0.058	-1.51c	-0.02
Lhouse	-0.758	-3.04a	-0.28
Discus	-0.889	-1.77b	-0.33
Visit	-0.101	-0.48	-0.04
Rosca	0.583	0.89	0.22
Basoc	-1.246	-3.82a	-0.47
Constant	9.899	2.76	

Log-Likelihood = -133.43
Correct Prediction = 66.70%
Breusch-Pagan LM test with 9 DF = 60.954

Note:

a, b and c indicate statistically significant at 1%, 5% and 10% level, respectively. *t*-table for 1% level of significance with N = ∞ 100 is 2.32; 5% is 1.64 and 10% is 1.28.
*The marginal effect is measured by $\Phi(-X'\beta)\beta_i$ calculated at the mean values of the regressors (see Greene, 2003).
Capital letter "L" in explanatory variables indicates computation of logarithm value.
Edu is education level (1 = primary school or below, 2 = junior high school, 3 = senior high school and 4 = university and diploma).
Lincome is monthly income in rupiah (Rp).
Laset is the amount of asset ownership in rupiah (Rp).
Lhouse is the size of house in M^2.
Visit is frequency of visits to relatives (1 = never, 2 = not so often, 3 = often, and 4 = very often).
Rosca refers to membership in a Rotating Savings and Credit Association (1 = yes and 0 = otherwise).
Basoc refers to membership in a business association (1 = yes and 0 = otherwise).
Discus refers to discussion with family members before borrowing (1 = yes and 0 = otherwise).

As expected, when poor people discuss borrowing plans with other family members, they are less likely to face credit rationing from formal MFIs. Sound familial relationships can reduce the probability of facing credit rationing as formal MFIs consider the familial stability of borrowers to secure loan repayments. Frequent visits to relatives are negatively correlated with the probability of poor people facing credit rationing. Maintaining kinship relationships enables the poor to overcome credit rationing, since relatives can provide information and assistance to access bank loans. Moreover, memberships in business associations increase the capability of poor people to overcome credit rationing from formal MFIs. However, involvement in ROSCAs does not lead to a reduction in the probability of facing credit rationing. This is not surprising as memberships in ROSCAs are restricted to a small group of neighbors. In contrast, business associations have a broader membership base, covering friends and business associates. By being involved in business associations, therefore, the poor can enhance networking access to formal MFIs. Burt (2005) argues that in broader networks such as in business associations overlapping information can be minimized, as they consist of individuals with diverse backgrounds who enrich information flows. In the context of microfinance, memberships in business associations facilitate knowledge acquisition of banking procedures among poor people from their interaction with other members. Hence, the poor can utilize business associates to expand their networking access to formal loans.

SOCIAL CAPITAL AND FINANCIAL PERFORMANCE

This section examines the relationship between social capital and loan repayment rates with MFIs. It is worth noting that data on loan repayment rates of MFIs are approximate as difficulties were involved in gathering information from the surveyed MFIs. The loan repayment rates of microbanks, for instance, cannot be accessed due to confidentiality. Because of inappropriate accounting reports, ROSCAs and moneylenders cannot provide data on loan repayment rates. To overcome this problem, MFIs were surveyed vis-à-vis a list of loan repayment rates. Each respondent chose one of the following scales of loan repayment rates: (1) 90-100 percent, (2) 80-90 percent, (3) 70-80 percent, (4) 60-70 percent, and so on through to 0-10 percent. The mean value of the selected scales was assumed to be the loan repayment rate of the MFIs. For instance, MFIs that selected the scale (1) 90 to 100 percent were assumed to have a loan repayment rate of 95 percent. In regression computation, then, loan repayment rates of MFIs (RRT) are a function of the following variables: average loan size (Avloan), size of loan installment (Instal), loan installment period (Period), loan interest rates (Intres), years of enterprise (Year), proportion of lending staff living in the area of business operations (LaborRatio), and perception of the importance of social capital as measured by an index for social capital (SCI). In a more simple form, the relationships can be expressed as follows:

RRT = F (Avlon, Instal, Period, Intres, Year, LaborRatio, SCI)..............(2)

At the community level, the index of social capital can be measured by the existence of social associations, memberships in such associations, political participation, etc. (See Putnam, 1995). This method could not be implemented here because the unit analysis of this study is individual levels of MFIs. Hence, an index of perceptions is provided on the importance of social capital in MFIs' lending decisions in which four indicators are considered: 1) personal knowledge of borrowers (X_1), 2) perceptions of the importance of familial stability among borrowers (X_2), 3) friendships with borrowers (X_3), and 4) perceptions as to the importance of community leaders in lending decisions (X_4). As each indicator has score values in the range of 1 to 4, the index of social capital for each MFI (n) can be calculated as the sum of score values divided by the total score (16) times 100, or simply as,

Social Capital Index/SCI_n = $(\sum_{i=1}^{4} X_{in})/16*100$..(3)

Suppose that an MFI has score values for each social capital indicator of $X_1 = 4$, $X_2 = 4$, $X_3 = 4$, $X_4 = 4$. The index of social capital for this MFI is 100. This is the maximum value of the index. The minimum value of the index will be 25, when MFIs have the score value of one (1) for each indicator. The index of social capital varies, depending on the perceptions of MFIs toward the importance of social capital. It increases as MFIs regard social capital as an important factor in their lending decisions. On the other hand, it declines as MFIs disregard the importance of social capital.

Table 7 reports the results of regression estimates using the ordinary least square method (OLS). Since the regression computation uses the logarithm value of the variables, the estimate coefficients indicate the marginal effects of explanatory variables on the dependant variable. The regression computations utilize three data sets: (1) full sample, (2) samples of formal and semi-formal MFIs, and (3) informal MFIs. Regarding the F-value, the explanatory variables considered in the regressions jointly affect the explanatory variable. In other words, the selected explanatory variables in the regressions are statistically acceptable. The Breusch-Pagan (B-P) LM tests indicate that the estimated regressions do not face heteroskedasticity problems. Considering the t-statistic, the average loan size positively affects the loan repayment rates of MFIs. The magnitude effect of the coefficients implies that a 10 percent crease in the average loan size gives rise to higher loan repayment

Table 7 *Estimate Regressions of Repayment Rates of MFIs in the Boyolali District*

Explanatory variable	Full sample (N=153)		Formal and semi-formal MFIs (N=97)		Informal MFIs (N=56)	
	Coefficient	t-Statistic	Coefficient	t-Statistic	Coefficient	t-Statistic
Lavloan	0.047	1.87[c]	0.043	1.80[c]	0.091	4.80[a]
Linstal	-0.028	-0.99	-0.011	-0.42	-0.045	-2.14[b]
Lperiod	0.246	3.79[a]	0.187	3.05[a]	0.050	1.12
Lintres	0.195	3.30[a]	0.307	4.22[a]	-0.028	-0.82
Lyear	0.070	3.01[a]	-0.002	-0.07	-0.008	-0.40
LlaborRatio	0.205	8.41[a]	0.048	2.02[b]	0.591	7.70[a]
LSCI	0.508	7.66[a]	0.577	7.25[a]	0.294	3.57[a]
F-ratio	9,409.68		11,339.03		33,581.56	
B-P LM test	12.32 (13 DF)		28.80 (13 DF)		15.864 (13 DF)	

Note:

[a], [b] and [c] indicate statistically significant at 1%, 5% and 10% level, respectively.
t-table for 1% level of significance with N = ∞ is 2.32; 5% is 1.64 and 10% is 1.28.
Capital letter "L" in each explanatory variable indicates computation of logarithm value.
Lavlon = Average loan size in rupiah (Rp).
Linstal = The size of loan installment in rupiah (Rp).
Lperiod = Installment period (1 = daily, 2 = weekly, 3 = fortnightly, 4 = monthly).
Lintres = Interest rate on loan (%).
Lyear = The period of undertaking financial business.
LlaborRatio = Proportion of lending officers living in the area of operation (%).
LSCI = Index of perceptions of the importance of social capital.

rates of MFIs in the order of 0.5 percent. However, an increase in the size of loan installments reduces MFIs' loan repayment rates, most likely because an increase in loan installments reduces the repayment capability of poor people due to their unstable income flows.

Loan installment periods have a positive effect on the loan repayment rates of MFIs. Longer periods (e.g., from fortnightly to monthly) increase the repayment capability of poor borrowers, giving rise to the loan repayment rates of formal MFIs. Thus, formal MFIs should consider loans with longer installment periods if the aim is to improve loan repayment rates. However, loan installment periods do not statistically affect the loan repayment rates of informal MFIs. This is probably the case as the loan installment of informal MFIs is relatively small, accounting to around Rp 10,000 or about US$1.05 weekly. As such, the frequency and period of loan installments will not reduce the capability of poor borrowers to repay loans from informal MFIs. The average loan installment of ROSCAs and moneylenders is usually less than Rp 50,000. Furthermore, an increase in loan interest rates has a positive impact on the loan repayment rates of MFIs. The magnitude effect of the coefficient is such that a 10 percent increase in interest rates of formal MFIs will be accompanied by a 3 percent improvement in loan repayment rates. On the other hand, an increase in interest rates may reduce the loan repayment rates of informal MFIs.

As expected, the period of business operations is positively correlated with the loan repayment rates of MFIs. A longer period of business operations facilitates MFIs learning more about the characteristics of poor clients. However, the magnitude effect of the estimate coefficient is small. Here, a 10 percent increase in the period of business operations will improve the rate of loan repayments by about 0.7 percent. This indicates that MFIs require a long-term process to recognize the characteristics of poor borrowers. For instance, the BRI-unit approach took more than 15 years to establish a sound microfinance business. The BRI program began in 1970 through the introduction of a subsidized credit scheme under Program Bimbingan/BIMAS or the Mass Guidance program. The financial progress of BRI-units has gained momentum since the early 1990s. This implies that to achieve sound lending practices, MFIs should recognize not only the economic characteristics of poor clients, but also their socio-cultural activities. This includes recognizing their social networks and the manner in which the poor utilize financial services.

The proportion of lending officers living in the area of business operations statistically affects the loan repayment rates of MFIs. The positive sign of the coefficient implies that an increase in the ratio improves loan repayment rates. As lending staff of MFIs live in the same network area as clients, they can maintain friendships with poor borrowers to closely monitor their financial performance. As a result, MFIs can minimize the probability of loan defaults. As expected, perceptions of the importance of social capital in lending decisions have a positive impact on MFIs' loan repayment rates. This implies that MFIs that consider the importance of social capital are more likely to have more optimal loan repayment rates, as they are encouraged to create lending innovations that link loans with borrowers' social networks. Such innovations can take the form of loans with support from community leaders and joint-liability loans. For instance, the success of BRI-units is associated with lending provisions that require borrowers to seek community leaders as witnesses as well as loans based on joint-liability between husband and wife. Proactive screening and monitoring efforts are carried out by the lending staff of BRI-units visiting the workplaces and homes of borrowers. Here, the lending staff of BRI-units can build mutual trust and friendship with borrowers, generating incentives to repay loans (Robinson, 2001).

Conclusion and Implications

This chapter has investigated the role of social capital in microfinance performance. It was found that social capital in the form of mutual trust and reciprocity facilitates the access of poor people to loans from socially close lenders, such as relatives, neighbors and friends. This access is made possible as the willingness to provide loans to the poor does not aim to maximize profits. As loans are delivered on the basis of social collateral, such as mutual trust, friendship and reciprocity, this collateral can substitute for the poor's lack of physical collateral. Social collateral matters in such informal loans as specific characteristics of lenders, such as income, education, gender and occupation, are not a major determinant of the willingness to provide loans to others. In contrast, norms of reciprocity are considered because socially close lenders expect to receive similar loans in the future and engage in self-help group mechanisms to cope with a lack of access to formal finance. Similarly, borrowers are willing to repay such loans because they recognize the norms of trust, friendships and reciprocity. Furthermore, social capital in the form of kinship relationships can enhance the access of poor people to loans from formal MFIs. Maintaining kinship relationships can lead the poor to obtain bank loans, through the role of relatives as loan co-signers or witnesses. Within a broader context, social and business networks enable poor people to access loans from formal MFIs. Through being members of business associations, for instance, the poor can gather knowledge of the borrowing procedures of banks from their business associates. This implies that the utilization of social and familial capital enhances the capacity of poor people to reduce credit rationing with formal MFIs.

This chapter has also examined the link between social capital and the financial performance of MFIs. It concludes that MFIs that consider the importance of social capital in lending decisions tend to have higher rates of loan repayment as MFIs are encouraged to create innovations by linking loans with borrowers' social capital. For instance, lending provisions with support from community leaders and joint-liability loans between husband and wife can reduce the probability of loan defaults. Lending officials of MFIs who live in the area of business operations also potentially reduce the probability of loan defaults, since they can closely monitor the financial performance of borrowers. Apart from the importance of social capital, an increase in average loan size further gives rise to higher loan repayments rates with MFIs. The longer the period of loan installment, the higher the MFIs' repayment rates. An increase in interest rates can improve the loan repayment rates of formal MFIs, but it adversely affects the loan repayment rates of informal MFIs. The number of years of business operations is positively associated with MFIs' loan repayment rates. However, MFIs need a long-term period to achieve higher rates of loan repayment. MFIs should not only recognize the economic characteristics of poor clients, but also their social networks and the way they utilize microfinance services.

Two lessons can be learned from this study from the view of microfinance practitioners, policymakers and scholars in Asia. First, the microfinance industry does not consist of homogenous institutions; instead it encompasses a variety of MFIs of a formal, semi-formal and informal nature. Each MFI has its own operational characteristics and clients. While some poor clients can access formal MFIs such as microbanks, many others utilize informal finance from relatives, friends, ROSCAs and moneylenders. Considering the heterogeneous characteristics of MFIs, the notion that the transformation of MFIs into commercial microbanks is the most appropriate approach for microfinance development (e.g., Charitonenko & Afwan, 2003; Charitonenko, Campion, & Fernando, 2004; Christen, 2001) should be challenged. Instead, pro-poor policies of microfinance in Asia should be undertaken through promoting operational linkages among formal, semi-formal and informal MFIs. An operational linkage, for instance, can be developed through encouraging microbanks to utilize cooperatives and other informal MFIs, such as ROSCAs, to channel loans to poor people. Being operationally close to the social networks of poor people, these MFIs can help microbanks overcome the information and enforcement problems of lending to the poor. This linkage benefits cooperatives and ROSCAs as microbanks can provide financial resources (e.g., loans), and transfer banking skills to these MFIs. Greater access to financial and business skills provided by microbanks can advance the financial practices of cooperatives and ROSCAs, which are vital for anticipating the needs of the poor for more sophisticated microfinance services.

Second, it is essential for microfinance practitioners, such as cooperative leaders, NGOs and microbank officers, to continuously create financial innovations for serving poor clients. Such innovations do not necessarily require the creation of new financial products and methods. Instead, they can involve adapting the existing business practices of informal MFIs such as moneylenders and ROSCAs. These informal MFIs have successfully coped with the high risks of lending to poor people through informal approaches. There is evidence that informal lending approaches enable cooperatives and moneylenders to harness the social networks of poor clients, leading to high loan repayment rates. Thus, microfinance practitioners should consider informal approaches as opposed to strictly formal borrowing procedures when dealing with the poor. Frequent visits of lending officers to the home and workplace of poor clients and simple procedures of borrowing are helpful in this regard. Close friendships with clients can generate reciprocal obligations of the poor borrower to repay loans. Lending innovations can also be developed through delivering loans to pre-existing networks of poor people, such as self-help groups (e.g., ROSCAs), religious associations, and other community organizations. As has been widely recognized, lending to groups of poor people enables MFIs to utilize social cohesion and peer pressure to minimize loan default rates.

Acknowledgements

The author gratefully acknowledges the valuable comments and suggestions of Professor Phillip Anthony O'Hara of Curtin University and audience members at the 3rd international conference of the Asia Association for Global Studies (AAGS) held in Kobe, Japan, March 28-29, 2008. Any remaining errors are my own.

Reference

Aleem, I. (1993). Imperfect information, screening, and the costs of informal lending: A study of a rural credit market in Pakistan. In K. Hoff, A. Braverman, & J. E. Stiglitz (Eds.), *The economics of rural organization: Theory, practice, and policy* (pp. 131-153). Washington, DC: World Bank and Oxford University Press.

Armendariz de Aghion, B., & Gollier, C. (2000). Peer group formation in an adverse selection model. *The Economic Journal, 110*(465), 632-643.

Banerjee, A., Besley, T., & Guinnane, T. W. (1994). Thy neighbor's keeper: The design of a credit cooperative with theory and a test. *The Quarterly Journal of Economics, 109*(2), 491-515.

Bardhan, P., & Udry, C. (1999). *Development microeconomics*. Oxford: Oxford University Press.

Baydas, M. M., Graham, D. H., & Valenzuela, L. (1997). *Commercial banks in microfinance: New actor in microfinance world*. Bethesda: Microenterprise Best-Practice.

Bebbington, D. H., & Gomez, A. (2006). Rebuilding social capital in post-conflict regions. In J. L. Fernando (Ed.), *Microfinance perils and prospects* (pp. 112-132). London and New York: Routledge.

Besley, T., & Coate, S. (1995). Group lending, repayment incentives and social collateral. *Journal of Development Economics, 46*(1), 1-18.

Besley, T., Coate, S., & Loury, G. (1993). The economics of rotating saving and credit associations. *American Economic Review, 83*(4), 792-820.

Burt, R. S. (2005). *Brokerage and closure: An introduction to social capital.* New York: Oxford University Press.

Charitonenko, S., & Afwan, I. (2003). *Commercialization of microfinance: Indonesia.* Manila: Asian Development Bank (ADB).

Charitonenko, S., Campion, A., & Fernando, N. A. (2004). *Commercialization of microfinance: Perspectives from South and Southeast Asia.* Manila: Asian Development Bank (ADB).

Christen, R. P. (2001). *Commercialization and mission drift: The transformation of microfinance in Latin America.* (Occasional paper number 5). Washington, DC: Consultative Group to Assist the Poorest (CGAP).

Collier, P. (2002). Social capital and poverty: A microeconomic perspective. In C. Grootaert & T. Van Bastelaer (Eds.), *The role of social capital in development: An empirical assessment* (pp. 19-41). Cambridge: Cambridge University Press.

Conning, J. (1999). Outreach, sustainability and leverage in monitored and peer-monitored lending. *Journal of Development Economics, 60*(1), 51-77.

Dercon, S. (2002). Income risk, coping strategies, and safety nets. *The World Bank Research Observer, 17*(2), 141-166.

Duong, P. B., & Izumida, Y. (2002). Rural development finance in Vietnam: A microeconometric analysis of household surveys. *World Development, 30*(2), 319-335.

Edgcomb, E., & Barton, L. (1998). *Social intermediation and microfinance programs: A literature review.* Bethesda: Microenterprise Best-Practices.

Fukuyama, F. (1999). *The great disruption.* New York: Simon and Schuster.

Ghatak, M., & Guinnane, T. W. (1999). The economics of lending with joint liability: Theory and practice. *Journal of Development Economics, 60*(1), 195-228.

Glaeser, E., Laibson, D., & Sacerdote, B. (2000). *The economic approach to social capital?* (NBER working paper no. 7728). Cambridge, MA: National Bureau of Economics Research (NBER).

Gomez, R., & Santor, E. (2001). Membership has its privileges: The effect of social capital and neighborhood characteristics on the earnings of microfinance borrowers. *The Canadian Journal of Economics, 34*(4) 943-966.

Greene, W. H. (2003). *Econometrics analysis* (5th ed.). New Jersey: Prentice Hall.

Guinnane, T. W. (2005). *Trust: A concept too many.* (Discussion paper no. 907). New Heaven: Economic Growth Center, Yale University.

Hermes, N., & Lensink, R. (2007, February 10). Impact of microfinance: A critical survey. *Economic and Political Weekly*, 462-465.

Hoff, K., & Stiglitz, J. E. (1997). Moneylenders and bankers: Price-increasing subsidies in a monopolistically competitive market. *Journal of Development Economics, 52*(2), 429-462.

Isaksson, A. (2002). *The importance of informal finance in Kenyan manufacturing.* (Working paper no. 5). Vienna: Statistics and Information Networks Branch of United Nation Industrial Development Organization (UNIDO).

Izumida, Y. (2004) *Rethinking the new approach on rural development finance.* (Working paper no. 04-F-01). Tokyo: Department of Agricultural and Resource Economics, University of Tokyo.

Johar, M., & Rammohan, A. (2006). *Demand for microcredit by Indonesian women* (mimeographed). Sydney: Discipline of Economics, University of Sydney.

Karlan, D. S. (2005). *Social capital and group banking* (mimeographed). New Heaven: Yale University.

Karlan, D. S. (2007). Social connections and group banking. *The Economic Journal, 117*(517), 52-84.

Karlan, D. S. (2004). *Using experimental economics to measure social capital and predict financial decisions.* (Working paper no. 082). Cambridge, MA: Bureau for Research in Economic Analysis of Development (BREAD).

La Ferrara, E. (2003). *Kin groups and reciprocity: A model of credit transactions in Ghana.* (Working paper no. 027). Cambridge, MA: Bureau for Research in Economic Analysis of Development (BREAD).

Meyer, R. L., & Nagarajan, G. (1999). *Rural financial markets in Asia: Policies, paradigms, and performance.* Oxford: Oxford University Press.

Mosley, P., Olejarova, D., & Alexeeva, E. (2004). Microfinance, social capital formation and political development in Russia and Eastern Europe: A pilot study of programs in Russia, Slovakia and Romania. *Journal of International Development, 16*(3), 407-427.

Mushinski, D., & Pickering, K. (2006). Heterogeneity in informal sector mitigation of micro-enterprise credit rationing. *Journal of International Development, 19*(5), 567-581.

O'Hara, P. A. (2006). *Growth and development in the global political economy, social structure of accumulation and modes of regulation.* London and New York: Routledge.

O'Hara, P. A. (2007). *The circuit of social capital – Dynamic linkages for individuals, networks, and governments.* Perth: Department of Economics, Curtin University of Technology.

Putnam, R. D. (1995). Bowling alone: America's declining social capital. *Journal of Democracy, 6*(1), 65-78.

Rankin, K. N. (2006). Social capital, microfinance and the politics of development. In Jude. L. Fernando (Ed.), *Microfinance, perils and prospects.* (pp. 89-111). London and New York: Routledge.

Reinke, J. (1998). Does solidarity pay? The case of the small enterprise foundation, South Africa. *Development and Change, 29*(3), 553-576.

Robinson, M. S. (2001). *Microfinance revolution: Lesson from Indonesia,* vol. 2. Washington, DC: World Bank.

Stiglitz, J. E. (1990). Peer monitoring and credit markets. *World Bank Economic Review, 4*(3), 351-366.

Stiglitz, J. E.(1993). Peer monitoring and credit markets. In K. Hoff, A. Braverman, & J. E. Stiglitz (Eds.), *The economics of rural organization: Theory, practice, and policy* (pp. 70-86). Washington, DC: World Bank and Oxford University Press.

Streeten, P. (2002). Reflections on social and anti-social capital. In J. Isham, T. Kelly, & S. Ramaswamy (Eds.), *Social capital and economic development: Well-being in developing countries* (pp. 40-57). Massachusetts: Edward Elgar Publisher Inc.

Uslaner, E. M. (2002). *The moralistic foundations of trust.* Cambridge: Cambridge University Press.

Wydick, B. (2001). Group lending under dynamic incentives as a borrower discipline device. *Review of Development Economics, 5*(3), 406-420.

Zeller, M. (2003). *Model of rural finance institutions.* Washington, DC: International Food Policy Research Institute (IFPRI).

Zeller, M., Schrieder, G., Von Braun, J., & Heidhues, F. (1997). *Rural finance for food security for the poor: Implications for research and policy.* Washington DC: International Food Policy Research Institute (IFPRI).

Part Two:
Gender and Development

• CHAPTER FOUR •

Negotiating Space and Gender: Female Street Entrepreneurs and Tongdaemun Market in Seoul, Korea

AYAMI NORITAKE
The Australian National University

This chapter explores the lives of female street entrepreneurs in contemporary Seoul, South Korea (hereafter Korea). Korea has experienced rapid economic growth and urban development since the 1960s. It is now the world's thirteenth largest economy in terms of GDP (World Bank, 2008, p. 1). Korea's program of economic development has been seen as an ideal model for developing countries. Seoul's recent urban development has also been promoted domestically and internationally as a "successful" way to create a "world city."[1] However, this development has marginalized people engaged in street entrepreneurship, a large proportion of whom are women.[2] Although women have been excluded from the conceptualization of and decision-making processes within urban development, scholarly attention to these subjects has been minimal. At the same time the relationship between gender and urban development has been largely ignored.

In this chapter, I will examine how spatial, social and gender relations affect emplacement among female street entrepreneurs and how such women negotiate space and gender in everyday life. My research contributes to a better understanding of the interrelationship between spatial, social and gender relations for those in disadvantaged social positions in newly developed countries by highlighting female subjectivities. Here, I consider "subjectivities" to be "the ensemble of modes of perception, affect, thought, desire, and fear that animate acting subjects," and "as the basis of 'agency,' a necessary part of understanding how people [try to] act on the world even as they are acted upon" (Ortner, 2006, pp. 106, 110).

Additionally, I aim to deconstruct the categorization of these women as "married female street vendors." Street entrepreneurs are widely referred to as *nojŏmsang* (street vendors) in contemporary Korea. When used by others, the term carries negative connotations. Such people labeled as such are considered "illegal" and "backward," as they occupy public space without licenses, do not pay sales tax, and are involved in "traditional" forms of business. They are officially called *pulbŏp nojŏmsang* (illegal street vendors). There are also legal street entrepreneurs who have licenses to run street stands. However, the term *nojŏmsang* is most commonly used alone to include even legal street entrepreneurs, and itself has connotations of illegality and backwardness. In addition, the women involved in street vending are dominantly and exclusively conceived of as married women and mothers. However, I argue here that they have diverse identities and perceive themselves differently from prevailing images. To rethink their experiences and also to envisage alternative forms of economic development for these women, it is necessary to highlight the dynamic and diverse dimensions of their sense of self. Therefore, I use the term "street entrepreneurs" although street vendors' organizations generally call themselves *nojŏmsang*.

This study focuses on a *chaeraeshijang*[3] (traditional marketplace), the Tongdaemun Shijang (Tongdaemun Market) in central Seoul. The *chaeraeshijang* are ideal sites for examining how changes in spatial, social and gender relations have affected women's lives. In *chaeraeshijang* areas, a large number of people engage in street business. The Tongdaemun Shijang is located in central Seoul and is one of the most popular *chaeraeshijang* and fashion markets in Korea. In recent decades, the Tongdaemun Shijang has been dominated by women as consumers, workers, and entrepreneurs. During the 1960s and 1970s, many young unmarried women worked as low-paid laborers in the garment manufacturing sector which had previously thrived in the area. It is often argued that the Korean labor movement gained momentum through the unionization and protests of garment workers, especially women, in the Tongdaemun Shijang (Chun, 2004; Koo, 2001, p. 73). At the same time, the area has attracted female merchants of garments and related goods, food services and street entrepreneurs. Small-scale garment manufacturers, also mostly women, are dispersed around the marketplace. Meanwhile, the area has witnessed repeated spatial changes through urban development, and this has precipitated struggles among female entrepreneurs, including street entrepreneurs, who have faced eviction.

This chapter addresses the following two sets of questions. First, how have economic, spatial, social and gender relations affected the development of the Tongdaemun Shijang in recent decades? Second, how do female street entrepreneurs perceive this development? What needs, desires and identities do female street entrepreneurs articulate in tandem with the forces that attach them to the area? How do female street entrepreneurs negotiate change? I will argue that the economic and spatial processes that have formed and transformed the marketplace have been highly affected by social and gender relations, including factors such as age, place of origin, class, education, and marriage. I also recognize that the women's needs, desires and identities are multiple, interrelated and changing over time. Further, female street entrepreneurs actively negotiate space and gender in diverse and creative ways, and this agency is a critical force in their understanding of their physical and social place. Importantly, the needs, desires and identities as well as the negotiations of the women have been formed through the spatial processes of the Tongdaemun Shijang and of the women's own lives.

I probe the above questions first by a discussion of the gendered spatial and economic processes through which the Tongdaemun Shijang has developed, and then by an analysis of the subjectivities of female street entrepreneurs who have become attached to the area. For this purpose, I draw on archival research, in-depth interviews and participant observation pursued during fieldwork in October 2006 and from April to August 2007.

TIME, SPACE AND GENDER IN THE TONGDAEMUN SHIJANG

Below, I present a history of the Tongdaemun Shijang in terms of the macro-level interaction of spatial and social relations. A place is a product of a particular articulation of social relations rather than being purely defined by its physical and administrative boundaries, and changes in spatial relations happen in close connection to social relations and vice versa. Places have their own history, and are ever-evolving. Any arrangement of social into a spatial form is temporary, just as a social subject takes a temporary form of being (Allen, Massey, & Cochrane, 1998; Massey, 1994; Massey, 2005). This conceptual framework leads to the understanding of the place called Tongdaemun Shijang as historically and socially constructed and always in a process of becoming. Spatial and gender specializations and divisions of labor have promoted the development of the Tongdaemun Shijang as a center of production and commerce of garment-related goods and of street businesses run predominantly by women.

Specialization of the Garment Sector

These specializations and divisions of labor and the changes that accompany them are intertwined with processes of national and regional economic and social development and the urban development of Seoul. Being inseparable from its location along the Ch'ŏnggyech'ŏn Stream in central Seoul (Map 1), Tongdaemun Shijang has developed approximately through four historical phases since the Korean War (1950-1953). The first phase was during and immediately after the war and lasted until the commencement of the nation's modern economic development. War refugees, including those from North Korea and other poor people, settled along the stream, creating a marketplace that flourished[4] through the trade of groceries and goods coming from US military camps. A common view is that during this period, which lasted until the 1960s, commerce was dominated by men and women's participation in trade was limited due to the legacy of Confucian ideology on commerce and gendered divisions of labor (P.-W. Chang, 1986, p. 262). However, in the 1950s there was already a noticeable presence of female street entrepreneurs in Seoul. Around the current marketplace area, many female street entrepreneurs sold groceries and ran small restaurants. In photographs of the 1950s, numerous women can be seen selling vegetables and other foodstuffs (City History Compilation Committee of Seoul, 2004, pp. 231-233). Peculiar to this area was the manufacturing and sale of garments. Clothes used by soldiers, among others, were remade and sold. However, since the use of the Ch'ŏnggyech'ŏn Stream for waste disposal by these businesses and nearby residents resulted in the spread of contagious diseases, the area became subject to local authorities' urban development controls. The area was reshaped in this period with the covering of the stream and clearing away of slums and illegal businesses.

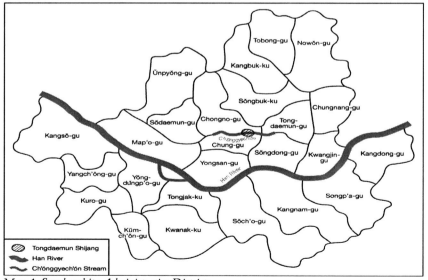

Map 1 *Seoul and its Administrative Districts*
Source: Cartographic Services, Research School of Pacific and Asian Studies (RSPAS), The Australian National University (ANU).

Gender Concentration of Garment Businesses and Street Entrepreneurship

The second phase of the development of the Tongdaemun Shijang occurred during the 1960s and 1970s, when the economic policies of the Park Chung Hee Regime (1961-1979) established a solid base for Korea's later economic, social and spatial development. In the 1960s, in pursuit of export-oriented industrialization, the government promoted labor-intensive light industry, especially textile and garment manufacturing. Between 1967 and 1971, the annual average growth of the sector was 28.5 percent. This increased to 36.2 percent in 1972 and to 39.9 percent in 1973 (World Bank, 1976, cited in Chun, 2004, p. 75). In the 1970s, however, shifts in government policy led to an expansion of heavy and chemical industries and investment in capital-intensive sectors such as steel, machinery, shipbuilding and electronics. This focus on urban manufacturing created large rural/urban income disparities and a massive rural-urban migration of people seeking wage work in urban industry. The regime also favored the development of specific regions in which the top leaders had family, political and/or military connections. Seoul and its neighboring regions were developed primarily for light and high-technology industries, and the southeastern region was targeted for heavy industry (J. Kim & Choe, 1997, p. 21). The Chŏlla provinces, on the other hand, were left largely underdeveloped because of the rivalry between their political leaders, most notably Kim Dae-jung (1998-2003), and the leaders from the Kyŏngsang provinces, notably Park Chung Hee and Chun Doo Hwan (1980-1988). Thus, many people from the Chŏlla provinces migrated to Seoul (Map 2).

The gender ideology of "Korean style capitalism" led to the feminization of the textile and garment sectors, the differentiation of women by age and marriage, and the concentration of female unskilled workers in Seoul. Coinciding with the myth that women are nimble fingered and the notion that the labor cost of women, especially young unmarried women, is low, women were mainly hired as unskilled low-paid workers in labor-intensive sectors. In 1966, more than 80 percent of female manufacturing workers were in light industry. The textile and garment sectors were the most feminized. In 1970, 62.8 percent of all textile and garment workers were women. As enterprises in these sectors were concentrated in the Seoul region, women dominated the capital's manufacturing workforce. In 1970, 23.1 percent of female textile and garment workers were employed in Seoul. The textile and garment sector was the second largest employer of women in Seoul, following the personal and household services sector (e.g., domestic helpers[5]), and followed by the retail trade sector (Economic Planning Board [EPB], 1973, pp. 94, 118). This trend continued until the mid-1980s. At the same time, while the number of job seekers drastically increased, Seoul could not offer sufficient jobs. The unemployment rate was high in Seoul at that time as a large number of people migrated from rural areas and small towns to Seoul "without any realistic prospects for jobs or housing" (J. Kim & Choe, 1997, p. 23). Numerous people turned to self-employment. Many of these people worked as shopkeepers and street entrepreneurs at that time.

Map 2 *South Korea and its Provinces*
Source: Cartographic Services, RSPAS, ANU.

During this period, the Tongdaemun Shijang and its vicinity became one of the centers of the capital industrialization and modernization project, while attracting small-scale garment manufacturers, traders and street entrepreneurs. The government-led urban development in the area was aimed principally at economic growth, and cities were made the center of light industry. The 1966 Development Plan, Seoul's first comprehensive effort in urban planning, developed the central area within the four main gates as a business district (J. Kim & Choe, 1997, pp. 62, 154-155). By that time, many refugees from North Korea and migrants from poorer regions had settled along the Ch'ŏnggyech'ŏn Stream. However, until the mid-1980s, the building of economic infrastructure took priority over people's needs for housing (J. Kim & Choe, 1997, p. 11; W. B. Kim, 1999, p. 13). The covering of the Ch'ŏnggyech'ŏn Stream throughout the 1960s and 1970s accompanied by the construction of new motorways contributed to the development of the Tongdaemun Shijang while clearing away riverside dwellers. The marketplace attracted numerous small-scale garment workshops and related businesses. While the marketplace of this period came under the spotlight as a site for the exploitation of young unmarried women[6] as unskilled cheap labor (Chun, 2004, pp. 121-134), a myriad of street entrepreneurs, most of whom were married women, also gathered and transformed the area.

Married Women and the Socio-spatial Divide
In the third phase, from the mid-1980s to the late 1990s, while the textile and garment manufacturing industry was less favored by government development policies, married female workers gravitated toward this sector of the economy. In the mid-1980s, continuing its emphasis on export-oriented industrialization, the government prioritized technology-intensive industries such as precision machinery, electronics and information technology. In the 1990s, the government focused on high-technology industries such as microelectronics, chemicals and bioengineering. The textile and garment sector lost the government's support and this allied with changes in the international garment industry caused people in the sector to lose their competitive edge. Although the Korean economy became more diversified, women's concentration in the labor-intensive sectors persisted. Meanwhile, married or middle-aged women after the mid-1980s were increasingly absorbed into the manufacturing sector due to a shortage of unmarried female workers. Married women's employment rate in the manufacturing sector, which was 13 percent in 1983, increased to 22 percent in 1992. In 1997, the rate of married, widowed and divorced women among all female workers was 77 percent (H. M. Kim, 2005, pp. 177-178). Thus, married women started to represent cheap labor and the textile and garment sector's workforce in place of unmarried young women.

At this time, the presence of the informal sector became more pronounced. According to Cho (1986), the division of the Korean labor market into a formal and informal sector was noted by researchers only at the beginning of the 1980s, and the informal sector grew as the formal sector developed (p. 158).[7] While young unmarried women's participation in the formal economy increased, a greater number of married women were engaged in the informal sector. In 1980, over 60 percent of female workers in urban areas were in this sector (Cho, 1986, p. 159). Part of the informal sector was comprised of married middleclass women (at least in the 1990s) (Lett, 1998, p. 61). Middleclass women's informal economic activities included transactions of real estate, group saving (*kye*), and home tutoring, among others. Informal economic activities such as street businesses also developed to provide low-cost commodities to the less affluent and to create income opportunities for those with fewer qualifications and limited access to capital.

At the same time, Korea was transformed into a consumer society, and Seoul became the nation's center of commerce. Domestic demand for consumer goods and services soared as wages and savings increased. With new economic opportunities arising and people demanding higher living standards, the government promoted import liberalization and the development of a distribution network of supermarkets and department stores. International events such as the 1988 Seoul Olympics and international tourism accelerated domestic and urban market development. Consumer goods' sales and service industries such as restaurants, hotels, insurance, health-related services, and entertainment grew rapidly. In 1986, the largest employer was the retail trade sector with 13.8 percent of the nation's workforce. The second largest was the textile and garment sector with 11.5 percent (EPB, 1987, p. 227). By 1991, the retail trade sector had become the largest employer, employing 12.5 percent of the workforce. The social services sector was second with 9.4 percent (the education services sector accounted for 60.6 percent of this sector), and in third place was the hospitality sector with 8.98 percent. The textile and garment sector accounted for 8.93 percent of workers (EPB, 1992, pp. 26-39). Although Seoul's service sector was already active,[8] the nation's overall economic development bolstered this sector, and wholesalers of manufactured goods became concentrated in Seoul.

The gender division in the labor market in Seoul also changed. Women were increasingly employed in the service sector of the economy. In 1970, women comprised 28.5 percent of workers in the wholesale and retail sectors (EPB, 1973, p. 64). In 1991, they comprised 45.5 percent of the workforce in retail, and 60 percent of those working in restaurants and hotels. The garment manufacturing sector was still the largest employer of women in Seoul, retail was the second, and hospitality third (EPB, 1992, pp. 40-53).

This transformation of Korea into a consumer society and Seoul's economic growth brought about social and spatial differentiation. While numerous shops, supermarkets and department stores boomed, the divide between these new enterprises and the older *chaeraeshijang* and street businesses became clear. By the 1980s, distinctions between the regions north and south of the Han River also became more acute in terms of class differences. The Han River is the largest river in Seoul and geographically divides the city into the southern part, Kangnam, and the northern part, Kangbuk (see Map 1). The Kangnam area developed mainly as a business and residential district for the middleclass. In contrast, the Kangbuk area, where the Tongdaemun Shijang is situated, included residential areas for low-income workers as well as for the middle- and upper-middle classes and *chaeraeshijang* together with large business and commercial districts. Following the 1987 democratization movement, urban development began to focus on people's basic needs such as housing. However, a flurry of government and private housing projects led to a drastic rise in land prices and more frequent government operations against illegal settlements and street entrepreneurs. The emphasis on economic growth was reinforced even after decentralization in 1995. With the commencement of direct elections at local levels, newly elected mayors, governors and council members focused even more on economic development.

Within the Tongdaemun Shijang, gender concentration and social and spatial divisions became more apparent. In the 1980s, many garment industries in the marketplace moved to cheaper production sites in China and other newly emerging Asian economies. The Tongdaemun Shijang changed from a site of both garment production and sales to one predominantly of sales, becoming one of the largest garment sales centers in Korea. Growing democratization from the late 1980s also influenced the trend of consumption of casual clothes, and the marketplace benefited greatly from the demands of an increased number of female and young consumers (Oh, 2001, p. 148). New wholesale complexes prospered, mostly selling women's garments, and increasingly attracted married female small-scale entrepreneurs and family workers discouraged from entering waged employment, especially in the formal sector. In the 1990s, with the development of modern fashion retail complexes, the Tongdaemun Shijang became one of the largest fashion markets in Asia attracting even more female entrepreneurs and consumers as well as foreign buyers. However, the marketplace started to be divided into new modern complexes with higher prices targeting wealthier and younger consumers, and the older arcades and buildings with lower prices targeting retailers, the less affluent and older consumers. At the time of my fieldwork, the divide between new complexes and older arcades was also apparent in the composition of owners and staff in shops. In the new complexes, most of the shop attendants were young female employees and the owner was not on site, while in the older arcades, the shops were mostly run by self-employed merchants and/or their family members, most of whom were middle-aged or older women.

Undeniably, the continuous struggles of street entrepreneurs as well as micro- and small-scale merchants against redevelopment forces have contributed to the current form of the marketplace. Especially after Seoul's nomination as host of the 1988 Olympic Games in 1981, crackdowns against street entrepreneurs in central Seoul intensified. Street entrepreneurs united to form the Korean Street-Vendors Confederation (KSVC) to protest for their right to earn a livelihood (*saengjonkwon*) alongside the labor movement, the urban poor and evicted residents – by demonstrating against and negotiating with local authorities. In contrast to developments in other commercial districts in central Seoul, the *chaeraeshijang* have not been "modernized" in the dominant way of small shops and street stands being replaced with established and larger-scale shops. Seoul's policy at that time was also to modernize the *chaeraeshijang* by keeping their original character while improving customer convenience through more access to parking areas, asphalt paths, and public toilets (see "Tongdaemuntŭng 10kaeshijang,"1983). Thus, the Tongdaemun Shijang remained open to many people for employment and consumption.

Post-crisis, Redevelopment and Gender

In the fourth phase of the development of the Tongdaemun Shijang, after the 1997 Financial Crisis, discrimination against women in the formal labor market was reinforced, and the number of street entrepreneurs as well as other informal workers appeared to increase. Korea's economy moved from a state-led model toward a more market-oriented one. When the government carried out financial and labor reforms, women were the first to lose their jobs. Although Korea's economy recovered quickly, women still had more difficulties in securing employment in the formal sector than men with the same qualifications.[9] Although there are no official figures to corroborate this, more people sought income opportunities in self-employment after the 1997 crisis such as street entrepreneurship in the *chaeraeshijang*. The number of customers seeking cheaper commodities in the *chaeraeshijang* also increased.

In particular, those unemployed and aged, especially women, have eagerly sought informal income opportunities, partly because of the lack of a social security system. The pension system established after the Korean War covered only civil servants, military officers and workers in private educational institutions. Until the late 1980s, the successive authoritarian regimes prioritized economic growth over social security (Okuda, 2005; Shin, 2006). In 1988, the national pension system covered firms with more than ten employees. By 1992 the coverage was extended to firms with more than five employees, and to the self-employed and workers in small firms in fishing and rural areas in 1995. The subscription rate of the total population was very low. It was 13.2 percent in 1990 and 18.6 percent in 1995 (Shin, 2006, p. 566). Two years after the 1997 Financial Crisis, the government made the national pension system compulsory for "all workers" by including the urban self-employed and workers in all types of small firms. This resulted in an increase of the subscription rate up to 58.8 percent in 2000. However, pensions did not cover those who were older than sixty at the time of the enactment of the system. Many people have also not paid the pension fees. The system allows people to hold membership without making contributions due to reasons of unemployment, low income and lack of fixed residence,[10] but people cannot receive a pension without contributing to the system. At the same time, full-time housewives who have not contributed to the system individually are provided with no more than a small sum (KRW150,000 annually) on the basis of their husband's contributions to the system. As a result, low-income people and housewives tend to depend on their income rather than the national pension system.

The move to a market-driven economy further accelerated the redevelopment of central Seoul and the displacement of street entrepreneurs. The Tongdaemun Shijang Area started to be redeveloped with the restoration of the Ch'ŏnggyech'ŏn Stream in 2002. The local authority forced street entrepreneurs to relocate from the riverside to the Tongdaemun Stadium within the marketplace in 2004 despite the predicted drastic fall in their daily income, and again planned to relocate them in favor of developing the stadium into a public park (as of November 2007). It also supported the redevelopment of a few garment complexes into a larger fashion mall by evicting female garment merchants and street entrepreneurs. These women are now fighting against their displacement in various ways.

THE TIME, SPACE AND GENDER OF FEMALE STREET ENTREPRENEURS

Here I develop an alternative history of the Tongdaemun Shijang through the subjectivities of local female street entrepreneurs. By examining how their narratives articulate their needs, desires and identities, I explore the ways in which spatial and social relations construct, and are constructed by, the women's sense of self and place. As will be shown, the women reconfigure their subjectivities and identities and eventually their spatial and social relations through their agency, reproducing, negotiating, and resisting spatial and social relations.

Employing women's narratives as a powerful means to inquire into the ways in which women evaluate their belonging to place and their life trajectories, I highlight the dynamism of self-identification and its diversity among women in their narratives. Following McNay (2000), I conceive of the act of self-identification in the form of narration as an attempt "to integrate permanence in time with its contrary, namely diversity, variability, discontinuity and instability" (p. 89). Women's narratives attempt to create coherent subjectivities across time and space and by bridging discontinuities and instabilities in women's sense of self and place. Women's narratives also mirror the diversity among female entrepreneurs, revealing the coeval nature and coexistence of multiple life trajectories.

Here, narratives include individual interviews and informal talks I conducted during my fieldwork. I interviewed eight female street entrepreneurs, five of whom are cited in this study. I asked them to tell me their life stories and to explain how and why they came to work in the Tongdaemun Shijang. I had informal talks also with six other female street entrepreneurs. These interlocutors can be clustered into three cohorts: those in their sixties, those in their fifties, and those in their forties. Most of the interviewees were the main breadwinners of their family. Table 1 shows some details of the women who are cited in this paper.

In my analysis, I focus on three dimensions of female entrepreneur's narratives. First, I focus on the differences between how the women are represented in dominant public discourses[11] and how they express their own needs, desires and identities. Their attachment to work and place is far more complicated than simple economic necessity. Second, I focus on the interrelatedness between their needs and desires to pursue several different life projects and the ways in which they embody multiple identities. The women represent diverse needs, desires and identities both simultaneously and along their life courses. Third, I focus on the diversity and commonality among women, and explore possible sources of difference. For example, historical events differentiate the subjects in their formation and interact with their personal life courses.

The needs, desires and identities expressed in the women's narratives largely relate to five aspects of their lives: family and economic relations, spatial relations and physical mobility, personal abilities and desires, collective identity, and tensions in gender. Although I use these categories in my analytical framework, the women's narratives consistently reveal the interrelatedness of different aspects of life as "webs of meaning within which humans act" (Personal Narratives Group, 1989, p. 19).

Family and Economic Relations

Family and economic relations are highlighted differently in dominant public discourses and interviewees' narratives. Dominant public discourses largely conceive of women as daughters or mothers devoted to their families. A dominant discourse on the workers mobilized for national economic development in the 1960s and 1970s is that many young

Table 1 *Female Street Entrepreneurs Cited in the Study*

Name	Age	Marital Status	Children	Education	Occupation	Period of Engagement	Monthly Income[12]
Hwang Sookja	Late 60s	Married	Two sons and three daughters	Did not finish primary school	Operates a used handbag stand	Over 30 years	US$540-980 (KRW500,000-900,000)*
Song Okhee	Mid-60s	Widow	Six sons	Did not finish primary school	Operates a sandwich stand	Over 30 years	US$760-870 (KRW700,000-800,000)
Bae Minsook	Mid-50s	Married	Two daughters and one son	Finished junior high school	Operates a food and juice stand	Over 25 years	US$2,720-3,040 (KRW2,500,000-2,800,000)
Shin Kyŏnghee	Mid-50s	Married	A son and a daughter	Graduated from university	Operates a combined sewing and home supplies shop	Over 10 years	US$2,170-2,720 (KRW2,000,000-2,500,000)
Moon Meejŏng	Late 40s	Married	A son and a daughter	Finished junior secondary school	Operates a street restaurant	Over 20 years	US$3,260-3,800 (KRW3,000,000-3,500,000)

* The exchange rate US$1 = KRW920, applicable in July 2007, is used here.

unmarried women migrated to cities, especially Seoul, to support their families' livelihoods, including their brothers' education (Chun, 2004, p. 147; Koo, 2000). A recent dominant public discourse is that women are engaged in street entrepreneurship in order to support their children's education. These discourses obscure the presence of different women like those I interviewed, some of whom migrated after marriage and others who were always based in Seoul, and motives for their migration and engagement in street entrepreneurship other than simple economic necessity.

As in the public discourses, the need to support children's education is a reality that these women have experienced. When I asked them why they had started to work in the market, all immediately recounted their need to support their households, and especially to pay for their children's education. Hwang Sookja, born in the early 1940s in Chŏllanam-do province, came to Seoul at 18 after marrying. She started a street business selling foodstuffs on the side of the Ch'ŏnggyech'ŏn Stream in the mid-1960s when her husband failed in his business and costs were rising for their five children's education. At that time, only primary school education was compulsory and free. Junior secondary school nationally became compulsory and free only in 2002. The desire for children's higher education has long been a strong feature in Korea as in other Confucian societies, and with national economic development employers demanded increasingly higher levels of education. In the 1960s and 1970s, junior secondary school was considered the minimum education required to obtain a "decent" position such as a white-collar job. In the 1980s, high school was the minimum qualification. Then, the desire of Koreans for children's higher education intensified in later decades to become a sort of national project. The percentage of elementary school graduates going on to middle school increased from 58.4 percent in 1969 to 99.9 percent in 1997. In the late 1980s and early 1990s the number of students studying abroad also increased drastically.[13]

Although family and economic relations were dominant features in my interlocutors' narratives, they articulated these relations quite differently from dominant public discourses. Until now, I have used the term "education" in a blurred sense. Before the interviews, I had the impression that for many Korean parents it meant "schooling," rather than a more abstract ideal about "education." However, quite a few interlocutors appreciated aspects of the quality of life and self[14] their children achieved rather than the length of schooling and the title or name of the school from which they graduated. Some conveyed their happiness in having helped their children gain experiences and discover new horizons, while others expressed their satisfaction with the fact that their children were living their lives eagerly and honestly.

Several needs and desires addressed in the women's narratives are absent in public discourses. For example, many of my interlocutors, especially older women, recounted their struggle against discrimination. Bae Minsook expressed the view that her disabled husband felt freer in the Tongdaemun Shijang. Born in the early 1950s in a farmer's family in Kyŏngsangbuk-to, she did not like to work in agriculture. At sixteen, she left for Seoul to stay in an uncle's house and help his family business. She married a disabled man despite her parents' opposition. She started a street business in her neighborhood to support her family. After her children reached school age – twenty years ago – she began running her food stand in the Tongdaemun Shijang. She received help from neither her own parents nor her parents-in-law. At the time of my fieldwork, her disabled husband sometimes minded the stand in her absence. In the Tongdaemun Shijang and other *chaeraeshijang*, a larger presence of disabled people, both visitors and street entrepreneurs, was observed than in other commercial places in Seoul.[15]

Another desire expressed by the interviewees related to their age. Most of the women, who were in their fifties and sixties and whose children were grown up at the time of the interviews, expressed their desire to be economically independent and autonomous. These viewpoints will be discussed later.

Many women also expressed concern about youth unemployment. This problem has long been an issue in public discourse. For example, in the early 1980s, the job shortage for university graduates was already reported as a critical issue in the nation ("Kogŭmillyŏk Suyong Mothae," 1982). The number of unemployed seems to have increased, especially with the 1997 Financial Crisis. This has led to a prolonged period of parental support for children and to a persistent concern about lifelong security among older street entrepreneurs.

Public discourses on the female street entrepreneurs' engagement in the marketplace concentrate on issues related to economic necessity. The following categories of needs, desires and identities are largely invisible in dominant public discourses, mainly because the discourses overlook diversity and changes in the women's situations and perceptions.

Spatial Relations and Physical Mobility

The women prominently discussed issues connected with spatial relations and physical mobility that are largely invisible in public discourses. The topics they felt important included their reasons for migrating to Seoul and the conditions within the residential and working area in terms of proximity to family networks and their workplaces, forced evictions and relocations, and traffic and communication networks. These issues were expressed as closely related to the women's corporeality and, in many cases, aging.

Proximity to economic support from a family network and to income opportunities was important for women's emplacement close to the marketplace. Many recounted their encounter with Seoul and the marketplace as an important phase of their married lives. None of them were engaged in street businesses before marriage. Most of them came to Seoul after marrying, associating the beginning of their lives in Seoul with their married lives. For Song Okhee, proximity to her brother and to the Tongdaemun Shijang was crucial. Born in the early 1940s in Chŏllabuk-to province, she lost her father when she was three. She lived with her grandmother, mother and elder brother. At ten, she started to work in an aunt's silk reeling workshop, staying in the aunt's home away from her own family. She often attempted to escape and was taken back to her own family home several years later. She married at twenty-one and came to live in her family-in-law's house in a neighborhood adjacent to the marketplace. She had six sons. Her family was evicted twice and relocated to a satellite city. After working in various kinds of informal positions, she set up a snack stand in the marketplace in the early 1980s. Three years later, her husband died. She and her sons moved to a neighborhood near the marketplace where her brother and his family lived, relying on his economic support and income generation in the marketplace.

Another common topic in the women's narratives concerned evictions and moving. Most of those in their fifties and sixties viewed their lives in terms of repeated relocations. Some were forced to move their businesses or were evicted from residential neighborhoods due to the area's redevelopment, and others moved to live in cheaper housing due to their families' economic situations. However, they remained attached to the marketplace area for their economic activities. Song Okhee, who was evicted twice and returned to the marketplace to start a snack stand, began her life story with the phrase, "An eviction was taking place so they could build apartments...." She recounted the eviction as the starting point of her attachment to the marketplace.

Female street entrepreneurs' experiences of crackdowns greatly affected their physical positions and feelings. Song Okhee recounted:

> With the crackdowns, they took things away, they took a parasol, a frying pan, and I cried. I often fell, and even though I fell down, those people were merciless. I lived this way.... As I said just a while ago, I ran a business...in the Yŏngdŭngpo area...in the Haebang-dong neighborhood for three months and stopped, and came to the street here, joined in the confederation, and came to start this street business. I've run [the business] till now.

After several crackdowns Song Okhee moved her stand to a safer place. She asserted that she preferred her current location despite a decrease in her income. Moreover, she attributed her moving to her age, saying that it was too tiring for her to continue working at the pace she used to work at in her former location. She remarked that in the previous place she had too many customers and also had to compete with other women selling similar things next to her. She also lacked space for her to even stand. Her current stand is far from other street entrepreneurs dealing with the same foodstuffs and spacious enough to seat several people. She asserted that this way of doing business suited her lifestyle better now that she was older and needed to earn only for herself.

Many women represented their daily mobility and sense of place as changing due to their age, the development of the area, and the local transportation and communication network. Most of the women who had been engaged in street business for more than twenty years stated that until 10 or 15 years ago they had moved their carts everyday between where they lived and their place of work so as to avoid crackdowns. At the time of my fieldwork, all the women left their carts at their workplace. Older women stressed that they were not strong enough to move their carts every day. They lived beyond walking distance from their businesses and commuted mostly by subway. The development of public transport surely facilitated their access to the area.[16] A few of the younger cohorts used their own cars. Song Okhee was unlike the others in that she used a bicycle. Bicycles were not popular in Seoul until the city government recently started to promote their use in order to ease traffic congestion.[17]

Spatial changes, such as the emergence of larger buildings in the area, have also affected the location and mobility of street entrepreneurs, who are concentrated in front of the most popular buildings. Moreover, access to water has been important for street entrepreneurs selling food. Most of those in their sixties remembered that in the 1960s and 1970s, when water and sewerage were not yet fully available in the area, they had to transport water over long distances. However, after the late-1980s, when many new buildings were constructed, the women have been able to obtain water from public restrooms in nearby buildings. The buildings are private property, but street entrepreneurs use their facilities. With changes in communication systems, street entrepreneurs can now obtain other supplies more easily. At the time of my fieldwork, all of my interlocutors used a mobile phone to order the delivery of business goods.

As the physical mobility of street entrepreneurs has decreased, so too have their interpersonal interactions. However, when crackdowns against them became severe in the late-1980s, they began to unite and appreciate their collective identity as "street vendors," as will be discussed later.

Personal Abilities and Desires

In discussing motives for engagement in the marketplace, street entrepreneurs' narratives highlight personal abilities and desires, both of which are invisible in public discourses. Among those who came to Seoul after marrying in the 1960s and 1970s, the discourse of searching for a new life was widely shared. Song Okhee emphasized that marriage had liberated her from a hard life in the countryside. Suffering greatly when working in her aunt's workshop, she had made several attempts to leave without success and considered marriage the only means of liberation. For her, married life in central Seoul represented a positive change.

Another common theme in the women's narratives was their ability or inability to carry out economic activities. A dominant public discourse about the informal sector, including street entrepreneurship, is that people engage in such work because of the lack of opportunities for them in the formal economy. Among my interlocutors, just a few articulated this sentiment. Shin Kyŏnghee recounted her attachment to the marketplace as a consequence of events related to her failure to become a school teacher after graduating from university. She gave her lack of ability as the reason for this failure. She was born in Seoul in the early 1950s. Her family moved a dozen times for economic reasons. She finished university hoping to become a teacher, but failed the exam and subsequently abandoned her dream. She worked from time to time sewing home decorations and bedding items (*homp'aeshŏn*) at home. Getting married at thirty, she then had a son and a daughter. Her husband worked in a company as an accounting manager. After five years of staying at home, she set up a small restaurant but the business failed. Next she opened a fabric street shop within the Tongdaemun Shijang. However, when her husband quit work ten years ago, she decided to open her current sewing stand for more earnings to make up for her husband's income loss. She mentioned her ability to sew as the reason for taking up her current job. She repeatedly said that she had chosen the work not because she liked it but because she had the appropriate skills.

Interestingly, most narratives suggest that in addition to having an economic need to work, the women also continued working because of a pleasure in and desire for business success. Hwang Sookja, for example, emphasized her satisfaction at being appreciated for her business performance. She cheerfully discussed her business after being relocated to the Tongdaemun Stadium in 2004:

> I came here with empty hands. There was nothing I could do, so I started a candy business. Within the market, everyone knows the *ajumma* (auntie) of the candy trade. When I was involved in the candy trade, customers said that my candies were delicious and told me to sell more.

Moon Meejŏng recounted that she loved her restaurant work because of the interactions with customers, and that for her the development of her business meant providing customers with better-quality foods and services rather than making it larger physically and financially. She was born in Seoul in the late 1950s as the youngest child of the family, with one brother and five sisters. After her father's death, she helped her mother in the family restaurant. Married at twenty-one, she had two children. Her husband ran a retail business. While her children were at primary school, she started a stand selling side dishes. Her business grew progressively and her stand turned into a larger-scale street restaurant employing four women. Hers was the only street restaurant I encountered that contained a full coffee stand. She remarked that she acquired her idea from customers' demands for a variety of coffee and fruit drinks after the flour-based meals she offered. After she invited a young man to run the coffee stand inside her restaurant, it became so popular that he employed three helpers. She spoke of her pleasure in looking at her customers' happy faces.

Most of my older interlocutors also conveyed a wish for autonomy in their old age. Autonomy is a different desire and need from that of economic necessity. Although it is widely believed that poorer people rely on their children (especially sons) when they have aged,[18] the women's narratives suggest a wish to be economically independent. For the women, economic independence means the freedom to make decisions for themselves. Song Okhee, who visited her first son's house in a satellite city every Saturday, repeatedly remarked that she preferred living alone to living with her son's family.

Collective Identity

The women interviewed also expressed a sense of collective identity, in contrast to a public image that street entrepreneurs are individualistic. While none mentioned the labor and democratization movements of the mid- and late 1980s, many recounted their sense of belonging to the KSVC. Most were members of the organization. Their motive for joining was mainly to resist crackdowns. Hwang Sookja, a long-time member of the KSVC, was recently evicted from the side of the Ch'ŏnggyech'ŏn Stream and relocated within the Tongdaemun Stadium together with over 800 street entrepreneurs. The KSVC insisted on the evicted street-entrepreneurs' relocation within the Tongdaemun Shijang.

Their narratives also asserted their identity as members of a "street vendors" community, different from the KSVC. This became clear every time a threat of displacement occurred. For example, Song Okhee was terrified when a rumor reached her on a hot day in July 2007 informing her that the local authorities were going to inspect street entrepreneurs in the area. The KSVC immediately appealed for members to be cautious and to have stores clean and safe. However, her fear was based on the fact that the authorities considered her a "street vendor" regardless of her membership in the KSVC. Her words "All the street vendors are family members" express her identification with all "street vendors" who face displacement.

I also observed the women's sense of belonging to an informal mutual-help network of street entrepreneurs and other people such as friends who were customers. For example, those who directly responded to Song Okhee's aforementioned uneasiness related to the local authority's inspection were her friends, including her neighboring street entrepreneurs and regular customers. They collectively provided her with a set of possible measures to deal with the inspection. When a local government official came, she was tense but ready to respond to him. The measures her colleagues and friends had suggested exactly met the demands of the official. She was relieved. Besides this, Song Okhee daily offered her friends who visited her stand a cup of instant coffee, and they often brought her foods and drinks, newspapers, clothes, and so on. She freely lent her bicycle to other street entrepreneurs. She even let visitors use her stand space as a baggage room. A street entrepreneur friend of hers told me that Song Okhee had innate virtue, *indŏk*. Song Okhee smiled happily. Such a network and mutual trust among friends and colleagues is an important source of energy and sustenance for female street entrepreneurs.

This collective identity, as a member of the "street vendors'" community and of an informal mutual-help network, seemed to be stronger among those in their sixties than in younger cohorts. This may be partly because the older women have had more experience of crackdowns and the risks associated with displacement as they have been engaged in street business longer. It may also be because the younger cohorts are more concerned with their need to earn enough for their children's education. Networks are not something which can be established in one day, but they are the product of a lengthy process of mutual engagement among people. Among the interviewees, Hwang Sookja and Song Okhee had established the strongest networks. Apart from their personalities, which enabled them to develop close friendships with many people, they commonly had more free time for interacting with neighboring street entrepreneurs and friends than others with busier stands. All day long, Hwang Sookja and Song Okhee continuously received friends' visits, and they spent a long time together.

Many of my interlocutors' narratives also reflect business-related interdependence among workers in the area. While catering for shoppers, street entrepreneurs also satisfied the business and daily-life needs of other workers in the area. Many workers spend long hours at their workplace. Especially since the lifting of the prohibition of night traffic in 1982[19] and since the new fashion malls in the area started to operate overnight in the 1990s, the number of street stands and their operating hours have increased. Food businesses usually operate with longer hours to cater for workers' varying hours. Song Okhee works from 5 a.m. to 6 p.m. Bae Minsook works from 10 a.m. to 7 p.m., and her employee works from 7 p.m. to 2 a.m. Restaurants are often open for twenty-four hours. Since many workers work until late at night or all night long, there are also businesses such as spas with sleeping rooms nearby. Street businesses need suppliers and service providers as well. Several such individuals drop in to street stands every day to ask if the proprietors need anything.

Tensions in Gender

Street entrepreneurs' narratives demonstrate that the gendered dimensions of women's lives are far more complicated than the ways in which gender is represented in dominant public discourses. Public discourses simply relate mothers' economic necessity to their engagement in street entrepreneurship. However, if the narratives are traced attentively, women's sense of gendered self emerges as far more complicated and multilayered. From childhood, the women had been discriminated against in various ways. In the 1960s and 1970s, education was still the most common arena of gender discrimination in Korea. Some interviewees stressed that they had not been given the chance at higher education because their parents or grandparents had prioritized boys' schooling. Moon Meejŏng, from the youngest cohort, was most direct and critical in talking about the gendered dimensions in her life. She differs from the other women in her greater economic success through her larger-scale business, and by the fact that she has one elder brother and five elder sisters and lived with her grandmother until she married. She expressed a strong desire to give her daughter an education as good as her son's, while criticizing her mother's and grandmother's prioritizing her brother's schooling over hers and that of her sisters. Her striving for self-realization in business may partly be a reaction to this deprivation of educational and other opportunities.

While public discourses also depict the women as confined to a marginalized workplace because of a lack of options, most of the women interviewed represented their work as a positive opportunity. Women's opportunities in the Korean formal labor market have been limited by their gender, age, schooling and marital status. Until the mid-1980s, wage employment was not easily available for married and older women. Most of the women had already started their street businesses by the 1980s and had not been interested in waged employment such as factory work.

Without the vocational skills required to participate in specialized industries, many had conceived of their engagement in street business as one of their best options because of its ease of entry and earning potential (at least at the time of their entry).[20] Later on they found other positive outcomes from the work. All also recounted that they had not sensed that street businesses discriminated against women, and that the marketplace had been always packed with female street entrepreneurs. Additionally, most of their businesses were related to food preparation and clothing, with which they were familiar as married women.

The narratives suggest that the street entrepreneurs experienced a tension between the different gender positions socially ascribed to them, namely those of the married woman and mother. All the women were married or widowed and had children. Until quite recently, it was assumed in Korea that women generally would get married and have children, preferably sons. Whenever the women in their fifties and sixties came of age, the responsibility and roles of a married woman and mother in the prevailing notion of womanhood were mainly of a homemaker and caregiver who nurtured family members. This was based on a clear gendered division of labor in which money-making was not women's responsibility. In fact, most women stayed at home while their children were young, despite the insecure economic position of their households. However, when their children reached school age, most of the mothers needed to earn money to support their children's education.

Most women linked their need to earn money with the inadequacy of their husbands' incomes to support the family, and some explicitly expressed a reluctance to work outside the home because it was against their role and wish to stay at home as married women. Most asserted that they had started to work as breadwinners because their husbands failed in business or did not want to earn more money. While some had worked to earn money within their home by doing piecework or occasional work when their children were young, their narratives show a tendency to consider their work as complementary to their husbands' income and working as breadwinners as a less desired option. Hwang Sookja explained her early years as the family's main breadwinner:

> My husband is from the North [Korea]. Coming here, well, he wasn't able to make a living, without skills, and didn't know how to do things. As he is aging, he can't do anything, he just sits. And so, while my husband looked after the children, I went out to do business.

At the same time, many women in their fifties and sixties longed to be homemakers. Song Okhee said:

> Do you want to know what I've wished to do?... It's the best if a woman just takes care of the home. That's the happiest, I think that way.

> Even now. If a woman can live [only] a family life at home, that's the best. That's the happiest [life].... Doing only housekeeping and working only at home, right? I think living at home doing this, this way is the happiest [way]. Isn't that right? It's the happiest if you were born as a woman not to do other things than staying at home with children and [living] morally. Where else is happiness other than that?

The tension between the desire to live an idealized womanhood and the need to fulfill an economic role as mothers becomes a heavy burden for women, especially when they are forced to become the main breadwinners of their families. Bae Minsook did not show much suffering from such tension. This could be explained by the fact that she actively opted for this alternative way of living as the main breadwinner. In contrast, Shin Kyŏnghee is the one who most strongly, albeit implicitly, expressed a resistance and reluctance to becoming the main breadwinner of the family. She did not recount any experience of gender-based discriminative attitudes on the part of her parents. She had only sisters and no brothers. Her narrative indicates she disliked working outside the home after she married, and that she reached a turning point when her husband became unable to sustain the family and provide their children with a higher education. When I asked her who had earned money while she was staying at home to rear her small children, she recounted:

> Now, in the situation of our country, women bring up children. Women also do housekeeping, and husbands go out to earn money. We have to do it. Naturally, I did housekeeping. While rearing children I also did all the housekeeping work. Having said that, it doesn't mean the other family members didn't work. They cleaned the house, and (pause). Since my mother-in-law lived with us at that time (pause). Well, such a situation, [if you ask such] a question, all women['s situation] is almost the same, women without a special profession. So, I, too, lived that way.

Shin Kyŏnghee started to run her sewing stand in the Tongdaemun Shijang when Korea was hit by the financial crisis. She told me that it was when her husband resigned from his company, although she did not mention the financial crisis. When I asked her why her husband had resigned his job as an accounting manager in a company, she was at a loss for words, in contrast to the fluent narrative she had been engaged in until that moment:

> (Long silence) Well, (a deep sigh) now, it's complicated (pause). What I say, what I say, my feeling [about it] (pause), it's very complicated (pause). Since I should talk about all humane deep feelings, then, (pause) he quit the job because the company's situation and his own situation and character didn't suit each other.

Although she avoided talking about her "complicated" feelings in this narrative, she told me later that the news about her husband's resignation was a shock to her. She was more upset that she had to be the main breadwinner than that her husband had lost his job *per se*. Her narrative as a whole implies that she was resistant to living her life differently from the dominant notion of a married woman as homemaker and caregiver. It emerged that she had considered her own income-generating work as complementing her husband's income to that time and that she had became the main breadwinner of the family against her own wishes.

Here, it is important to note that Shin Kyŏnghee's gender identity has been neither static nor uniform. Although she has accepted the conventional idealized model of married womanhood, she has also been engaged in a process of negotiation to accommodate different and new needs and desires in her daily life. She recounted:

> In our country, well, there is a thought, which has come from the old times, that is that women have to support men. By the way, with my character, my thought is also fundamentally so, that fundamental idea. I believe a little, well, in the thought that we have to support men. But, compared to other women, I tend to insist on my opinions. I tend to insist on taking action. I tell these things [to my children]. Even if you are a woman, even if you are a man, you have to do certain things. I have to do that. My children are from a different generation than me, and [a woman] cannot survive without an education and only supporting men. A daughter-in-law will come to us later, and they (she and my son) will [have to support] each other.

The women's narratives also indicate that the women are conscious of a gendered division of labor, even among street businesses. Based on the notion that some kinds of work should be done by men, Song Okhee told me that she did all types of work for her business, including "men's work" such as the transportation of heavy goods.[21] Her remarks expressed complicated feelings of regret, resignation and pride. Shin Kyŏnghee sewed at her stand while her husband attended customers, procured business supplies, and cut fabrics for her. Even though she considered her husband's work as inferior to the ideal kind of work for men, compared to his former position as an accounting manager, she expressed her appreciation of his role in her business. She did so in order to assert her gender identity in which her desire to live as a homemaker and caregiver would otherwise conflict with the need to support her children's education as their mother.

CONCLUSION

I have shown the interrelatedness of spatial, social and gender relations in the formation of the Tongdaemun Shijang through the representation of two histories of the marketplace: one from a macro-level dynamic of spatial, economic and gender relations and the other constructed through female street entrepreneurs' sense of self and place.

The first history explored space-gender concentrations and divisions of labor in national, regional and local economic and urban development. It revealed that space and gender worked to remap the physical and social location of women in street entrepreneurship in a *chaeraeshijang*. Various factors such as age, origin, class, education, and marriage highly affected the women's lives and spatial trajectories and the creative processes of the marketplace. From the 1960s to the 1970s, with state-led export-oriented industrialization, the gender ideologies of "Korean style capitalism" mobilized young unmarried women into labor-intensive light industry in urban areas, especially into the textile and garment manufacturing sectors in the Seoul region. The Tongdaemun Shijang was one of the sites where small firms in these sectors and street entrepreneurs were concentrated. From the mid-1980s, married women started to be employed in the garment manufacturing and other labor-intensive sectors as unskilled laborers. At the same time, the urban service sector developed rapidly with women's active participation as entrepreneurs and employees. In this period, the Tongdaemun Shijang developed as a commercial center and attracted numerous female street entrepreneurs – predominantly mothers. In recent decades, economic and urban development have led to an increase in the number of street entrepreneurs owing to the potential of income-earning opportunities, limited access to the formal labor market, and insufficient social security for the poor, the aged, and women. After the 1997 Financial Crisis, street entrepreneurship functioned as a safety net for those who suffered a loss in income. In the process of becoming one of the largest fashion markets in Korea and Asia, the Tongdaemun Shijang continued to attract female street entrepreneurs, particularly because of its specialization in garment-related trade and the potential for earning an income in food-related businesses.

The second history contrasts with the aforementioned one in the representation of female street-entrepreneurs' engagement in the process of making the Tongdaemun Shijang. In the first history, being wives and mothers without competitive qualifications, female street entrepreneurs tend to be seen as passively confined to their current place due to limited access to the formal labor market. However, in the second history, in which I sought to highlight their subjectivities, female street entrepreneurs emerged as social agents who created their own meaning and place in the marketplace and wider society.

Their narratives indicate that their attachment to the marketplace has been shaped by multiple interrelated and changing needs, desires and identities and through diverse ways of negotiating space and gender. At the same time, the women's different needs, desires and identities and ways of negotiation have been formed through the spatial processes of the marketplace and of the women's own lives through marriage, migration, redevelopment, evictions, government crackdowns, aging, and interactions with other street entrepreneurs and friends.

There were as many common concerns as there were differences in the women's articulations of their sense of self and place. Regarding economic and family relations, their narratives highlight experiences of discrimination and increasing needs for children's schooling, stressing their family's wellbeing as their priority. Spatial relations were portrayed as migration to Seoul, proximity to family networks and income opportunities, daily physical mobility, aging, changes in access to space and other business resources, crackdowns and eviction. These spatial relations and physical mobility led to interdependence among diverse actors. Personal abilities and desires were related to the search for a new life, inability to realize a dream at a young age, and business abilities. Collective identity was expressed in a variety of ways: as members of the KSVC, feeling part of a community of "street-vendors," or that of an informal mutual-help network, and as interdependent on other entrepreneurs and workers of the area.

Female street entrepreneurs' narratives represent the market as a place where they have formed new desires and identities, such as those associated with developing their enterprises and becoming autonomous older citizens, as well as developing a collective identity as members of a street vendors' community and mutual-help network. These desires and identities contribute to their self-esteem, interdependency and inspire them to work every day as well as to continue with the process of making the Tongdaemun Shijang, or contributing to the development of the marketplace.

Further, the women's narratives express their gender identities as complicated and multi-layered. The most common issue was the tension between polarized gender positions: the desire to play the roles of homemakers and caregivers to follow the conventional ideal of married women in Korea and the additional desire to fulfill their economic responsibilities as mothers. Despite active engagement in street entrepreneurship, many have retained a desire to be their family's homemakers and caregivers. The extent to which they suffer from the tension varies.

Most notably, their ways of negotiating such contradictions are diverse. In part, this diversity derives from the variation in the extent to which they are dominated by these gender identities. For example, younger women are evidently freer from traditional gender ideals and have been developing different processes of gendered self-formation. Some women negotiate tensions by forming other identities. Bae Minsook has a strong sense of being the main breadwinner of her family, asserting that it was her own decision to act as such. Hwang Sookja expressed her identity as a member of a street entrepreneurs' community, her wish to be appreciated for her business performance rather than her earning power, and her desire to be an autonomous aged person. In comparison, Song Okhee without hesitation expressed her yearning to be a homemaker. She asserted her happiness as being appreciated by family members and friends for her entrepreneurship, caring for others and having a humane sense of being, playing a role in developing an informal mutual-help network, and being autonomous. In contrast, Shin Kyŏnghee, who expressed her suffering most strongly, has not developed such a positive sense of self, separate from the realm of being a wife and a mother. However, she has also been negotiating her sense of gendered self by promoting a different set of gender ideals to her children and appreciating her husband's role as a co-worker in her business.

Diversity was observed not only among different age cohorts but also among different groups of street entrepreneurs, according to whether their children were already economically independent or not; whether they had migrated to Seoul before or after marriage, or grew up in Seoul; whether or not they were the main breadwinners of their families; whether or not they considered themselves successful in business; and whether or not they had developed mutual-help networks. All these differences affected their sense of belonging to the Tongdaemun Shijang as a place as well as their gendered selves.

This examination of female street entrepreneurship has destabilized certain fixed concepts of the place called Tongdaemun Shijang and of "married female street vendors." The Tongdaemun Shijang, like other *chaeraeshijang*, is not merely a traditional and static entity being modernized in a unilinear fashion. On the contrary, it is a place which has been formed and transformed with ever-changing, interacting, and diverse identities of people, who transcend and mutually interact across the boundaries of this market and other places daily and over time. Furthermore, female subjectivities and identities were subjected to change through the processes of the becoming of this place (Tongdaemun Shijang) and of the women's lives, not limited by the monolithic identities of "married women" or "mothers." Street entrepreneurship in contemporary Seoul continues to be a form of work which offers people, especially women who have limited access to formal income opportunities, a viable physical and social place. Seoul's *chaeraeshijang* have developed to attract female street entrepreneurs because of their resilient, creative and diverse economic practices in which diverse subjects are actively involved. It would be more productive to reconceptualize urban development to take account of such a notion of place, work and people.

Acknowledgements

The research for this study was supported by funding from the Australian National University and a 2007 Korea Foundation Fellowship for Field Research. The author gratefully acknowledges the help of street entrepreneurs in the Tongdaemun Shijang, the Korean Street-Vendors Confederation (KSVC), the Korean Women's Institute, Ewha Woman's University, and friends in Seoul. I would also like to sincerely thank Tamara Jacka and Ruth Barraclough for their very thoughtful and extremely valuable feedback. My sincere thanks go as well to Carolyn Brewer and Pyone Myat Thu for their dedicated proofreading. An early version of this article was delivered at the 3rd international Asia Association for Global Studies (AAGS) conference in Kobe, Japan in March 2008, and another version was published in *Intersections: Gender and Sexuality in Asia and the Pacific*, Issue 17, July 2008 [available at: http://intersections.anu.edu.au/issue17/noritake.htm].

Note on Romanization

This study mainly adopts the 1984 McCune-Reischauer-based romanization system. As an exception, this study uses "*shi*" for the letters "시" for the benefit of English speakers. For example, "시장" (marketplace) is written as "*shijang*." For the names of well-known people and places, I follow the most widely used romanization. For the names of authors, I use the romanization that the authors themselves have used.

Notes

1 The Seoul Metropolitan Government and the local mass media have recently promoted Seoul as a "world-class" city (see, for example, "Sudokwŏnchŏngch'aek Shidaee Matke," 1998). *The Basic Urban Planning of Seoul 2020*, published in 2003, highlighted the objective of making Seoul a world city with "harmony between nature and people, and between history and the cutting-edge" (K.S. Ryu, "2020 Seoul Toshi Kibonkyehwoek" Naeyoung, 1998). The urban redevelopment project of Seoul which has most appealed to the national and international community as a model has been the restoration of the Ch'ŏnggyech'ŏn Stream, completed in 2005. As Massey (2005) notes regarding London, this view of a "successful" city is problematic (pp. 156-157). The success based on prioritizing certain sectors such as finance and high technology depends on increasing poverty and exclusion.
2 A demographic picture of Korean street entrepreneurs has not been compiled due to the dearth of reliable data.
3 The term *chaeraeshijang* is used both in singular and plural forms.
4 The Kwangjang Shijang, a part of the current Tongdaemun Shijang, was officially organized in 1904 for grocery trade and for textile and garment trade in later periods.
5 House helpers including nannies, predominantly women, have been in high demand in Korea's informal labor market. The Korean terms referring to these work positions have changed over the last four decades. In the 1960s and 1970s, employment advertisements in major newspapers used the terms *shikmo* (cook-maids) and *yumo* (nannies). In later decades, they have used *kajŏngbu* (housekeepers).
6 In general, women quit their job upon marriage, or were forced to leave the workplace around the age of 22.
7 Cho (1986) defines the informal sector as "marginalized," "subordinate" and "composed of petit bourgeoisie and marginal workers" in contrast to "the more advanced capitalist corporate sector" (p. 158).
8 In 1960, primary industry employed 2.2 percent of Seoul workers, secondary industry 24.9 percent, and tertiary industry 71.6 percent (EPB, 1963, p. 16).
9 According to Korean feminist critiques, while the number of female part-time and

casual workers has increased in the process of recovery from the crisis, women's employment has been practiced not by meritocracy but by a patriarchal culture which discriminates against women in the formal labor market by defining them not as individual laborers but as a collective whose main social roles consist of being wives and mothers (e.g., H. M. Kim, 2001, pp. 64-66).

10 As of July 2007, 56 percent of the subscribed self-employed and workers in small firms have not paid full subscription ("Mitppajin Kukminyŏn'gŭm," 2007).

11 Here "public discourses" are those of local officials, leading newspapers, scholars and middleclass people, including those of leaders of the KSVC.

12 The figures are calculated based on the information my interlocutors gave me during my fieldwork. They run their businesses for more than twelve hours per day for six to seven days a week. In 2006, a household in Seoul earned US$3,440 (KRW3,200,000) per month on average while spending US$2,784 (KRW2,590,000, exchange rate US$1=KRW930 applied) (Seoul Metropolitan Government, 2007). Employees in shops and restaurants in the Tongdaemun Shijang were paid US$3.30-4.30 (KRW3,000-4,000, exchange rate US$1=KRW920 applied) per hour on average in July, 2007.

13 With the liberalization of overseas travel in 1989, the number of Korean students studying abroad increased from 18,000 in 1983 to 84,700 in 1992. In 1994, the media estimated up to 100,000 students were studying abroad ("Haeoe Yuhak 5wolbut'ŏ Chayulhwa," 1994).

14 By "quality of life and of self" I stress the mental and spiritual dimensions rather than the material dimensions of life.

15 There is no official figure to corroborate this account. However, one can easily note a larger presence of disabled people in the *chaeraeshijang* than in other commercial places in Seoul. Subway areas are other places where disabled people are more visible as merchants.

16 As of August 2007, there were four subway stations and many city bus routes in the area.

17 According to my observations, women riding motorbikes started to be visible only in 2005 or 2006 in the Tongdaemun Shijang. This absence of women riding motorbikes was related to the absence of female delivery agents. Most suppliers to street entrepreneurs were men who rode motorbikes to deliver goods. The gender norm that men transport heavy things has given rise to this gendered division of labor and gendered mobility. The exception is the delivery of meals from small restaurants in the area, which is mostly done by middle-aged women on foot.

18 Korea has a long tradition of aged parents' dependence on their first sons. However, this trend has been changing in recent decades. In 1979, a decade before the introduction of the national pension fund, it was reported that 52.6 percent of respondents in a survey preferred their dependence on sons to a government pension (2.5 percent) ("Adŭle Ŭt'ak 52.8% Ch'aji," 1979). In 1990, 34.5 percent of survey respondents preferred to be dependent on the retirement grant and pension from employers, 22.0 percent on earnings and property, and 6.8 percent on children and the government fund ("Nohusaenghwalbi Wŏl 21man~40manwŏn Yesang," 1990).

19 The curfew was established by the US government in 1945 following the Koreas' separation

20 In contrast, some women who had worked in the garment manufacturing sector in the 1960s and 1970s gained advanced sewing skills and established their own garment subcontract firms in the neighborhoods of the marketplace. Most of the women I interviewed did not have such specialized skills.

21 At least in Seoul at the time of my fieldwork it was still a predominant gendered cultural practice for women to order men to carry heavy things and men did so.

References

Adŭle ŭt'ak 52.8% ch'aji [52.8% dependent on sons]. (1979, November 30). *Chosun Ilbo*.
Allen, J., Massey, D., & Cochrane, A. (1998). *Rethinking the region*. London: Routledge.
Chang, P.-W. (1986). Women and work: A case study of a small town in Korea. In S.-W. Chung (Ed.), *Challenges for women: Women's studies in Korea* (pp. 255-281). Seoul: Ewha Womans University Press.
Cho, H. (1986). Labor force participation of women in Korea. In S.-W. Chung (Ed.), *Challenges for women: Women's studies in Korea* (pp. 150-172). Seoul: Ewha Womans University Press.
Chun, S. (2004). *Kkŭnnaji anŭn shidaŭi norae* [Unfinished songs of apprentices]. Seoul: Hankyoreh.
The City History Compilation Committee of Seoul (2004). *The launch of Seoul as the capital of the Republic of Korea (1945-1960)*, Seoul through Pictures 3. Seoul: Mayor of Seoul.
EPB. (1963). *1960 Population and housing census of Korea*, vol.1, Complete Tabulation Report, 11-2 Seoul City. Republic of Korea: Economic Planning Board.
EPB. (1973). *1970 Population and housing census report*, vol. 2, *10% sample survey, 4-1 Economic activity*. Republic of Korea: Economic Planning Board.
EPB. (1987). *Korea statistical yearbook*. Republic of Korea: Economic Planning Board.
EPB. (1992). *1991 Report on establishment census*, vol. 2, Region, Rep. Korea. Republic of Korea: Economic Planning Board.
Haeoe yuhak 5wolbut'ŏ chayulhwa/kochulisang oekukŏshihŏm ph'yeji [Automization of studies abroad from May: Abolition of the foreign language test for students for high-school graduates and higher-level students]. (1994, April 15). *Seoul Shinmun*, p. 3.
Kim, J., & Choe, S. (1997). *Seoul: The making of a metropolis*. London: Wiley.
Kim, H. M. (2001). Work, nation, and hypermasculinity: The "woman" question in the economic miracle and crisis in South Korea. *Inter-Asia Cultural Studies, 1*(1), 54-68.
Kim, H. M. (2005). The formation of subjectivities among Korean women workers: A historical review. In P. Chang & E.-S Kim (Eds.), *Women's experiences and feminist practices in South Korea* (pp. 177-204). Seoul: Ewha Woman's University Press.
Kim, W. B.(1999). Developmentalism and beyond: Reflections on Korean cities. *Korea Journal, 39*(3), 5-34.
Kogŭmillyŏk suyong mothae [Can't accommodate high-level labor force]. (1982, September 4). *Dong-A Ilbo*, p. 5.
Koo, H. (2001). *Korean workers: The culture and politics of class formation*. Ithaca and London: Cornell University Press.
Lett, D. P. (1998). *In pursuit of status: The making of South Korea's "new" urban middle class*. Cambridge, MA: Harvard University Asia Center.
Massey, D. B. (1994). *Space, place and gender*. Cambridge: Polly.
Massey, D. (2005). *For space*. London, Thousand Oaks, and New Delhi: Sage Publications.
McNay, L. (2000). *Gender and agency*. Cambridge: Polity Press.
Mitppajin kukminyŏn'gŭm: Ch'enapaek 7ch'o 2766ŏk [National pension shortfall: Total nonpayment of 7,276,600 million]. (2007, October 25). *Segye Ilbo*, p. 5.
Nohusaenghwalbi wŏl 21man~40manwŏn yesang/Kagujutaesang chosa [Living expenses of old age, 210,000~400,000 wŏn monthly: Survey for householders]. (1990, January 23). *Dong-A Ilbo*, p. 7.
Okuda, S. (2005). Kankokuniokeru shoushikoureikato nenkinmondai [Issues on Korea's falling birthrate-aging and pension]. In S. Okuda (Ed.), *Keizaikikigono Kankoku: Seijukukini muketeno keizai-shakaiteki kadai, Kenkyuukai Chuukan Houkoku* [Post-economic crisis Korea: socio-economic challenges towards maturation. Research Council Interim Report](pp.143-167). Chiba: Institute of Developing Economies.
Oh, Y. S. (2001). Ch'ŏnggyech'ŏnkwa Tongdaemun Shijang [Ch'ŏnggyech'ŏn Stream and Tongdaemun Shijang]. In U. Y. Chŏn, K. H. Kim, T. Y. Song, U. W. Kang, Y. S. Oh, Y.

G. Chin, I. H. Song, *Ch'ŏnggyech'ŏn; Shigan, changso, saram – 20segi Seoul pyŏnch'ŏnsa yŏngu* [Ch'ŏnggyech'ŏn Stream; Time, Place and People – Studies of transition from Seoul in the 20th Century I] (pp. 117-159). Seoul: Research Institute of Seoul Studies, Seoul City University.

Ortner, S. B. (2006). *Anthropology and social theory: Culture, power, and the acting subject* (pp. 106, 110). Durham and London: Duke University Press.

The Personal Narratives Group (Ed.) (1989). *Interpreting women's lives: Feminist theory and personal narratives*. Bloomington and Indianapolis: Indiana University Press.

Ryu, K. S. (1998, April 4). "2020 Seoul toshi kibonkyehwoek" naeyoung ["2020 Seoul Basic Urban Plan" contents]. *Seoul Shinmun*, p. 20. Seoul Metropolitan Government (2007). *Seoul statistical yearbook 2007*.

Shin, D. H. (2006). *Kankokuno kokuminhoshouseido* [The National Pension System of Korea]. *Journal of The Medical Welfare Association of Kawasaki, 15*(2), 565-569.

Sudokwŏnchsŏngch'aek: Shidaee matke [Metropolitan area policy: To suit the times]. (1998, June 17). *Seoul Shinmun*, p. 2.

Tongdaemuntŭng 10kaeshijang 「taep'yoshijang」 ŭro josŏng [Development of 10 marketplaces such as Tongdaemun as representative markets]. (1983, March 4). *Dong-A Ilbo*, p. 10.

World Bank (2008). World Development Indicators. Retrieved July 22, 2008, from http://siteresources.worldbank.org/ DATASTATISTICS/Resources/GDP.pdf

• CHAPTER FIVE •

On Identity and Development: Filipino Women Entertainers in Transition in Japan[1]

MA. LEDDA B. DOCOT
University of Tokyo

Classified by the United States government in 2002 as belonging to the Tier Two Watchlist,[2] Japan has engaged in a major crackdown on illegal migrants, raiding entertainment bars and tightening immigration rules as a means to prevent human trafficking and the exploitation of foreign workers, especially women. Recently, talks concerning the entry into Japan of Filipino nurses and caregivers as part of the ongoing negotiations for the Japan-Philippines Economic Partnership Agreement (JPEPA) have effectively covered the issue of remaining Filipino entertainers, married or divorced women in Japan, and their children. At this stage, when we have yet to see the implementation of laws and programs for the integration and reintegration of migrants, for the "development" of the lives of foreigners in Japan, peoples' efforts at community organizing have shown potential in introducing and lobbying for change.

Japan has become a site of struggle and negotiation for Filipino women who aim for self-development. After years of work in the sex and entertainment industry, Filipinos who are former and even current entertainers hope to reclaim lost skills for upward mobility. It has also been reported that migrants in general experience tensions or problems in labor-receiving countries due to "undercasting" or seclusion in their places of destination. True enough, migrants in Japan are still treated merely as a part of the "foreign labor problem" (Chan-Tiberghien, 2004). Labor migrants may be considered part of the lowest strata of the absorbing community because they become occupiers of the so-called "3D" (dirty, dangerous, difficult) or "3K" (*kitanai, kiken, kitsui*) jobs. As foreigners, they may also experience difficulty in integrating into a culture "alien" to them (Nowotny, 1981). Thus, understanding a specific migrant-oriented organization's conceptualization of development for Filipinos in Japan, as seen in a particular project for women, remains the main task of this chapter.

The life stories of Filipino women in Japan, as well as the characteristics of organizations which seek to assist them, of course vary in many ways. To avoid hasty generalizations about women and organizations, I take the case of a particular program for Filipino women in Japan – the training of current and former Filipino women entertainers to become English teachers for Japanese children – initiated by a Filipino-run community organization in Tokyo called the Center for Japanese Filipino Families (CJFF). By looking at this program, I aim to show how complex issues in migration – of governmentality and neocolonialism – surround, penetrate and comprise a specific development project for a group of Filipino women in Japan.

FRAMEWORK

Conway (2006) suggests that all forms of collective action, or perhaps all social processes, need to be partly understood in terms of identity formation (p. 8). Feminist views on identity construction (Abu Lughod, 2006), meanwhile, suggest that the international dispersal of peoples may be understood as configured by history and crafted according to nations' contemporary politics of governing. Thus, I first attempt to illustrate how issues of Filipino contemporary migration and its feminization intersect with and relate to the Philippines' colonial legacies. While previous studies have established that the migration of Filipinos for work purposes can be explained according to the fluidity and personal desires of migrants (as agents) to seek social mobility, this study looks at issues of neocolonialism as intricately connected to contemporary Filipino migration. I also concur with McGovern (2006) that colonialism continues to echo in the politics of neoliberal globalization in the Philippines.

To contextualize Philippine migration and to show that contemporary migration reflects the country's compliance with supposedly internationalist trends in policymaking, I further borrow Foucault's (1991) concept of "governmentality." As interpreted by Ferguson and Gupta (2005), governmentality refers to the processes by which the conduct of a population is governed by institutions and agencies, including the state; by discourses, norms, and identities; and by self-regulation, techniques for the disciplining and care of the self (p. 114).

As the program of CJFF for Filipino women in Japan contains the English language and education as its primary components, this chapter provides a discussion of both as (1) products of neocolonialism related to the Philippine state's persistence in nurturing colonial legacies, and (2) as possible cultural products used by organizations which simultaneously "resist" (protest) and "accommodate" (negotiate and reconfigure) remnants of colonialism. The Philippine state, in the face of its determination in cultivating these legacies, is seen here as that which legitimates a kind of "economic coercion" (San Juan, 2000) in the form of governed migration.

Further, I explore CJFF as an organization in two ways. First, to give weight to the importance of concepts of identity in creating and maintaining communities, I qualify CJFF as a kind of self-reflexive and identity-oriented "new social movement organization" characterized by: (a) a membership that includes actors who continuously practice the organizational objectives they pursue; (b) actions which serve as expressions of the global interdependence of our world, such as submersion in networks where new meanings are created and practiced; and (c) actions which have both visible and less visible results such as community construction, institutional change and cultural innovation (Melucci, 1995, pp. 113-114). Second, I also borrow from Clifford's (1997) use of the term as involving "contact zones of nations, cultures, and regions" (p. 238). As a "contact zone," a migrant-oriented organization as part of a diasporic community or overseas-based Filipino civil society becomes a space where its members negotiate through and engage in political struggles "to define the local, as distinctive community, historical contexts of displacement" (p. 238).

NEOCOLONIALISM, GOVERNMENTALITY, AND MIGRATION

The Americanization of Philippine Education

At first glance, the occupation by the United States of the Philippines from the end of the nineteenth to the middle of the twentieth century seems to have been more liberating than the Spanish colonial experience, with the Americans promoting free public education, in contrast to the Spanish policy of non-education of the Filipino "indios." As Smith (1945) advises, it is wise to bear in mind the fact that the essential purpose of the educational system has been, since 1901, political rather than cultural (p. 140). Finding the Philippines in political turmoil and convinced that the country was incapable of managing its own affairs, the Americans implemented "benevolent assimilation" as an approach to colonizing the Philippines. Deprived of systematic education under Spanish rule, Filipinos from every walk of life, as Smith observes, "have always felt that the key to political and social advancement was to be found in embracing the American ideal of popular education" (p. 140). This comparatively benign American colonial policy, at least as contrasted with that of Spain, served to win Filipino loyalty and gratitude (Meadows, 1971, p. 338).

The educational system configured by the United States in the Philippines vastly expanded the social, political, and economic horizons of Filipinos, bringing more and more Filipinos into the mainstream of Western knowledge as well as increasing their self-knowledge – thus inflating their material and aspirational levels with a whole new range of "wants" (McHale, 1962, pp. 337-338). San Juan (2002) criticizes the US for its "gospel of capitalist rationality," for its "civilizing" discourse of governance and for its "worldview of evolutionary progress" (p. 51). Propped up by a rhetoric of development, the Americanization of Philippine education proved to be successful, for the country continued to echo American education in its school curricula long after it was given independence by the United States.

It should however be noted that the Americans did not completely ignore the use of the Philippine national language by the Filipinos. Tagalog as a lingua franca was to be used in the actual teaching of democracy and nationalism to Filipinos, after the Philippines acquired the tools from Americans by which the country could be self-administered by educated Filipinos (Smith, 1945, p. 142). The success of the Philippine Commonwealth Government's encouragement of the development of Tagalog literature and the usage of the native language, however, remains a contentious issue, for until today the clamor of a small number of nationalists to eliminate English as an official language of instruction in all educational levels is continually being ignored by the government.

In the American postcolonial situation after the Philippines gained its independence from the US, the use of the English language has already found a place in the country's educational system as a standard language. After the Philippine Commonwealth and the declaration of the country's independence from the US, the Philippine government under former president Ferdinand Marcos (1965-1986) gradually restructured the Philippine educational system towards greater integration of the country into an increasingly globalizing world. From Marcos to the present, governments have repeatedly argued in favor of promoting the English language, as this is believed to be a condition for the global competitiveness of millions of Filipino overseas workers now deployed to about 200 countries worldwide. As President Arroyo (2003) has said, "the great comparative advantage of the Philippines is our rich human resources: highly skilled, well-educated, English-speaking."

Not only has the government paid no heed to the calls of nationalist politicians and members of academe to de-emphasize the use of English as the main language of instruction, the agenda of Philippine education was also used to educate Filipinos in English in preparation for their future overseas. In 2006, President Arroyo issued Executive Order No. 210, entitled "Establishing the Policy to Strengthen English as a Second Language in the Educational System." This policy further strengthened the place of English as a second language through the following provisions: "*English shall be taught as a second language starting with the First Grade;*" "*The English language shall be used as the primary medium of instruction in all public and private institutions of learning in the secondary level,*" and "As the primary medium of instruction, *the percentage of time allotment for learning areas conducted in the English language is expected to be not less than seventy percent (70%) of the total time allotment for all learning areas in the secondary level* [my emphasis]."

Education, Arroyo (2006) admits, is "part of the legacy of America's involvement in the Philippines" and in this age "never has the mastery of the english (sic) language been more important to (the Philippines') national well-being." As Executive Order No. 210 further states, its objective is "to develop the aptitude, competence and proficiency of all students in the use of the English language to make them better prepared for the job opportunities emerging in the new, technology-driven sectors of the economy." From the period of American colonial rule, the English language was transformed from being a mental and cultural colonizing tool to becoming an "accepted" component of Philippine education. In the area of migration, the English language is being branded as a valuable colonial legacy which the Philippine state effectively uses in the promotion of the global competitiveness of the Filipino workforce. In the last five decades, the Philippines has seen the transformation of the English language as a developmental tool imposed by the Americans to push forward Western knowledge and rationality to becoming a "comparative advantage" in the global labor market.

Labor Policy and Colonial Legacies

The development of the countries' labor exportation, like the evolution of its educational system in relation to the English language, may also be traced by looking at colonial legacies which have defined the kind of economic opportunities and ventures that the Philippine state has pursued (Guevarra, 2006, p. 524). Postcolonial/neocolonial Philippines, which has been run by elites who share American-dominated paradigms of "development," continues to be export-oriented and has failed to resolve structural problems related to land issues remaining from the Spanish colonial era.

Programs for local agriculture after independence reflected the new Western rationality of the global marketplace. Quite similar to other former colonies in Asia such as India, traditional agricultural practices in the Philippines were widely replaced by commercial farming while home and community industries were replaced by feudal enterprises which were economically disadvantageous to locals. Also resembling the situation in other former colonies, infrastructure development in the Philippines was aimed towards integration into the world capitalist system, without much sensitivity towards the cultures and traditions of local communities.

In over three hundred years of Spanish rule, the Philippines saw the solidification of its capitalist-oriented infrastructure, providing a base for the further US-led liberalization of Philippine policies. During the 1970s, the Marcos government carried on agribusiness programs such as the so-called Green Revolution, an American-led program which sought to end world hunger through the use of modern technology, genetically improved seeds and fertilizer. This caused the country to be more dependent on the global economy and Western technologies, undermining self-sufficiency, ignoring the widening urban-rural divide, and causing the accumulation of debts among farmers (Collins, Lappe, & Rosset, 2000). In this situation, the cost factors associated with agriculture have been too expensive for small-scale farmers, leaving the only options of joining the labor force through local employment, or internal or international migration.

Colonialism and Filipino Migration
We recall that Filipino women in the pre-Spanish occupation period worked in the fields, raised livestock, and participated in trade with their male counterparts (Infante, as cited in Lauby, 1988, p. 474). It was the Spanish Code of Laws implemented in the Philippines that confined Filipino women to the home, forbidding women to transact business or dispose of property (Rojas-Aleta, as cited in Lauby, 1988, p. 474), bolstering a patriarchal foundation and instilling in the Filipino consciousness the notion that women's main role is to maintain the household. Earlier literature has also identified the worsening economic conditions in the colonial period as a factor forcing women to engage in sex work.

Some literature suggests that American colonialism brought prostitution into the Philippines, since there was no record of its pre-colonial existence. It was during the American colonization of the Philippines when the configuration of gender and class was articulated in the sexual commodification of poor women pushed into prostitution by the economic pressures of poverty (McGovern, 2006, p. 4). During the American period, women's sexuality was turned into a source of profit in entertainment halls which catered to Americans in the Philippines. This gendering of entertainment work became prevalent in particular cities and towns in the Philippines where US military bases were located. From then on, entertainment work became an "easy escape" from poverty, and in the 1970s, the entertainment industry was "developed" to support the country's tourism program which seemingly included in the package the four S's – sun, sex, sea and sand (Matthews, as cited in Crick, 1989, p. 308) – to a generally Japanese clientele.

Beginnings of Filipino Women's "Forced Migration" to Japan

As a measure to combat deflation and to increase dollar remittances in the country, the Marcos administration resorted to a labor policy which created state agencies charged with the deployment of Filipino workers overseas (introduced under Presidential Decree 442 or the Labor Code of the Philippines). The objectives as stipulated by Article 12 of the Labor Code include: (Section c) to facilitate a free choice of available employment by persons seeking work *in conformity with the national interest*; (Section d) to facilitate and regulate the movement of workers *in conformity with the national interest*, and (Section f) to strengthen the network of public employment offices and rationalize the participation of the private sector in the recruitment and placement of workers, locally and overseas, to serve *national development objectives* [my emphasis].

Following the decree, the Philippines witnessed the rapid exodus of Filipino men and women to the Middle East, Europe, and the US, initially as construction workers and medical personnel. From reliance on neoliberal trade backed up by American economic rationality, the Philippines shifted to a strategy of exporting human labor. Filipino activists from the late 1960s to the present have provided critical analyses of the extensive Filipino overseas migration nurtured during the Marcos period and propped up by American imperialism. Quoting San Juan (2000):

> There was no real Filipino diaspora before the Marcos dictatorship in the 1970s and 1980s. It was only after the utter devastation of the Philippines in World War II, and the worsening of economic and political conditions in the neocolonial set-up from the late 1960s to the present, that Filipinos began to leave in droves. During the Marcos martial law regime, the functionality of overseas contract workers (OCW) was constructed and/or discovered by the elite and its hegemonic patrons as a response to both local and global conditions. (p. 232)

Three decades later, after the institutionalization of labor exports from the Philippines, what started as an interim strategy for debt payment and response to inflation has become a permanent and legitimized government program. The movement of Filipinos to Japan in the 1970s, apart from explanations which center on the Western-oriented internationalism adopted by Japan and the rest of Asia, may also of course be seen according to economic developments inside Japan, particularly the Izanagi boom (1965-1970) and the Heisei boom (1986-1991) – the upsurges of which caused labor shortages in the country. The Filipinos who first came to Japan were generally young females – and obviously, they migrated not to provide the much-needed labor for Japan's heavy industries.

Earlier studies suggest Filipino women were "pulled" to Japan by an income gap. Ventura (2006) notes with frustration that people have often in the past written about Filipino migrant workers as if the issue was one of simple economic need (p. 162). The movement of Filipinos to Japan may have also been driven by the goals and dreams of individuals to upgrade their economic status for themselves and their families. As a former Filipina entertainer relayed to me when asked about her decision to come to Japan: "Gustong-gusto ko talaga no'n!" (I really, really wanted [to come here]!).

While it may hold true that women are themselves agents who can act on their own aspirations, it can also be remembered that it was during this same period that Japanese sex tourism in Asia was at its peak, and tourist spots like beach resorts and golf courses in the Philippines catered to a group that Ventura (2006) has called the "Japanese underground" (p. 165). The development of tourism to facilitate the needs of this underground market, as Sellek (1996) writes, was established in response to the internationalization of the sex industry (p. 166). The Marcos government propagated this local entertainment industry through outright promotion despite the common knowledge that what was really happening was prostitution hidden under the cloak of tourism. When civil society started to protest against this situation, the underground entertainment industry catering to the Japanese was legitimized under the banner of international migration and cooperation. As the Philippine Labor Code states, "recent local and international developments have imposed new demands and challenges on the existing delivery systems for labor and labor-related services." Such policy re-prioritizations contributed to the feminization of Filipino migration, through which the "needs" of both countries – lack of workers in Japan's entertainment sector and lack of jobs in the Philippines – were met.

Governmentality of Migration in the Neocolonial Situation

The present art of governmentality makes use of migration, far from being an interim strategy, but as a "pillar of the government foreign policy" (Soriano, 2007, p. 13). During the time of Marcos, the internationalizing policies on migration were used by the Philippine state as rhetoric to support the right to self-determination of its citizens. In fact, the idea of women being the new breadwinners in whichever type of work they are engaged (including entertainment) is also used by the government to support their rhetoric of "female empowerment."

Governments after Marcos continued to cultivate overseas migration, and now Filipino overseas workers have been accorded various heroic names: They have been called "modern-day heroes" (de Guzman, 2003) by the Aquino administration, "citizens of the world" by the former

Chair of the Commission of Filipinos Overseas, Dante Ang (2005), "economic saviors" by Estrada (1999), and "overseas Filipino investors" by Arroyo (2001). To give credence to the contributions of Filipino overseas migrants to the country's economy, to recognize their status as somewhat accomplished citizens, and to laud their crucial roles in international diplomacy, they have been called the "new aristocrats" (Guevarra, 2006) and the new "ambassadors of goodwill" (Guevarra, 2003).

Also part of this governmentality of migration is the state's action of instituting protective laws supposedly to ensure the welfare of Filipino overseas workers. The Migrant Workers and Overseas Filipinos Act of 1995 (Republic Act 8042), which "aims to wind back the protective function of the state vis-à-vis its overseas workers," has been criticized as based on an endorsement of neoliberal, free trade thinking underpinned by the notion of deregulation and a manifestation of the adoption of a "victim discourse" with respect to the broader process of globalization (Ball & Piper, 2002, p. 1018).

The institutionalization of overseas labor migration, a policy direction which was deemed a necessary response to the global trend towards internationalization, continues to the present as a governmental program of poverty alleviation, employment and national development. As seen in the overview of Filipino migration I have outlined above, the massive migration of Filipinos characterized by the significant participation of women became effectively normalized by seemingly inevitable tendencies towards economic progress. So far, I have illustrated the Philippines' context of feminized migration as an assemblage of issues related to the country's colonial legacies and neocolonial situation. Before I proceed to discuss how these issues of Philippine education, migration, and colonialism may intersect in looking at a particular organization's program for Filipino women in Japan, I provide some background on the emergence of Filipino civil society from the post-American period.

DEVELOPMENT THROUGH COMMUNITY ORGANIZATIONS

Filipino Civil Society

In discussing a project for development initiated by a non-governmental organization, it remains important to recall that it was under the Marcos administration, during a time of heightened internationalism in Philippine diplomacy and policies, that the country witnessed the emergence of a mass-based, nationalist social movement. Meadows (1971) traces this growth of the civil society from the 1950s, the period when a "new generation of Filipinos" emerged with a background and outlook quite different from those of an earlier generation, which had been framed by the experience of war and continued dominance of the United States in Philippine politics. In the face of neocolonialism, nationalists launched "an intense and emotional search for a national identity" (p. 338). During this period, a mass-based civil society emerged, manifesting in their actions the growth of a so-called "anti-Americanism" and anti-neocolonialism as frameworks for social action (p. 338).

It is likewise important to discuss the role of religion in Philippine social movements, due to the influence of Catholicism and religious groups in the country. In the early 1970s, the world saw better coordinated social action addressing issues in civil rights, and in the case of the Third World, protests against American-led dictatorships. "Liberation theology" or "peoples' theology" likewise emerged. During the 1960s, it was in fact in the Philippines and Brazil that mission-oriented "Basic Ecclesial Communities" or self-reliant sub-units of parishes were first created, long before liberation theology became a prominent framework for the community organizing of church workers (Nadeau, 2002). This activism bore fruit in 1986, when social actors within civil society called for the ouster of Marcos after nearly two decades of dictatorial rule. Since then, these actors have played important roles in the national affairs of the Philippines, and the country has been tagged as having a "weak government" but a "strong civil society" (Tigno, 1997, p. 117).

The social activist movement in the Philippines which emerged in the late 1960s did not only produce grassroots organizations and lobby groups; it was in itself a training ground for social entrepreneurs. Some veteran social movement actors continue to fill leadership roles in civil society or community organizations in the Philippines. I establish here that networks of civil society organizers, with roots that can be traced back to early organized social movements in the Philippines, also now comprise a portion of the labor migrants from the Philippines. The state-sanctioned movement of Filipino migrants has not only led to the sustained movement of Filipinos to many parts of the world and the formation of Filipino communities overseas, but also the exportation of groups of community workers and missionaries who now assume lead roles in organizing Filipino communities abroad. I call this group of leaders deployed overseas the "exported community workers" or "expert community workers" which then fill a portion of the "exported Filipino civil society."

Professional or expert community organizers are now being sent by organizations from the Philippines and other countries of migration, or being recruited by specific organizations in the destination country, as a part of a larger social movement project by groups in the Philippines or elsewhere. Apart from organizing Filipinos in the destination country, the presence of these community workers-cum-migrants in the international migration system also creates and strengthens transnational social movement networks, as we shall now see in the case of CJFF.

CJFF's Beginnings

It is first important to note that CJFF's executive director Cesar Santoyo did not come from the "rank and file" of Filipino migrant workers in Japan, but was a *padala*,[3] dispatched as an "expert community worker" whose leadership background includes extensive experience in local (mass-based, grassroots and Church-based organizations in the Philippines) and overseas community-based organizing of Filipinos (for an organization for domestic workers in Hong Kong). CJFF is neither a registered non-profit organization in Japan nor a registered non-governmental organization in the Philippines, but a "sent mission" of the United Church of Christ Philippines (UCCP) to the United Church of Christ Japan (UCCJ). From its inception in 2001, the CJFF remains the only organization in the whole of Japan affiliated under the banner of UCCJ that serves foreign migrants.

CJFF receives contributions from groups with various church affiliations (Catholic, Protestant, Methodist): as a mission program, it is being hosted by UCCJ; it receives financial donations from the United Church of Christ Canada and the Global Ministry for Global Mission of the United Methodist Church; and a Japanese activist who worked with Santoyo in the past to coordinate Filipino and Japanese activists for a campaign against the implementation of an Official Development Assistance (ODA) project of Japan to the Philippines supports CJFF by providing free housing to Santoyo.

CJFF has adopted a general motto of ecumenical movements that acknowledges diversity: "That they may all be one." The network within which CJFF operates, grows, and survives shows its cooperation with varied political lines and religious dominations. It receives organizational and institutional support as well as material and financial contributions from Protestant and Methodist Churches while still co-implementing migrant-related projects with Anglican-supported organizations in the Tokyo area. CJFF also maintains friendships with community workers from Catholic and Muslim faiths both in Japan and the Philippines, and, finally, it keeps its strong links with political activists from the mass-based nationalist social movement from the 1970s as well as "mainsteam" Japanese activists. Santoyo's approach to his "mission" for Filipino migrants in Japan was based on what he learned from his long-time exposure to Church-based organizing grounded on the concept of liberation theology. The CJFF used Basic Ecclesial Communities/Basic Christian Communities – applying different faiths in community organizing, matched with political activism – as its reference framework in drafting its "mission" for its development programs for Filipino women and their families in Japan.

CJFF's Vision, Mission and Practices as Ideological Frames

With the word "families" included in the organization's name, CJFF's vision of the Filipino community in Japan is one which transcends differences in religious denominations and cultures. While the use of the terminology may imply a firm grounding in "traditional" Filipino "family-oriented" conceptions of morality and social values (which were embedded in the Filipino psyche during the Spanish colonial period) or of gender relations (where the female is expected to play subjugated roles within the family), CJFF's conception of the term "family" has evolved. The prime consideration is that Filipino women have become "economically active persons" (Bohning, 1981, p. 28) in international migration, and thus more active agents within the family as a basic social unit. Further, CJFF's usage of the term "family" mostly de-emphasizes the role of the father because of the situation of Filipino families in Japan, where 40 percent of their marriages end in divorce (C. Santoyo, personal communication, March 2007). To further understand how CJFF puts its mission and vision into practice, I will outline some issues which the organization faces as it promotes the economic empowerment of Japan-based Filipino women.

On "indoctrination." The general aims of CJFF are to promote Filipino migrants' rights and welfare, and to contribute to the eventual multiculturalization of Japan. To quote the mission statement of CJFF in full:

> We envision members of Japanese-Filipino families as a strong community, actively living in harmony with all people for the promotion of their rights and welfare, contributing their creativity for the enhancement of life's faith, culture and arts, advancing solidarity and cooperation with migrant support organizations and institutions in Japan and in the Philippines, and participating in building a multicultural society of Japan.

Grounded in Christian ecumenism, the CJFF practices a kind of counseling that acknowledges religious pluralism and cultural diversity, avoiding the practice of "mythical" applications of theology (Forrester, 1988, p. 57).

While it is a joint project of the United Church of Christ in the Philippines and Japan, CJFF downplays the religious indoctrination of its participants and instead opts for the creation of programs which seek to "invite" Filipinos as active participants in Church activities. An example of this project would be the Christmas Lantern (*parol*) Campaign initiated by CJFF. It is a tradition in the Philippines during Christmastime to display *parol*, which symbolize the star of Bethlehem that guided the Three Kings to find the Baby Jesus. According to Santoyo, the campaign, which invited women to create lanterns, was not only an income-generating project but a "very subtle way of evangelization." For instance, after a pastor displayed six pieces of *parol* outside her church in Hokkaido, six Filipino women visited for the first time.

On program framing. Some organizations in Japan, according to Santoyo, tend to provide merely an "ambulance service." For example, in cases of domestic violence, one who takes a superficial view of the issue may think that all that has to be done is to fetch the victim and bring her to the hospital so that she can be treated for her injuries. He points out that in some cases women's shelters can be likened to this kind of temporary – and reactionary – service. According to Santoyo, even some members of the police force do not know many of the new Japanese laws on domestic violence, and only send women home after they report abuses. He says that the role of NGOs and other support organizations in this situation now should be to spread awareness and further strengthen the implementation of these laws. Acknowledging the efforts of civil society organizations in Japan, he says: "These laws did not emerge out of nowhere; they were [created] because of the efforts of NGOs and lobby groups."

On Filipino migration. Regarding how contemporary Philippine migration should be viewed, Santoyo says that one should look back at the US colonial period in the Philippines, when workers were first gathered for deployment to Hawaii, California, and other American states. According to him, an important factor connected to the international migration of Filipinos is the feudal or *hacienda* system in the Philippines, which concentrated the control of land into the hands of very few families. Hence, he says, "the tendency now is for people to look for other opportunities." Acknowledging that there was internal migration throughout the Philippines before the Americans came, Santoyo adds: "If you look at the case of migration deeply, the highlight should be on the lack of land reform and industrialization."

On women's empowerment. Asked about how he perceives empowerment, Santoyo replies: "You cannot separate economics from politics." To further elaborate his views, he differentiates the approaches of two other Filipino-run organizations in Japan which were created to promote the so-called "empowerment" of Filipino women, particularly the former group known as "Japayukis."

Organization A, he says, concentrates more on networking rather than on organizing. Organization B, on the other hand, is a community organization that operates under the assumption that empowerment has a political dimension. Empowerment as defined by Organization A is "to help the migrants" while avoiding the concept of political organization. This same organization recently published a book claiming that women are empowered from the anger they feel due to the oppression and aggression they regularly experience. Santoyo comments, "It is not about anger. Anger is mere result and effect." Instead, he says that the notion of empowerment should be understood through the concept of justice and that "one has to be organized to be empowered." He cites lobbying for policy reforms, skills and economic development, empowering of the oppressed and the weak, as important components for women's empowerment. In implementing projects aimed at empowerment, Santoyo says: "We should ask who the real actor in empowerment is. I think that the best person to rely on is yourself."

With the ideological framework of CJFF and its leaders' orientations stated, I now proceed to discuss how these are applied in praxis. I first provide an overview of the organization's recent activities.

On political activism. Since the organization operates with scarce financial resources, CJFF's structure came to be composed of a single full-time leader or executive director (Santoyo), who uses his skills in mass organization to gather and work with various sub-groups who are pursuing similar aims as CJFF. In fact, CJFF's uniqueness as an organization lies in its capacity to initiate the creation of grassroots organizations and to coordinate social actions through transnational networking.

While the CJFF plans and implements activities for Filipino migrant families in Japan, it has other activities centered on political issues in the Philippines. Santoyo clarifies that not all of his actions are carried under the banner of CJFF. Being "somewhat" church-based, Santoyo says that he prefers to participate in more political activities "only in his own [personal or individual] capacity."

One example of this is his personal participation in campaigns against the extrajudicial killings of political activists in the Philippines. Not necessarily "carrying the flag" of CJFF, Santoyo assisted in the dissemination of information about the issue to both Filipino and Japanese communities in Japan. This involvement, which may not "directly" involve Filipinos "locally" (i.e., those currently living in Japan), is linked to Santoyo's continued engagement with his earlier established networks in the Philippines, Hong Kong and Japan. As part of the said campaign, Santoyo was in charge of inviting Japan's Social Democratic Party leader and Senator Misuho Fukushima to serve as one of the judges for the People's Tribunal Hearings held in March 2007.

Meanwhile, the political involvements of Santoyo like the campaign mentioned above, or poll-watching in the last Overseas Absentee Voting elections in Japan "to guide the integrity of the votes of migrants," are not necessarily actual CJFF projects but self-expressions of his political beliefs. Nonetheless, his involvements in such activism lead to the shaping of his and the organization's character as figures in the arena of community action of Filipinos in Tokyo. As another church-based worker commented on the apparent political activism of Santoyo, "He is Bonifacio while I am Rizal." Bonifacio, in Philippine history, was the hero who led an armed revolution against Spain. The Philippine national hero Rizal, on the other hand, advocated a more propaganda-based and reform-oriented type of resistance. The NGO worker adds: "When you mention Cesar's name (to the embassy staff), they'll run away because they think that there is another signature campaign."

To further examine the manifestations of issues which were discussed in the earlier sections – of governmentality, neocolonialism, identity and social movements – I now focus on one of the biggest, and perhaps most well-received, projects of CJFF since its inception.

DEVELOPMENT PROGRAM FOR FILIPINO WOMEN IN JAPAN

The Mission Program: Filipino Women as English Teachers

In 2006, Santoyo organized a gathering of former and current Filipino women entertainers in Tokyo involved in various informal language tutorials in their respective neighborhoods. Initially, he got in touch with the women whom he had already met through CJFF's counseling service and networks. A group of interested women responded and organized themselves into what is now known as "Community and Home Based English Teachers" (CHOBET).

As I have understood during my volunteer work for CJFF, the term "CHOBET" refers to both of the following: 1) an organization of mostly Filipino women interested in English teaching as an "alternative trade" and career, and 2) education and training programs which serve as "contact zones" for the interaction of women who share the same goals of "skilling" and "re-skilling" through the development of capacity in the English language as a tool for teaching.

CHOBET's organizational mission gives particular emphasis on skills acquisition as a source of empowerment, and on education as a means of developing mechanisms for collective action and lobbying aimed at greater and structural social change. As a program for skills training and development, CHOBET found as a useful component the capacity of Filipino women in the English language.

The training program given by CHOBET comprises a two- or three-day workshop which includes in its repertoire the following: the teaching of prominent educational philosophies (e.g., Steiner and Waldorf schools), lectures on various kinds of teaching methods which can be applied to community and home-based education, role-play activities concerning the teaching of English, and, lastly, actual demonstrations of lesson plans participants have been asked to design after learning teaching philosophies and methods.

Some say that most Filipino women in Japan have now "aged" – the majority having arrived in the late 1970s and onwards, working in the entertainment industry and later on staying to marry in Japan. As reflected in the demographic data of 73 participants who attended seven different CHOBET workshops from May 2006 to July 2007, around 61 percent (average age of 36) are, or have been, married. The data gathered through CHOBET indicates that 64 percent of all participants are from Manila and its surrounding vicinities, and 78 percent have finished or entered college. Ninety-four percent of the CHOBET participants were female, a figure which supports earlier claims of the highly feminized migration of Filipinos to Japan (Anderson, 2003; Philippine Migrants Rights Watch, 2004).

Interestingly, most participants seem to have intentionally left out the section of the questionnaire where they were asked to indicate their former and current occupations both in the Philippines and Japan. Of all the women, only four wrote that they were formerly entertainers in the Philippines, while not even one person wrote that she works in Japan as an entertainer. This omission or declaration of their experience in entertainment work may be an indicator of women's valuation of their status as migrants in Japan. CHOBET trainings allow time for group work, where women are able to share their problems and experiences in Japan. Not only does this provide a space for a discussion with an expert counselor (Santoyo), it also opens a chance for the sharing of thoughts among women who often find themselves in strikingly similar situations.

CJFF was established at a significant turning point, when the condition of Filipino women in Japan was slowly moving in a different direction. While the issues of domestic violence and trafficking of women which were massively reported by the media in the early 1990s still exist, Santoyo has also heard women discuss "new" problems that they are now experiencing in Japan. Women now talk about upgrading, rediscovering, and learning skills lost after a long period of engagement in the entertainment industry. They also look for venues where new capacities can be acquired or where forgotten skills can be recovered. Filipino women in Japan, therefore, were/are "in transition."

The materialization of these new or re-born aspirations expressed by women themselves, however, has proved to be difficult. Entertainment work remains an easy source of money, with women receiving from ¥1,500 per hour or from ¥10,000 per night. While some women are eager to "move on," this has been difficult because of issues such as remaining obligations to their families. Often, they are mothers of Japanese-Filipino children, breadwinners for their families in the Philippines, or both – making the option of shifting to a different kind of work sometimes almost unimaginable.

The CJFF has identified two general problems that women face as they try to embark on skills training: difficulty in comprehension and economic insecurity. Filipino women who have worked in occupations other than entertainment have not only lost "touch" with their abilities; their experience as migrants in Japan has stripped them of their self-confidence as well.

Such is the case of Maria, who, before coming to Japan as an entertainer, worked as a teacher in a public school in the Philippines. Aspiring to go back to her former profession, Maria is now experiencing difficulty as she has been de-skilled during long years of entertainment work. When she attended the CHOBET training, she exclaimed that she "cannot even construct a decent sentence in English." Other women are also discouraged by stories of discrimination by Japanese employers. One of the participants who graduated from a private university in the Philippines had been admitted as tutor in an *eikawa* (English conversation) school, only to be fired when the administration discovered that she still works at night as an entertainer to augment her salary.

To provide a better idea of the actual experiences of women as they seek to redefine and rejuvenate their identity and to reclaim a place in society, I provide below a case of one CHOBET member named "Rosa."

Rosa

Rosa recalls that English teaching and other jobs in the *kaisha* (offices) were not yet open to non-native speakers of the English language in the 1990s. Thus, despite being a fresh graduate of a medical course in the Philippines, there was no other job available to her in Japan besides entertainment work. Prior to coming to Japan, Rosa worked at the front desk of a hotel in Manila, and she noticed that her workmates began to leave for overseas work, one after another. Her sister, who was already in Japan at that time, encouraged her to come to Japan as well.

Rosa then found a "conservative" snack bar in the Tokyo area where she stayed to work. She was content with earning thousands of yen less than the other entertainers. Her work in the snack bar was only to sit in front of customers – unlike other *omise* (bars) where women's salaries are dependent on the customers they "recruit" and the drinks they order.[4] She came to Japan only with a three-month tourist visa, but with better financial prospects before her, she decided to overstay her visa. She became involved with one of her customers, who then got her pregnant. However, she could not stay with her partner because the man was already married. For the next six years, she continued to work in the same snack bar until she decided to surrender herself to the Immigration Bureau so that she could finally go back home with her child.

At first, she intended to stay in the Philippines for good, finding opportunities where she could invest her savings. However, there were not many options back home. She decided to try a clothing retail business. With a friend, she traveled to Taiwan to purchase clothes wholesale and resell them in the Philippines. Still, she was not content with the meager earnings from her business, especially after being accustomed to a more comfortable lifestyle in Japan. The environment was not good for business, either. At the Customs section of the airport, it is a common practice among Customs officials to overcharge taxes once they learn that the goods are being brought in for business, no matter how small the business may be. Hence, she decided to return to Japan in 1997, using another name and overstaying her visa once again.

She returned to the same *omise* to work, and by 1999 she had saved enough money for the airfare of her mother and son. A friend had encouraged her to bring her child back to Japan so that they could appeal for him to be granted official status as a Japanese national. The process takes a long time, however, and although she visited many organizations to request assistance, most of them only gave vague advice or even discouraged her.

In 2001, she was referred by a Filipino-run women's shelter to an NGO specializing in cases related to Japanese-Filipino children. With the help of the NGO, she and her family were able to receive a special permit to stay in Japan. The permit was granted just in time, for her deportation was already being arranged. She was already in detention as a police officer patrolling the neighborhood had stopped her on her bicycle to ask for her documents.

Her involvement in volunteer work started with the Japanese NGO which assisted her with the visa procedures. With eight other Filipino women, she became a key player in the "Nationality Campaign," a lobby program that has led to the filing of a petition now pending in the Supreme Court. Also at that time, she started to volunteer to teach her son's classmates in the daytime while still working at the club at night. She wanted to be involved in other jobs because according to her, "I was never satisfied even if I was well-compensated as an entertainer. I knew that it was not the kind of job that I wanted." Like other entertainers, she knew that she is qualified to be hired for other jobs, but sometimes the earnings in entertainment work are too attractive to give up.

At the time she started volunteering almost a decade after she first came to Japan, non-native speakers were still not widely accepted as English teachers. For her once-a-week work as an English teacher to her son's classmates, she only charged ¥500 per child. This was the reason why no one questioned her being given the position, because technically, she was only a volunteer teacher. Still, "I could sense then that something good would come out of it," she said.

Rosa also recalls that there were no seminars then for learning how to teach English, and even the Filipinos she met who came to Japan as teachers seemed unwilling to share their knowledge. She attributes this to a prejudiced notion that entertainers are unqualified for such professional occupations. Bookstores became her refuge. She searched for materials that could be used and figured out how to make lesson plans on her own. Eager to learn, she flew to Hokkaido for a teaching seminar which cost her over ¥200,000.

She learned mostly by herself, often just trying to recall what she had learned in her grade-school years in the Philippines. Expressing how she felt while attempting to teach, she stated: "I would evaluate myself after each class, and I would feel bad if I did not perform well…. I loved and enjoyed what I was doing, very much unlike my job in the *omise*, which I hated until the end."

For Rosa, becoming a teacher has also given her a somewhat "refreshed," if not new, identity. Before, she was aloof towards the rest of society because of the indifference of the Japanese towards night workers. Being a *sensei* [teacher], though, was different. She happily related how "Even the mothers of the children began calling me *sensei*. It's a sign that I have finally been accepted."

Like Rosa, many other Filipinos are now taking up English-teaching jobs in Japan, some in formal educational institutions. In 2006, about 100 Filipinos were hired as assistant English teachers in public elementary and junior high schools. In Ibaraki Prefecture, 40 percent of the foreigners employed by Selti, a placement agency, are Filipinos. The evaluation of teachers by the prefecture's Board of Education has also given positive feedback on Filipino teachers, saying that they fare well even in comparison with native speakers and are able to relate effectively with children (Tutor, 2006). In recent years, placement agencies have mushroomed all over Japan. Since the terms of employment for English teachers are on a "non-quota" basis, the number of Filipinos employed as English teachers has increased significantly.

CHOBET also cites the following as its purposes: to serve as a groundbreaker to properly understand the situation of Filipino women in Japan and the ways and means to empower them; to develop consciousness among women and foreign migrant women on building social movements; to provide skills development and upgrading for English language teachers; and to promote the protection of women's rights and welfare. The "balance" of CJFF shows notions of women's development grounded in "economic empowerment" through skill acquisition and re-acquisition. At the same time, women are invited to "subtly" participate in activism by being encouraged to organize themselves and become active agents of their own empowerment through skills training which they can use to improve their economic situation.

The CHOBET program pursues its goal of grassroots organizing by leaving important tasks related to CHOBET to an already active group of women leaders. For the early sessions of CHOBET, CJFF hired a Filipino woman who teaches in an international school in Tokyo to serve as the main educator for women wanting to start this so-called "community and home-based teaching." However, while she was knowledgeable in the field of education as a professional teacher, the concepts of formal education and alternative community education are different. This somewhat displaced the original idea of providing women with an unconventional approach to teaching the English language. Thus, at the end of 1996 Santoyo invited Rosa to become one of CHOBET's main community organizers-cum-trainers.

Upon review of the ideological framework of CJFF as reflected in the views of Santoyo as its leader and as seen in its involvement in what could be seen as forms of "contentious politics" (Tarrow, 1998, p. 20), it can be stated that CHOBET as a program for women shows an interesting mix of priorities and ideology. The program uses the idiom of "global competitiveness" – signifying the current situation of Filipino women as speakers of the English language and of Japan as a country which has taken the route of internationalizing its educational system. The venture of the CJFF in training women to teach English further responds to the propagation of English usage as part of Japan's internationalist policies. Such policies aim to support, through new approaches to education, the cultivation of "Japanese with English Abilities." In addition, this new policy thrust is aided by the liberalization of the Worker Dispatch Law, broadening the scope of labor deployment to fill positions in the English teaching profession.

Some entertainers who have joined CHOBET, and even those who are already working in educational institutions, admit that their English skills may not be sufficient to be teachers of the language. A CHOBET graduate shares her struggles coming up with lesson plans:

> I asked my mother to send me teaching materials from the Philippines. So before, I would use "Made in the Philippines" materials. One time, I told my students, "'A' is for *atis* (sugar apple)." It was only when the children asked, "Sensei, *atis* tte nani?" (Teacher, what is *atis?*) that I realized I still have a long way to go.

The same CHOBET member, who, even before participation in CHOBET had established her own community-based teaching program, says that it is not really because of the English language that she and other former entertainers are being trusted by Japanese mothers to provide an alternative education for their Japanese children. The fee of ¥500 per child, which is the suggested fee to be charged for a 50-minute community- or home-based teaching session (¥5,000 for every 50 minutes, for a group of ten students), is not a bad deal for the Japanese. While the children attend lessons, their mothers can leave for work or do some errands. In a way, this type of teaching becomes a less costly alternative to daycare. Santoyo adds that CHOBET is also a venue where women "can express care and concern for people, most especially children." Hence, the CHOBET curriculum for teaching uses the English language in addition to what else teachers can offer the children. The English language "adds spice" to the program, but is not necessarily its central feature.

The use of the English language as an "empowerment tool" for women, as seen in the case of the CHOBET program, may also be viewed as a creative reinterpretation of the Philippines' neocolonial legacy. In its one year of existence, CHOBET has attracted the attention of Filipinos who have all been educated in English as a second language – hoping that their long years of being educated in English in the Philippines can at least be used in Japan. Filipino women in Japan, at least those whom I met through CJFF, see English teaching as a possible alternative to night work.

This development shows that organizations which in some ways have a progressive orientation can find new means of transforming normally contentious issues into "options." To paraphrase Santoyo, "If we were in the Philippines, our cry would be 'No to the English language!'" Indeed, protests against the propagation of English in the Philippine educational curriculum continue today. However, the context of the organization is more complex. It is located in a migration destination, and its clients face difficulties related to issues of identity, such as having low self-esteem due to stereotypes attributed to them. As seen in the case of CHOBET, the English language is perceived by Filipino women migrants as a "realistic" empowerment tool, a form of capital which they can control (and improve), depending on their aspirations. This indicates that the ideologies of leaders and organizations, in the context of migration, are sufficiently fluid to accommodate and negotiate with enduring realities.

CONCLUSIONS

I have argued in this chapter that the institutionalization of the massive and highly feminized overseas labor migration from the 1970s was the Philippines' response to an earlier era of US-led internationalization. While proclaimed by former presidents of the country as inevitable interim strategies that lead to economic progress, migration policies more realistically reflect the neocolonial politico-cultural configurations of the Philippines. In the face of continued labor exportation from the Philippines to other countries, transnational linkages among non-governmental organizations, such as those in Japan, have developed and led to the formation and strengthening of an overseas-based Filipino civil society. I have provided here an illustration of what now comprises a fraction of the Filipino diaspora – the leaders of migrant-organizations who may have not necessarily risen from the ranks but are "expert" or "professional community workers" who leave their "home" (the Philippines) to represent or work for groups of Filipinos living overseas. I have also illustrated that a portion of today's migrants-cum-community leaders are being "dispatched" on a particular mission or involved in advocacy related to the propagation of social movements. I have contended that although community leaders may be, or may have been, affiliated with a particular social movement or form of activism, the knowledge created through and out of program framing, dynamics within community organizations, and the methods by which goals are sought and conceptions of development are understood, remain largely context-specific.

This was seen in the case of the CJFF's CHOBET program, which introduces English language teaching as an alternative option and career opportunity for former and current Filipina entertainers in Japan. In the context of migration and the particularities of the migrant experience, ideological frames are negotiated to accommodate the needs of members seeking an organization's direction, particularly those connected to the transformation of their image as foreign women in Japan.

Moreover, while CJFF's leader is apparently rooted in, and partly identifies with, the nationalist and anti-imperialist tradition of a certain sector of Philippine civil society and thus adopts a critical view towards internationalist educational policies, CJFF has subverted one of the main manifestations of American neocolonialism and transformed it into a tool for the empowerment of migrants. While the use of the English language as a medium for protest against neocolonial domination is not a new development within social movements in the Philippines, it has interesting implications within a context of labor migration. Rather than indicating the migrants' further submission to the capitalist global order and/or the community organization leaders' co-optation into the very system that they are challenging, it can instead be seen as a radical subversion of a cultural product – originating in the home country's colonial past, reinforced by current economic realities, and promoted by the government in its labor and educational policies – from an instrument for the preservation of hegemony into a tool for active and sustained resistance. By serving as a means for the migrants' upward social mobility, English language skills, in effect, facilitate the empowerment of Filipino migrants as a community, strengthen their capabilities for organizing, and increase their opportunities for political engagement in an international arena.

With regard to the impact of gender and the intersection of gender issues with migrants' concerns, it may be said from this study that the gendered terrain of Filipino migration, particularly to Japan, has necessitated a particular approach towards actions within civil society. Just as the feminization of migration has implied that women are now taking more active roles in the economic sphere (in a sense, transgressing the traditional gender-based public/private divide), the proliferation of new social movements has likewise allowed women to emerge as key players in political advocacy on a transnational scale.

While CJFF's leader is, notably, a male, the organization has recognized from the beginning that it needs to consider gender in mapping out its goals and programs. In its emphasis on empowerment, it has encouraged women to organize among themselves and engage in concerted action on issues affecting Filipinos, both abroad and back "home." The heightened participation of Filipino women in transnational social movements may yet become a significant factor in the evolution of issues within the international migration context – one that could have a profound effect on the politics and processes of social movement organizations, both at the micro level and as part of broader political and economic developments.

Notes

1. This chapter is based on my master's thesis, "NGO Micropolitics: An Ethnographic Case Study of a Filipino-run Community Organization in Tokyo," submitted to the University of Tokyo in February 2008. All interviews with NGO workers and other ethnographic data were gathered during one year of volunteer work with CJFF from October 2006 to October 2007.
2. Those classified under Tier Two are countries whose governments do not fully comply with the Trafficking Victims Protection Act's minimum standards but are "making significant efforts to bring themselves into compliance with those standards" (United States Department of State, 2006). There are critics of this classification system, however. A multinational poll conducted by World Public Opinion (2007) indicated that many people feel the US should not act as a self-declared "global cop" on this issue.
3. *Padala* literally means "sent." The term is often used by Filipinos to refer to "gifts" sent from abroad to the Philippines. For instance, a *balikbayan* (homecoming) box full of imported goods can be called a *padala* from migrants for their families. I use the term here to refer to people being sent by organizations to another organization or another country to fulfill a particular mission.
4. Some women find this kind of "competition" rather challenging. A former entertainer who is married to a Japanese man and who owns a *sari-sari* (general merchandise) store in Kanagawa says: "Madaling pagkakitaan ang club kasi konting bola-bola lang, may pera na" (It is very easy to earn money in clubs. You get money out of fooling Japanese). Some scholars in the past have focused on such "opportunism" of women entertainers. However, as I learned from the women whom I interviewed, most of them have actually adopted this kind of attitude as a survival strategy. As one former entertainer explained, "Kung ikaw ang maloko ng customer, malas mo. Kung ikaw ang makaloko, swerte mo" (It's too bad if a customer fools you. If you're the one who is able to fool the customer, then you're lucky).

References

Abu-Lughod, L. (2006). Writing against culture. In E. Lewis (Ed), *Feminist anthropology: A reader* (pp .153-169). Malden, MA: Blackwell.

Anderson, J. N. (2003, June). *A gendered diaspora: Filipinos in Japan*. Paper presented at the Hawaii International Conference on Social Sciences, Honolulu, Hawaii, USA. Abstract retrieved June 5, 2007, from http://www.hicsocial.org/Social2003Proceedings/James% 20N.%20 Anderson.pdf

Ang, D. A. (2005). *The Filipino as citizen of the world*. Angana, Guam. Retrieved August 2007, from http://www.cfo.gov.ph/daainguam.pdf

Arroyo, G. M. (2001, September). *PGMA's speech for the overseas Filipino workers of Japan*. Tokyo, Japan.

Arroyo, G. M. (2003, March). *PGMA's speech during the dinner hosted by the US-ASEAN Business Council*. Washington, DC.

Arroyo, G. M. (2006, October). *PGMA's speech during the National Competitiveness Summit*. Malacañang, Philippines.

Ball, R., & Piper, N. (2002). Globalisation and regulation of citizenship: Filipino migrant workers in Japan. *Political Geography, 21*, 1013–1034.

Bohning, W. R. (1981). Elements of a theory of international economic migration to industrial nation states. In M. Kritz, C. Keely, & S. Tomasi (Eds.), *Global trends in migration: Theory and research on international population movements* (pp. 28-43). New York: Center for Migration Studies.

Collins, J., Lappe, F. M., & Rosset, P. (2000). *Lessons from the Green Revolution.* Retrieved October 5, 2007, from http://www.foodfirst.org/node/230/print

Chan-Tiberghien, J. (2004). *Gender and human rights politics in Japan: Global norms and domestic networks.* Palo Alto, CA: Stanford University Press.

Clifford, J. (1997). Diasporas. In J. Rex (Ed.), *The ethnicity reader: Nationalism, multiculturalism and migration* (pp. 257-290). Cambridge: Polity Press.

Conway, J. M. (2006). *Praxis and politics: Knowledge production in social movements (New approaches in sociology).* New York: Routledge.

Crick, M. (1989). Representations of international tourism in the social sciences: Sun, sex, sights, savings, and servility. *Annual Review of Anthropology, 18*, 307-344.

De Guzman, O. (2003). *Overseas Filipino workers, labor circulation in Southeast Asia, and the (mis)management of overseas migration programs.* Retrieved March 2007, from http://kyotoreview.cseas.kyoto-u.ac.jp/issue/issue3/article_281.html

Estrada. J. E. (1999, July). *State of the nation address: A poverty-free Philippines. Delivered by His Excellency President Joseph Ejercito Estrada.* Quezon City, Philippines.

Ferguson, J., & Gupta, A. (2005). Spatializing states: Toward an ethnography of neoliberal governmentality. In J. X. Inda (Ed.), *Anthropologies of modernity: Foucault, governmentality and life politics* (pp. 105-134). Oxford: Blackwell.

Forrester, D. (1988). *Theology and politics.* Oxford: Blackwell.

Foucault, M. (1991). Governmentality. In G. Burchell, C. Gordon, & P. Miller (Eds.), *The Foucault effect: studies in governmentality* (pp. 87-104). Chicago: Chicago University Press.

Guevarra, A. P. (2003, August). *Governing migrant workers through empowerment and sustaining a culture of labor migration: The case of the Philippines.* Paper presented at the annual meeting of the American Sociological Association, Atlanta Hilton Hotel, Atlanta, GA. Retrieved July 7, 2008, from http://www.allacademic.com/meta/ p107225_index.html

Guevarra, A. P. (2006). Managing "vulnerabilities" and "empowering" migrant Filipina workers: The Philippines' overseas employment program. *Social Identities, 12*(5), 523-541.

Guevarra, A. P. (2006, August). *The "New aristocrats": Filipino nurses, cultural capital, and the nurse shortage.* Paper presented at the annual meeting of the American Sociological Association, Montreal Convention Center, Montreal, Quebec, Canada. Retrieved October 2, 2007, from http://www.allacademic.com/meta/p104975_index.html

Lauby, J. (1988). Individual migration as a family strategy: Young women in the Philippines. *Population Studies, 42*(3), 473-486.

McGovern, L. (2006, July). *Colonialism/neocolonialism in the context of neo-liberal globalization: Impact on Filipino women and implications for decolonization.* Paper presented at the annual meeting of the American Sociological Association, Montreal Convention Center, Quebec, Canada. Retrieved October 3, 2004, from www.allacademic.com/meta.p105564_index.html

Meadows, M. (1971). Colonialism, social structure and nationalism: The Philippine case. *Pacific Affairs, 44*(3), 337-352.

Melucci, A. (1995). The new social movements revisited: Reflections on a sociological misunderstanding. In L. Maheu (Ed.), *Social movements and social classes* (pp. 107-119). London: Sage Publications.

McHale, T. (1961). The Philippines in transition. *The Journal of Asian Studies, 20*(3), 331-341.

Nadeau, K. M. (2002). *Liberation theology in the Philippines: Faith in a revolution.* Westport, CT: Praeger.

Nowotny, H. (1981). A sociological approach toward a general theory of migration. In M.

Kritz, C. Keely, & S. Tomasi (Eds.), *Global trends in migration: Theory and research on international population movements* (pp. 64-83). New York: Center for Migration Studies.

Philippine Migrants Rights Watch. (2004). *Philippine migration: Challenges to hurdle (An alternative report)*. Retrieved May 22, 2007, from http://www.pmrw.org/images/Reportto GCIM.pdf

San Juan, E. (2000, July). Trajectories of the Filipino diaspora. *Ethnic Studies Report, 18*(2), 229-238.

San Juan, E. (2002). Toward a decolonizing indigenous psychology in the Philippines: Introducing *sikolohiyang* Pilipino. *Journal for Cultural Research, 10*(1), 47-67.

Sellek, Y. (1996). Female foreign migrant workers in Japan: Working for the Yen. *Japan Forum, 8*(2), 159-175.

Smith, P. (1945). A basic problem in Philippine education. *The Far Eastern Quarterly, 4*(2), 140-147.

Soriano, J. (2007). *The Filipino diaspora: A historical and critical perspective*. Retrieved July 8, 2007, from www.soriano-ph.com

Tarrow, S. (1998). *Power in movement: Social movements and contentious politics*. London: Cambridge University.

Tutor, B. (2006). *Filipino Assistant English Teachers (AET's)*. Retrieved March 19, 2007, from http://www.philippinestoday.net/index.php?module=article&view=4

United States Department of State. (2006). *Trafficking in persons report*. United States: Office to Monitor and Combat Trafficking in Persons.

Ventura, R. (2006). *Underground in Japan*. Manila: Ateneo de Manila University Press.

World Public Opinion. (2007). *World publics reject US role as the world leader*. Retrieved June 3, 2007, from http://www.worldpublicopinion.org

Part Three:
Culture and Development

• CHAPTER SIX •

Imagining Others: A Study of the "Asia" Presented in Japanese Cinema

KINNIA SHUK-TING YAU
The Chinese University of Hong Kong

After the Meiji Restoration in 1868, Japan went through a process of modernization and transformed itself into a world power. During the nineteenth century, Japan achieved its imperialistic ambitions through a series of wars with China and Russia and the annexation of neighboring regions such as Okinawa, Taiwan and Korea. Though defeated in the Second World War, Japan managed to recover quickly and develop its economy. Japan's success in obtaining the right to host the Olympic Games in 1964 symbolized its "full re-entry into the international community" and "provided an opportunity to display Japan's industrial and technological achievements" (Tipton, 2002, p. 179). From the 1970s to 1980s, Japan continued to enjoy rapid economic growth, raising its status on the world stage.

Compared to other Asian countries, Japan industrialized at a faster pace; therefore, it often considered itself superior to its neighbors. This sense of superiority is reflected in the movies in which "Asia" was portrayed as inferior and less civilized. However, the burst of Japan's "bubble" economy and economic recession in the 1990s, coinciding with the rise of Asia (particularly China and South Korea), prompted Japan to rethink its relations with other Asian countries as well as its position in Asia. Consequently, more and more Asian topics and Asian elements found their way into Japanese films and the portrayal of Asians changed in a drastic way.

The purpose of this chapter is to investigate the portrayal of Asian elements in Japanese films as well as analyze Japan's changing perceptions of Asia from the Second World War period to the present. As cultural viewpoints do not arise in a vacuum but are at least partly shaped by surrounding socioeconomic conditions, an attempt is made throughout to relate changing Japanese perceptions of Asia to the development of Japan and the Asia region. "Asia" here refers to Japan's immediate neighbors, China, Hong Kong, Taiwan and South Korea.

DURING THE WAR

In the mid-nineteenth century, the arrival of the Black Ships of Commodore Matthew Perry marked the opening of Japan by which Japan realized its military development compared poorly to the West's. While impressed with the modernized West, Japan also felt inferior at the same time. To erase this feeling of inferiority, Japan aimed to become an influential state equal to the Western powers by quickly following a path of westernization. The expression *Datsu-A Ron* (Leaving Asia) reflected Japan's endeavor to separate itself from Asia, as it considered its Asian neighbors to be backward, less civilized, and hence inferior.[1] Nevertheless, as Japan hoped to emulate the Western powers by means of colonialism, Asia became Japan's target for its colonial activities. As an excuse for its expansion into Asia, Japan advocated the concept of *Dai-to-a Kyoeiken* (The Greater East Asia Co-prosperity Sphere). Its objective was to unite the East Asian regions to create a "Greater East Asia" to counter Western aggression and influence. Japan's egotism was reflected in the films produced at the time.

During the Second World War, Japanese feminized China (including Hong Kong and Taiwan) through romance films, so as to produce a superior, masculine image of Japan. For instance, Li Xiang-lan (a.k.a. Yamaguchi Yoshiko) was the designated actress in *tairiku eiga* (movies about mainland China) directed by Japanese. In *Song of the White Orchid* (1939, Kunio Watanabe), *China Night* (1940, Fushimi Osamu), and *Vow in the Desert* (1940, Kunio Watanabe), which were known as the *tairiku eiga* trilogy, Li starred as a young Chinese woman receiving help from a Japanese man of a higher social class. These films attempted to foster the impression that the Japanese were the saviors of China. *China Night* was especially controversial because Li's character is beaten by a Japanese sailor played by Hasegawa Katsuo. Instead of resisting him, she thanks him for "enlightening" her and immediately falls in love with him.

On the other hand, the Japanese intended to use the Hong Kong actress Zi Luo-lian as a Japan-Hong Kong goodwill ambassador. Similar to the characters played by Li Xiang-lan, Zi played a Chinese woman in *The Attack on Hong Kong* (1942, Tanaka Shigeo) who falls in love with a Japanese soldier but is killed by the British army in the end. The purpose of the film was to arouse anti-British sentiments in its viewers as Britain and Japan were at war from December 8, 1941.

Besides representing China in the *tairiku eiga* trilogy, Li Xiang-lan also represented Taiwan in *Sayon's Bell* (1943, Shimizu Hiroshi). Here, she played a Taiwanese aborigine girl, Sayon, who drowns while helping her Japanese teacher carry his luggage in a storm. The Office of the Government-General in Taiwan praised her courageous act by setting up a memorial bell, the Sayon's Bell, at the site of the accident. The movie was based on a true story and the Japanese government used it to enhance Japan-Taiwan ties. The commendation of Sayon called on Taiwanese to be loyal to Japan just like Sayon. Similar to her image in *tairiku eiga*, Li once again represented Japan's ideal colonial subject.

Japanese ethnocentrism is evident in the above movies, where the heroes of higher social status represent the "superiority" of Japan and the lower-class heroines represent the "inferiority" of its conquered races. Such films, with little subtlety, strove to promote the delusion that Japan was proffering goodwill to its Asian neighbors, doing so in a fashion akin to what Edward Said termed "Orientalism."[3] Said wrote how, in colonial and post-colonial contexts, the "superior" country fabricates illusory images in its media regarding the "inferior" country to enforce relations of dominance over the latter (Wang, 2004, p. 524). Although geographically situated in Asia, Japan perceived its Asian neighbors from a colonizer's point of view. It was through colonialism that Japan endeavored to achieve parity with the Western powers.

THE POST-WAR PERIOD

After the war, Japan initiated the establishment of the Southeast Asian Motion Pictures Producers Association to reverse its image as a "conqueror," open up Asian markets to its products, and strengthen Asian film networks to counter Western cultural influences. During this period, due to marketing concerns, the distance between "superior" Japan and "inferior" China[4] was reduced. Under such circumstances, a certain level of "equality" between Japan and other Asian regions could be observed in a series of film co-productions including *A Night in Hong Kong* (1961, Chiba Yasuki), *Hong Kong Star* (1962, Chiba Yasuki), *Honolulu-Tokyo-Hong Kong* (1963, Chiba Yasuki), *White Rose of Hong Kong* (1965, Fukuda Jun), and *A Night in Bangkok* (1966, Yasuki Chiba).[5] Most of these transnational romantic dramas were inspired by Hollywood pictures such as *Roman Holiday* (1953, William Wyler), *Terminus Station* (1953, Vittorio De Sica), *Love is a Many Splendored Thing* (1955, Henry King), and *The World of Suzie Wong* (1960, Richard Quine). Hong Kong actress You Min, who starred in *A Night in Hong Kong*, *Hong Kong Star*, and *Honolulu-Tokyo-Hong Kong*, was one of the first Chinese actresses with an international image.[6] When she retired, she was replaced by Taiwanese actress Zhang Mei-yao who starred in *White Rose of Hong Kong* and *A Night in Bangkok*. Unlike the characters played by Li Xiang-lan, these actresses no longer starred as low-class

Chinese women who needed to be educated or rescued by Japanese men from a higher social class. Instead, they were multilingual, highly educated, and sometimes wealthier than the Japanese heroes, namely Takarada Akira and Kayama Yuzo.

According to the casting, however, the images of a "masculine" Japan and a "feminine" Asia were still present in the above movies. Obviously, Japan still considered itself superior because the Chinese regions at that time were economically and technologically backward to Japan.

Meanwhile, the 1960s saw the rise of Japanese cross-border *yakuza eiga* (gangster films). They similarly displayed Japan's superiority by demonizing Asian elements. In *Narazu mono* (The Rogues) (1964, Ishii Teruo), and *Gang 9, Tokyo Gang versus Hong Kong Gang* (1964, Ishii Teruo), Japanese filmmakers projected stereotypical images of Chinese people as gang members and prostitutes. This demonization of Chinese characters served to distinguish the Chinese as "aliens" and enhance the "goodness" of the Japanese. It was another means of conveying a conception that Asians were inferior to Japanese. Interestingly, the villains in the films were often played by Japanese actors and actresses, such as Abe Tooru, Ohki Minoru and Mihara Yoko, and their Chinese (Mandarin or Cantonese) was far from accurate.

In the above movies, Hong Kong was portrayed as a city of crime and poverty. The depiction of the Kowloon Walled City[7] highlighted this evil image. Takakura Ken, who starred in most of the *yakuza eiga*, was the epitome of masculinity and loyalty. He represented the chivalrous *yakuza* hero protecting his community, and more importantly traditional Japanese values, against the onslaught of foreign forces.

CHINESE STARS IN JAPAN DURING THE 1970S AND 1980S

From the 1970s onwards, the kung fu boom, spurred by the rising popularity of Bruce Lee, changed Japanese attitudes towards Hong Kong and its cinema. The first Bruce Lee picture released in Japan was *Enter the Dragon* (1973, Robert Clouse), which depicted Hong Kong as a center attracting martial arts fighters from around the world. Together with *The Big Boss* (1971, Luo Wei), *Fist of Fury* (1972, Luo Wei), and *Way of the Dragon* (1972, Bruce Lee), these movies inspired Japanese to produce their own *wasei kanfu eiga* (Japanese-made kung fu films), such as the *Satsujin ken* (Street Fighter) series (1974, Ozawa Shigehiro) and the *Onna hissatsu ken* (Sister Street Fighter) series (1974-1975, Yamaguchi Kazuhiro), which became a trend in the 1970s. Chiba Shinichi and Shihomi Etsuko starred in most of the *wasei kanfu eiga*, becoming cultural icons in this genre. From that time onward, kung fu or martial arts represented a new Chinese element in Japanese cinema. However, Japanese stereotypes of

Hong Kong can still be observed in some of the films. For instance, in *Gekitotsu! Satsujin ken* (The Street Fighter) (1974, Ozawa Shigehiro), Hong Kong is portrayed as an old city with people still wearing *changshan* (long Chinese garments); in *Golgo 13: Assignment Kowloon* (1977, Noda Yukio), Hong Kong is portrayed as a city of crime and drug trading, which is a reminiscent of the city's image depicted in *yakuza eiga* from the previous decade.

Nevertheless, Bruce Lee's movies also contributed to the rising interest in Hong Kong movies in Japan. Japanese film distributors began to import more Hong Kong movies, paving the way for the success of Michael Hui and Jackie Chan. Hui's satirical comedies, known as the "'Mr. Boo!' series" (released between 1979 and 1985 in Japan), enabled Japanese audiences to appreciate an alternative Hong Kong film genre. On the other hand, Chan brought in a new style of martial arts movies by combining comedy and kung fu. His *Drunken Master* (1978, Yuen Wooping) was a big hit in Japan, and he soon became an international star thereafter. Both Hui and Chan were able to grab the attention of the Japanese because they displayed a novel form of acting.

Japanese entertainment companies made early efforts to attract Asian stars in the music industry. In the 1970s, Japanese record companies were aware of the rising popularity of Chinese singers in Hong Kong and Taiwan. These companies sent representatives to different Asian regions, searching for potential artists to promote the Japanese music industry (Hirano, 1997, p. 50). Under such circumstances, Hong Kong and Taiwan singers such as Agnes Chan and Teresa Teng successfully broke into the Japanese market and achieved stardom. Aside from their talent, it was their "foreignness" that attracted the Japanese. However, these artists had to adjust their image to cater to the tastes of their Japanese fans.[8] This manipulation of the image of Chinese stars reflected a sense of Japanese supremacy.

The year 1973, the end of the fixed currency exchange rate with the US dollar, marked the beginning of the yen's floating exchange rate. The rising value of the yen stimulated Japanese to travel abroad. Asian regions such as Hong Kong, Taiwan and South Korea became popular destinations due to their proximity.[9] Low production costs and cheap labor in Asia also attracted Japanese investment. With the opening of China in 1978 and the permission of foreign investment in the retail sectors of East and Southeast Asian regions in the 1980s, Japan began to develop overseas retail businesses in these areas, opening Japanese department stores in regions selling Japanese products. The infusion of Japanese-style retail services and management practices into Asia was a reflection of Japan's desire to re-experience a sense of colonialism through the economic sector.

The 1970s and 1980s also witnessed a change in relations between China and Japan. The two countries established diplomatic relations in 1972 and signed a treaty in 1978.[10] New trade agreements were forged which spurred Japanese businesses to invest in China. This led to a "China boom," which aroused an interest in China among Japanese.[11] Subsequently, Chinese martial arts films such as *Shaolin Temple* (1982, Zhang Xin-yan), starring Jet Li, became very popular and gave rise to a second kung fu craze.

Although establishing diplomatic relations with China would mean that Japan had to break off its ties with Taiwan,[12] non-governmental interactions between Japan and Taiwan continued and the two still remained closely connected to each other.[13] Some Japanese saw China as a potential competitor, and they wanted to use Taiwan to curb China's development into a world power.[14] Japan's awareness of China becoming a potential threat to its leading position in Asia indicated the beginning of a shift in Japanese attitudes towards Asia.

FROM THE HEISEI ERA

The Heisei period began in 1989 after the end of Showa period, with Prince Akihito becoming the new emperor of Japan. With the beginning of this new age, Japan underwent drastic political, social and economic changes. It also marked a new page of Japanese relations with Asia. *Beijing Watermelon* (1989, Obayashi Nobuhiko) was the first Japanese movie with Chinese characters released in the Heisei era. It indicated a change in Japanese attitudes towards China, although it still exhibited a certain sense of Japanese "superiority." In the movie, Haruzo (Bengal), a vegetable shop owner, starts out disliking the Chinese students who come to his shop, but when he sees one collapse from malnutrition, he begins to treat the students nicely by offering discounts to them. In fact, his Good Samaritan behavior escalates to the point that he almost bankrupts his business. In the end, the Chinese students return the favor by voluntarily working for Haruzo. The story depicts friendship between Japanese and Chinese; however, it mainly signifies a growing interest in Asia on the part of Japanese, and contains an underlying message that Japan is still China's "savior."

Hong Kong Paradise (1990, Kaneko Shusuke) praises Hong Kong as a "paradise" for Japanese tourists. However, the movie's depiction of tourist attractions, such as the Jumbo Floating Restaurant, Cantonese operas and magic shows, stereotypes Hong Kong in a fashion similar to Ishii Teruo's *Gang 9, Tokyo Gang versus Hong Kong Gang*, indicating that Japan's understanding of Hong Kong was still superficial. Nevertheless, an evident shift in Japanese perceptions of Hong Kong occurred, with Hong

Kong portrayed positively as an exciting and adventurous place rather than a crime-ridden city.

In the 1990s, the burst of the bubble economy in Japan was accompanied by economic and social problems in the nation. Economic recession led to a rise in bad debts, causing many large financial corporations to go bankrupt. High school and college graduates experienced difficulties in securing employment. Salarymen were laid off. Worse yet, a series of government scandals were disclosed, including corruption within Tokyo Sagawa Express, a parcel delivery firm.[15] The administration was in a shambles and the nation witnessed a constant change of prime ministers.[16] The 1995 sarin gas attack by Aum Shinrikyo reflected the serious instability of Japanese society.[17] Japan's leading position in Asia was also challenged by the rise of Asia, especially China and South Korea. While Japan was undergoing economic recession, China[18] and South Korea[19] were experiencing rapid economic growth. Facing these internal and external problems, Japanese began to treasure their glorious past, an attitude which was reflected through movies about reunion with the dead, such as *Love Letter* (1995, Iwai Shunji), *Crying out Love in the Center of the World* (2004, Isao Yukisada), and *Be with You* (2004, Doi Nobuhiro). Meanwhile, with "Asia" becoming a new land of opportunities, Japan began to reconsider its relations and position with the region. As pointed out by Iwabuchi (2000), "the Asia which Japan encounters in the 1990s…is no longer contained by the image of traditional, underdeveloped, backward neighbors to be civilized by Japan" (p. 14).

Under such circumstances, Japanese media presented a very different Asia than previous. In the 1990s, with rapid economic development in the ANIEs (Asian Newly Industrializing Economies), namely Singapore, Hong Kong, Taiwan and South Korea (McCormack, 1996, p. 156), Japanese women magazines began to introduce these regions as Asian "metropolitans" to its readers (Okada, 2003, p. 126). Another example was the song *Ajia no junshin* (The Purity of Asia), sung by the pop duo Puffy in 1996.[20] It depicted Asia as pure and enchanting, appealing to Japanese youth to open their hearts to this newly discovered Asia.

In the meantime, popular stars such as Kaneshiro Takeshi, Faye Wong, Michele Reis and Kelly Chen strengthened a modern image of Asia in the minds of Japanese.[21] Unlike Agnes Chan and Teresa Teng, who had to adjust their images to fit into Japan's show business culture, these young idols appealed to Japanese with their unique looks and charismatic personalities. They appeared to represent a more cosmopolitan Asia in terms of their appearances, styles, tastes and beliefs.[22]

The above examples signified a re-evaluation of Asia on the part of Japanese. Compared to earlier images of Asia, this shift in perceptions was reflective of a more positive attitude towards Asia. This appeared to be the case as the "Asia" Japan was willing to approach was now a purer, cleaner, wealthier, more civilized and more modern region in Japanese eyes. Furthermore, Asian characters or customs were praised in the movies as a means of showing discontent and disappointment with Japan among Japanese.

FASHIONABLE AND DYNAMIC ASIA

In the 1990s, Japanese filmmakers also took a different approach in their portrayal of Asians. The pureness of Asians was often contrasted with the materialism of Japanese, who "lost sight of values that made them human" (Schilling, 1999, p. 50). In *Swallowtail, The City of Lost Souls* (2000, Miike Takashi), and *Calmi cuori appasionati* (Calm Passionate Hearts) (2001, Nakae Isamu), Asians were no longer depicted as inferior outsiders. Instead, they were appreciated by the directors for their energy and dynamism. Overseas Japanese in the "Yen Towns" in *Swallowtail*, or Japanese-Brazilians in *The City of Lost Souls*, insist on their self-identity and way of life, despite the fact that they are despised by most Japanese in Japan. In contrast to their self-perceptions of confidence and integrity, Japanese people (including policemen and triad gang members) are portrayed as cowardly and sly.[23]

Iwai Shunji and Miike Takashi were two forerunners who showed sensitivity towards Asians in their films.[24] Compared to their predecessors, these new wave directors of the 1990s held a more open-minded view of other Asians. In their movies, various Asian elements can be found and these elements are no longer depicted as evil or inferior.[25]

Calm Passionate Hearts is a cinematic adaptation of two best-selling novels by Eguni Kaori and Tsuji Jinsei respectively. It depicts the love story of Junsei (Takenouchi Yutaka) and Aoi (Kelly Chen). Most of the movie takes place in Florence, Italy, a city of art and romance that is, importantly, "foreign" to both of them. Having a Japanese father and growing up in Hong Kong, Aoi and her cross-cultural identity make her an embodiment of "internationality." In addition to the exotic locale of Florence, Kelly Chen and her designer fashions from Salvatore Ferragamo, Christian Dior, Kenzo, Fendi and so forth, endeared the film to thousands of Japanese "office ladies."[26] Chen came to symbolize a fashionable and cosmopolitan woman with a flare for life similar in outlook to the character Carrie Bradshaw (Sarah Jessica Parker) in *Sex and the City*.[27]

Asian stars in the above Japanese movies are multilingual. In other words, the Japanese language is less dominant, since it is no longer the main spoken language in these films. For instance, the dialogues of *Swallowtail* are mostly in English or Mandarin. Ageha's (Ito Ayumi) attempts to learn Mandarin reveal the growing influence of China. Meanwhile, *The City of Lost Souls* consists of dialogues in Japanese, Portuguese, Mandarin and Cantonese. In this sense, Chinese or other foreign languages (no longer limited to English) have become the hallmark of fashion. This multilingual outlook can also be applied to the youth drama *Bounce ko gals* (1997, Harada Masato), since Mandarin pop serves as the background music to the activities of contemporary high school girls in Japan.

FRIENDLY AND MASCULINE ASIA

Many post-1990 Japanese movies suggest friendships are possible between Japanese and their Asian counterparts, with some films reversing the traditional romantic pattern of "Men are from Japan, and women are from Asia."[28] Examples can be seen in *Perfect Education 3* (2002, Sam Leong)[29] and *About Love* (2005, Shimoyama Ten, Yee Chin-yen and Zhang Yibai). In these movies, transnational couples eventually overcome their language and cultural barriers, and suffering Japanese heroines are rescued and assuaged by Chinese heroes.[30] The movies alter the pattern of Japanese men rescuing Asian women, materially or mentally, which was earlier employed to confirm the masculinity and superiority of Japan. This change thus contributed to a new image of Asia in the eyes of Japanese related to heroism and remedies for broken hearts.

The friendly image of Chinese people in the films can also be considered as a side effect of *zanryu koji* (Japanese orphans in China). The orphans became more well-known in Japan after 1981 when China opened its doors to trade, prompting the mass media to focus on the problem. For example, the Japan Broadcasting Corporation (NHK) produced the popular TV series *Daichi no ko* (The Son of Earth) (1995), which was adapted from the best-selling novel of Yamazaki Toyoko. Zhu Xu, who played the "Chinese" father of Kamikawa Takaya, was welcomed by the Japanese audience and improved the image of Chinese people in their minds. *The Bell of Purity Temple* (1991, Zhe Jin), a Chinese movie on *zanryu koji* starring the well-known Japanese actress Kurihara Komaki was also acclaimed at the time it was released in Japan. All of the above movies romanticized the relationship between Chinese and Japanese through encounters between Japanese orphans and their Chinese foster parents. Although the protagonists in both stories were able to reunite with their Japanese families, they both chose to remain in China and to repay the kindness to the country where they grew up.

KOREAN CINEMA UNDER THE JAPANESE OCCUPATION

In early twentieth century Korea, films were used for propaganda purposes by the Japanese government. Japan's occupation of Korea officially began in 1910, with the Japan-Korea Annexation Treaty, and lasted until

1945. During this period, the Korean film industry was very much in the hands of Japanese who had full control over distribution and exhibition rights and owned most theaters in Korea. There are very few written accounts on Korean films during this period as films made before 1943 have not been recovered (Kim, 2002, p. 20). The first Korean film was *Uirijok gutu* (Royal Revenge) (1919, Kim Do-san), a *kino*-drama (a combination of motion picture and stage play) financed by Park Sung-pil, the only Korean film businessman at that time. Due to a shortage of equipment and his limited experience, the director had to hire a Japanese cameraman to shoot the film (Min, Joo & Kwak, 2003, p. 27).

In 1919, 2 million Koreans gathered to protest against the Japanese, establishing the March First Movement. The Japanese army suppressed the riots and killed more than 7,000 Koreans. In the wake of the riots, the Japanese government adopted a relatively "lenient" policy of allowing Koreans to publish their own newspapers and advocated public education (Min & Kwak, 2003, p. 28). A number of films were made during the 1920s including a Japanese-directed film *Chun-hyang jon* (The Story of Chun-hyang) (Hashikawa Koju),[31] which was based on a famous Korean folk story.[32] Like *The Story of Chun-hyang*, most movies made at that time were adaptations of Korean folktales that were highly successful at the box office. Several film production companies were formed, of which Choson Kinema was the most prominent. Founded by Japanese merchant Yodo Orajo, the company brought in technicians from Japan and produced films using Japanese directors and Korean actors. Korean filmmakers managed to produce a few nationalistic films including *Arirang* (1926, Na Un-gyu), *Sarangul chajaseo* (Looking for Love) (1928, Na Un-gyu), and *Imjaobnun narubae* (Ferryboat with No Ferryman) (1932, Lee Gyu-hwan). However, Koreans did not enjoy much freedom in the film industry as the Japanese still had strict control over Korean film productions.

In 1924, Japan censored imported films, fearing that liberal Western ideas might influence Koreans to rise up against the Japanese colonial government (Min & Kwak, 2003, p. 29). Censorship became more severe which led to the decline of film productions in the 1930s as many Korean filmmakers fled to China. Japan endeavored to turn Koreans into Japan's imperial subjects under the slogan of *Naisenittai* (Unification of Japan and Korea). Under the policy of *Soshikaimei* (Adoption of Japanese-style Names), Koreans were forced to abandon their Korean names and were conscripted into the Japanese army (Ryang, 2000, pp. 2-3). In 1938, Japan banned the use of the Korean language. In 1940, under the Chosun Motion Picture Law, all ten Korean film companies were closed down and the Japanese colonial government established one company called the Chosun Film Co., which mainly produced Japanese propaganda films to enhance the concept of *Naisenittai* (Min & Kwak., 2003, p. 32). As a result, there were no Korean language films between 1938 and 1945, and film productions were fully controlled by Japanese for propaganda purposes (Wade, 1983, p. 177).

During the 1930s and 1940s, few Japanese films depicted the lives of Koreans. Monma Takashi (1994) points out that, during this period, Japanese filmmakers were compelled to act in accordance with the policies of the Japanese imperial government. Japanese movies that included Korean characters had to convey a message that Koreans were under the benevolent protection of Japanese (p. 214). Therefore, movies such as *Kono haha wo miyo* (Behold this, Mother) (1930, Tasaka Tomotaka) and *Renga joko* (Women Workers in the Brickyard) (1940, Chiba Yasuki) were censored by the Japanese government due to their portrayal of the hardships of Korean immigrants, which implied Koreans were not well protected by Japan.[33] In *Arigato-san* (Mr. Thank You) (1936), Shimizu Hiroshi used a more objective approach in portraying the conditions of Korean workers. By capturing the Korean workers as part of the scenery in the movie, Shimizu simply let viewers draw their own conclusions.

When the Second World War began, films became an important tool for Japanese propaganda. *Boro no keshittai* (Watchtower Suicide Squad) (1943, Imai Tadashi) praises the heroic acts of the border guard forces fighting against anti-Japanese partisans at the Manchuria-Korea border. Shimizu Hiroshi's short film *Tomodachi* (Friends) (1940) depicts Korean children getting along well with Japanese children, which was intended to promote *Naisenittai*.

KOREA BETWEEN THE 1950S AND 1980S

The Japanese occupation of Korea ended with Japan's defeat in the Second World War. With memories of the occupation still fresh in Korean minds, tensions soon rose between Japan and South Korea. In 1952, South Korean president Rhee Syng-man established the "Syng-man Rhee Line" (a.k.a. "Peace Line" in South Korea) on the Sea of Japan (East Sea),[34] banning fishing boats other than those of Koreans from entering the area around the Liancourt Rocks.[35] The problem of the "Syng-man Rhee Line" is addressed in the movie *Arega minato no hi da* (The Light of the Harbor) (1961, Imai Tadashi) which tells the story of a Japanese fishing boat captured by South Korea and rising tensions between Korean residents and Japanese in Japan.[36] Diplomatic relations between the two nations were re-established through the "Treaty on Basic Relations between Japan and the Republic of Korea" in 1965, by which Japan recognized South Korea as the only legitimate government on the Korean peninsula.[37] However, most Koreans, especially the older generation who directly experienced hardships under the Japanese, remain antagonistic towards Japanese. Anti-Japanese sentiment was enshrined in laws prohibiting

Japanese cultural imports into South Korea, laws which were only overturned in 1998.[38]

During the early years of Japanese occupation, large numbers of Koreans moved to Japan to work as laborers as most agricultural lands were confiscated by the Japanese and pro-Japan Koreans.[39] Until 1916, there were about 1,000 to 2,000 Koreans moving to Japan every year. This figure surged to 14,501 in 1917 owing to Japan's rising demand for workers to aid in its industrial development (Chapman, 2008, p. 17). The hardships suffered by Korean migrant workers are portrayed in Japanese films such as *Nianchan* (My Second Brother) (1959, Imamura Shohei) and *Kyupora no aru machi* (A Street of Cupolas) (1962, Urayama Kiriro). When the war ended, there were 2 million Koreans in Japan; within the following seven months, about 1.4 million Koreans returned to Korea, leaving about 600,000 Koreans in Japan (Chapman, 2008, p. 24). In 1952, the San Francisco Peace Treaty officially deprived Japan of the territorial ownership of Korea, which also meant that Koreans' Japanese nationality was no longer valid.[40] With the normalization of diplomatic relations between Japan and South Korea in 1965, Koreans who applied for South Korean nationality were allowed to obtain permanent residency in Japan.[41] However, Koreans living in Japan were not allowed to vote and they also faced discrimination in schools and in workplaces. Many chose to use Japanese names to hide their Korean identity in order to avoid prejudice (Iwabuchi, 2000, p. 58).

Japanese movies at that time often portrayed Koreans as victims of discrimination and most of them have a tragic ending. For instance, in *The Light of the Harbor*, the main protagonist, Kimura, is a resident Korean who has concealed his Korean identity from his colleagues. When a fishing boat is captured by South Korea, Kimura faces the dilemma of whether to reveal his true identity or not. When he tells his colleagues his secret, they start to distrust him, suspecting he is a spy. When their fishing boat crosses the "Syng-man Rhee Line" again, they are attacked by Koreans. While they try to escape, Kimura is shunned by his colleagues, and in the end he is killed by Koreans who think he is Japanese. Despite his death, his colleagues still blame him for the incident. *Death by Hanging* (1968, Oshima Nagisa) is based on the "Komatsukawa Incident," the murder of a Japanese girl at the hands of a resident Korean teenage boy in 1958. It was believed that the boy's poverty-stricken living conditions in Japan led to the crime. The movie attempts to understand the boy's mentality and suggests that his action was a reflection of resident Koreans' dissatisfaction with their treatment in Japan.

While Korea was divided into North and South, Koreans living in Japan were also divided into two groups, namely *chongryon* (pro-North Korea) and *mindan* (pro-South Korea). At first, the Koreans supported *chongryon* more than *mindan* because they believed that communism would lead to the unification of their country. *Chongryon* built Korean schools where resident Koreans could receive North Korean style education. The political difference between the North and South was highlighted in a Japanese movie *Ihojin no kawa* (The River for Aliens) (1975, Lee Ha-gin). The director, the cinematographer and the main actors were all resident Koreans. The movie depicted a young resident Korean working in Japan under a Japanese name. His encounter with a Korean girl rouses nationalist feelings in him and he decides to use his real name instead. However, towards the end the young man is attacked by the KCIA,[42] who suspect he is a dissident and cut his ear off.

South Korea began to develop its economy in the 1960s under economic reforms carried out by the military government of Park Chung-hee.[43] By emphasizing an export-oriented industrialization strategy, the nation achieved an average annual economic growth rate of 8 percent per year between 1962 and 1999.[44] This rapid economic development became known as the "Miracle on the Han River." With the democratization of the political system in 1987[45] and the 1988 Seoul Olympics, South Korea began to receive worldwide recognition as a rising economic power.

Concomitant with Korea's rising economic status, a slight change in the portrayal of Koreans in 1980s Japanese films became evident. Instead of merely portraying Koreans as victims, Japanese films in this period also tended to portray them as alienated individuals who attracted misfortune. For example, in *Kayako no tameni* (For Kayako's Sake) (1984, Oguri Kohei), Japanese women who fall in love with or marry Koreans are portrayed as unfortunate people.[46] These portrayals reflected Japanese prejudice against Koreans by associating Koreans with hardship and regrets, implying there were no "happy endings" to Japanese-Korean love relationships and signifying Japanese's resentment towards Koreans.

KOREA FROM THE 1990S

As South Korea's economy matured in the 1990s, Korean companies such as Samsung, LG and Hyundai shared the world market that was once dominated by the Japanese.[47] This period also witnessed the rise of the "386 generation,"[48] those who played a vital role in the cultural and economic sectors of South Korea. This "new" generation, who had not experienced Japanese occupation and the Korean War, were relatively more sympathetic towards North Korea and less resentful towards Japan. The cultural sector at this time played an important role in improving relations between South Koreans and Japanese. In 2002, the two countries co-hosted the World Cup, an event which greatly improved their relations.[49] That year was also the year of Japan-South Korea National Exchange, which witnessed a series of collaborations between the two nations in movies such as *Seoul* (2002, Nagasawa Masahiko), starring Nagase Tomoya and Choi Min-su; *2009 Lost Memories* (2002, Lee Simyung), starring Jang Dong-gun and Nakamura Tooru; and the television drama *Friends. Seoul,* directed by Japanese, was filmed in South Korea and most of the actors were Korean.[50] *Friends* was a two-episode special television drama co-produced by South Korea's Munhwa Broadcasting Corporation (MBC) and Japan's Tokyo Broadcasting System, Inc. (TBS). It starred pop idols from both nations, such as Fukada Kyoko and Won Bin. It was also the first time that Japan and Korea co-produced a television show. One of the latest collaborations[51] between Japan and South Korea can be seen in Kimura Takuya's *Hero* (2007, Suzuki Masayuki). It was partly shot in Pusan and Lee Byung-hun, a popular Korean actor in Japan, made a guest appearance as a significant figure helping Kimura solve a crime.

With the lifting of the ban, Japanese cultural products such as Japanese music, comics, anime and television dramas became "openly" accessible to South Koreans.[52] In the same period, with the blessing of the Korean government, Korean pop culture began to spread into Asia and achieved success in China, Hong Kong, Taiwan and Japan respectively.[53] Apart from singers such as BoA, K and Se7en, who scored hits in the Japanese music charts,[54] Korean television dramas also became popular in Japan. Two of the most significant examples were *Winter Sonata* and *Dae jang-geum* (A Jewel in the Palace), which brought stardom for Bae Yong-joon, Choi Ji-woo and Lee Young-ae in Japan.[55] Furthermore, Korean cinema also developed very rapidly from the 1990s. With the critical and box-office successes of *Shiri, JSA: Joint Security Area* and *My Sassy Girl* (2001, Kwak Jae-yong), Korean films received accolades from both Japanese critics and audiences.[56]

Unlike most Japanese movies before the 1990s that depicted resident Koreans as tragic characters, a different portrayal of resident Koreans appeared in films such as *All under the Moon* (1993, Sai Yoichi), *Asian Blue ukishima maru sakon* (Asian Blue: Ukishima Maru Incident) (1995, Horikawa Hiromichi), *Go* (2001, Yukisada Isao), *Yoru wo kakete* (Through the Night) (2002, Kim Su-jin), *Blood and Bones* (2004, Sai Yoichi), and *Break Through!* (2004, Izutsu Kazuyuki). These movies offered glimpses of the daily lives of resident Koreans from the 1940s onward.

All under the Moon and *Blood and Bones* were directed by Sai Yoichi,[57] a resident Korean in Japan. Both of these films were adaptations of the novels of the resident Korean writer Yang Sok-il,[58] who wrote his books based on his personal experiences. *All under the Moon* was based on his experience as a taxi driver; and *Blood and Bones* was based on his father's life. *All under the Moon* is about the daily life of a resident Korean taxi driver, Tadao (Kishitani Goro), who falls in love with a Filipino girl, Connie (Ruby Moreno). This movie challenges "the conventional representation of resident Koreans in Japan" (Iwabuchi, 2000, p. 55) by breaking the usual stereotype of resident Koreans as an oppressed group. The movie focuses on the reality of the lives of resident Koreans, instead of depicting them as victims of Japanese colonialism. Tadao does not care much about politics and instead he uses the history of Japanese occupation of Korea as a way to gain sympathy from Connie, lying that his brother was killed in the war. *Blood and Bones* is about a Korean called Shun-pei (Kitano Takeshi) who immigrated to Japan in the 1920s. His hard life in his early years in Japan turns him into a self-centered and vicious man. Through making money and engaging in wanton sex and violence, he assures himself and others that he is powerful and important.

Other movies raised awareness of the exploitation of Koreans under Japanese colonial rule. *Asian Blue: Ukishima Maru Incident* covers the Ukishima Maru Incident of 1945, in which a Japanese passenger ship carrying thousands of Korean forced laborers exploded and 500 Koreans were killed. Just as the movie describes, most Japanese are unaware of this incident. The movie examines the helplessness of the Korean forced laborers at that time and how their lives were manipulated by the Japanese. The ending does not answer certain unclear questions concerning the tragedy; however, it allows Japanese to rethink their country's treatment of Koreans during the Second World War. The sufferings of the forced laborers are also presented in the movie *Mitabi no kaikyo* (Three Trips across the Strait) (1995, Koyama Seijiro).

In 2001, Emperor Akihito made a statement on his 68th birthday, claiming that the Japanese royal family contains Korean royal blood. In the same year, the movie *Go* was released and became a big hit, by which the hero Kubotsuka Yosuke rose to stardom. These all reflected a change in Japanese attitudes towards Koreans and stressed intercultural ties between the two. *Go* was adapted from a novel by Kaneshiro Kazuki about a third generation resident Korean, Sugihara (Kubotsuka Yosuke), who decides to leave his North Korean school and study at a Japanese high school. Although he faces discrimination, he is able to fight back and becomes the best fighter in school. He encounters Sakurai (Shibasaki Ko), a Japanese girl, and they soon fall in love with each other. The movie shows that intercultural marriage and love relationships are common in Japan; for instance, Jong-il, Sugihara's best friend, is the son of a Japanese mother and a resident Korean father. Although Sakurai once could not accept Sugihara's Korean identity, in the end she realizes that she loves Sugihara for who he is and his ethnicity is irrelevant. The "happy ending" of Sugihara and Sakurai stands in contrast to the 1980s movie *For Kayako's Sake* in which Japanese-Korean love relationships are associated with remorse. The frequent depictions of Japanese-Korean couples in movies are reflective of Japanese society, as marriages between Japanese and Koreans have been rising steadily. In 1994, of the total marriages involving resident Koreans, 81.7 percent were with Japanese (Ryang, 2000, p. 6). Other movies that depict intercultural love relationships include *Break Through!* and *Summer of Chirusoku* (2003, Sasabe Kiyoshi).[59]

The above movies also reflect the fact that the question of nationality has become less and less important for Koreans in Japan. For example, those who had earlier supported North Korea no longer hold to such political viewpoints. Instead, most resident Koreans are more concerned with their futures in Japan (Ryang, 2000, p. 7). In *Go*, Sugihara's parents switch their nationality to South Korean for the sake of their son. In *Haruko* (2004, Nozawa Kazuyuki), a documentary film on the life of a Korean woman named Jeong Byeong-chun (a.k.a. Kanamoto Haruko), the mother suffers years of hardship to raise her seven children. At the age of 87, she gives up her North Korean nationality and becomes a South Korean. After living in Japan for seven decades, she cares more about her children and grandchildren than politics and nationality.

Concurrent with changing Japanese attitudes towards Koreans, a number of resident Koreans, particularly second and third generation residents, have begun using their real names in the Japanese entertainment industry, becoming famous in the process. Some examples include the directors Sai Yoichi (Choi Yang-il), Lee Sang-il,[60] and Kim Su-jin, as well as the producer Lee Bong-ou[61] and voice talent Park Romi.[62] These second/third generation resident Koreans were born and raised in Japan. Sonia Ryang (2000) has pointed out how the younger generation "became interested in identity politics, not from the angle of the north-south binary opposition, but with an eye to questioning their future in Japan" (p. 6). This mindset is expressed in *Go*, by Sugihara, who is frustrated for being alienated by Japanese. This movie also shows that second/third generation resident Koreans are more open-minded, and have their own thoughts about how they should live their lives. They are willing to accept who they are and are keen on finding their own "place" in Japanese society.

Japanese war films produced during the Heisei period also contain Korean elements that are quite different from war films produced before. *For those We Love* (2007, Shinjo Taku) was produced under the supervision of Ishihara Shintaro, who also wrote the script and is famous for his rightwing beliefs.[63] The movie is set in the Second World War, where a group of young pilots is about to conduct suicide attacks on Allied troops. Although the movie romanticizes the act of *kamikaze tokubetsu kogekitai* (best known as "kamikaze" in the West),[64] a positive portrayal of Korean elements can be found in the movie. One of the kamikaze pilots, Kanayama, is a Korean who on the night before his mission sings the Korean folk song *Arirang*, claiming that he is fighting for his homeland (Korea). *The Firefly* (2001, Furuhata Yasuo), although produced earlier than *For those We Love*, seems to be a continuation of the latter. The movie is set in modern times. Yamaoka (Takakura Ken), a former kamikaze pilot who survived the war, is asked by a Japanese woman called Yamamoto to return some belongings left by a deceased lieutenant to his family. The lieutenant was a Korean named Kanayama, and Yamaoka has to bring his belongings to his family in Korea and tell them that Kanayama had fought for his homeland and the woman he loved. These movies recognize the sacrifices that Koreans made for Japan during the war and highlight the brotherhood between Japanese and Koreans. They differ markedly from war films produced before the Heisei period in which Koreans were rarely mentioned.

JAPAN AND NORTH KOREA

While relations between Japan and South Korea have improved, Japan's relations with North Korea remain tense. Japanese attitudes towards North Korea continue to be negative, owing to such issues as the abduction of Japanese by North Koreans as well as nuclear research and missile tests conducted by the Pyongyang government. North Korea's economy now appears underdeveloped compared to the economies of South Korea and China.[65] In the 1990s, when North Korea lost subsidized imports from Soviet Union and China and experienced series of floods and droughts, its economy nearly collapsed, leaving the North even further behind South Korea. In 1996, North Korea sought international food aid. In response, both Japan and South Korea made contributions. Nevertheless, the discovery of North Korea's development of nuclear energy in 1993 had previously stirred up tensions between Japan and North Korea. Suspicions of North Korea deepened further when the North's abduction of Japanese citizens was brought to light in 1997.[66] Japanese mistrust of North Korea worsened yet again when North Korean missiles had reportedly traveled over Japan during a test launch.[67]

Most Japanese news reports portray North Korea very negatively.[68] In Matsumoto Hitoshi's *Big Man Japan* (2007), North Korea is depicted as an evil red monster whose appearance resembles North Korean leader Kim Jong-il. The monster represents the Japanese public's general impression that North Korea is a menace to Japan's security. Japan and South Korea share similar official viewpoints on North Korea. This is because both nations share the abduction issue[69] and, as they are both situated near North Korea, North Korea's possession of nuclear weapons poses threats to both countries. Japan also wishes to accommodate South Korea to ensure stability on the Korean peninsula (Ducke, 2002, p. 162).

Although the volume of film production in North Korea is limited with only one to two movies produced each year, Japanese collaborations with North Korea can still be observed. Kim Jong-il is known to be a movie fan, and there are rumors that his favorite Japanese movies include *Godzilla* (1954-2004) and the "*Tora-san*" series (1969-1995). In 1985, he invited the special effects team from Japan's Toho Studio to film a monster movie called *Pulgasari*, which was similar to *Godzilla*. The movie was directed by South Korean director Shin Sang-ok, who was kidnapped to North Korea as part of Kim Jong-il's plan to develop North Korean cinema.[70] Other efforts in promoting North Korean cinema can be seen in the establishment of the Pyongyang Film Festival of Non-Aligned and Other Developing Countries in 1987, and the screening of *The Schoolgirl's Diary* (2006, Jang In-hak) at the Cannes Film Festival in 2007, which witnessed the first time a North Korean film was shown at a major international film festival.

Portrayals of North Korea are not commonly included in Japanese movies. The closest Japanese films come to mentioning North Korea are through depictions of *chongryon* supporters and North Korean schools in Japan, which are shown in *Go* and *Break Through!*. A glimpse of North Korea is displayed in the final scene of *Blood and Bones*, where Shun-pei kidnaps his son and takes him to North Korea. In this film, the two live in a ramshackle home in bleak conditions, revealing Japanese perceptions of North Korea as an impoverished, desolate and depressing place.[71]

CONCLUSION

As discussed above, Japanese attitudes towards Asians have long corresponded to Japan's perceptions of its place in Asia and the world. When Japan rose to power in the early twentieth century, its sense of superiority during the Second World War was reflected in *tairiku eiga* in China and propaganda films in Korea. Although this sense of superiority declined somewhat after Japan's defeat in the war, Japanese still held superficial views of Asians, portraying places such as Hong Kong as impoverished and crime-ridden. Nevertheless, in the early years of the Heisei period, when Japan was faced with various economic and social problems from within and external challenges from China and South Korea, the Japanese realized they no longer dominated Asia. The rise of Asia spurred Japan to reconsider its relations with its neighbors and its position in Asia.

Japanese films made during the Heisei period reveal Japan to have a different perception of Asia than before. Japanese filmmakers no longer depict Asia as inferior or evil; instead, Asia today is often seen as fashionable and dynamic. To Japanese, Asian stars such as Kaneshiro Takeshi, Faye Wong, Michele Reis, Bae Yong-joon and Choi Ji-woo represent "modern

Asia" in their looks and styles. Japanese filmmakers have recently also used Asian elements to criticize Japan. In *Swallowtail* and *Seoul*, the image of the yen is used to signify the fading influence of Japan in Asia and the world.[72] An increasing number of collaborations between Japanese and Asian filmmakers have taken place during the Heisei period, indicating that many Japanese now respect and admire Asian cultures.

Some Japanese films even encourage Japanese to take the initiative in communicating with other Asian people. In movies such as *Perfect Education 3*, *Seoul* and *Break Through!*, Japanese characters attempt to learn a foreign language to communicate with non-Japanese Asians. This new attitude suggests a wish on the part of Japan to befriend its Asian neighbors, signifying its desire to re-enter the Asia that it once aspired to separate from.

Although recent movies imply Japan wishes to amend its relations with other Asian nations, in reality some distrust still exists between Japan and its Asian neighbors. The history textbook issue,[73] Japanese officials' visits to the Yasukuni Shrine,[74] and the comfort women issue[75] are still unresolved problems that strain Japan-Asia relations. In January 2008, rightist Japanese director Mizushima Satoru released his *Nankin no shinjitsu* (The Truth about Nanjing), which claims the Nanjing Massacre is a hoax created by the Chinese Communist government.[76] In the same year, Japanese right-wing politicians denounced the documentary *Yasukuni* (2007, Li Ying) as anti-Japanese because it displays photos of the Nanjing Massacre.[77] These right-wing voices will certainly affect Sino-Japanese relations.[78] To promote the positive relations portrayed in Japanese films of the Heisei period, Japan and Asian countries will clearly have to strive harder to solve their problems through mutual sincerity and understanding.

Acknowledgements

The author gratefully acknowledges the support of the Sumitomo Foundation, who provided a Fiscal 2006 Grant for a Japan-Related Research Project.

Notes

1. "*Datsu-A Ron*," an article written by Fukuzawa Yukichi, was first published in the newspaper *Jiji shimpo* on March 16, 1885. It stated that Japan could only achieve modernization and civilization through modernizing its military.
2. For reasons of clarity and brevity I use the official English titles of Japanese films throughout this chapter. Where an official English title is not available I use the Japanese title and the English translation.
3. Said's *Orientalism* referred to the academic, ideological and historical discourses of the "Orient" used by Europeans during the nineteenth century and early twentieth century. The "Orient" referred to Arabs, Islam and even Egypt as perceived by Europeans. According to Said (1978), Orientalism is a "political doctrine willed over the Orient because the Orient was weaker than the West, which elided the Orient's difference with its weakness" (p. 204).

4   China here refers only to Hong Kong and Taiwan. After the establishment of the People's Republic of China (PRC) in 1949, mainland China isolated itself from the rest of the world (except from other communist nations) and did not participate in the Southeast Asian Motion Pictures Producers Association.
5   *A Night in Hong Kong*, *Hong Kong Star*, and *Honolulu-Tokyo-Hong Kong*, known as the "Hong Kong series," were co-produced by Japan (Toho) and Hong Kong (MP & GI), while *White Rose of Hong Kong* and *A Night in Bangkok* were co-produced by Japan (Toho), Hong Kong (Cathy), and Taiwan (Taiwan Zhipian).
6   The image of You Min in the Hong Kong series was westernized and civilized. Her intelligence was conveyed by her proficiency in English, Japanese and Chinese. The mass media in Japan indicated that she was as popular as American heroines and even the Princess of Japan. As her popularity rose, You also played a guest role in two Toho movies: *A Trip to the West of the President* (1962, Sugie Toshio) and *Three Gentlemen from Tokyo* (1962, Sugie Toshio).
7   This was an area that was not under British rule during the colonial period. It became a haven for criminals and drug addicts, as the Hong Kong government had no right to enter and the Chinese government (Communist or Kuomintang) refused to administer it. The area was associated with mystery and intrigue until it was torn down in 1993.
8   Agnes Chan appeared as a folk singer in Hong Kong, but in Japan she was transformed into a Japanese teen idol who wore mini-skirts and sang pop songs. While Teresa Teng used a Chinese singing tone in Japanese *enka* and had an imperfect Japanese accent, she enjoyed great appeal among Japanese audiences (Komota, Shimada, Yazawa, & Yokozawa, 1980, p. 90). However, Teng had to dress maturely and elegantly to suit her Japanese *enka* songs, which differed from her "girl-next-door" image in the Chinese community (Hirano, 1997, pp. 52-55).
9   Japanese government statistics indicate that Hong Kong, Taiwan and South Korea were the top overseas destinations for Japanese tourists from 1973 (Sorifu, 1976, p. 33).
10 In 1972, China and Japan signed the "Joint Communiqué of the Government of Japan and the Government of the People's Republic of China." US President Richard Nixon's visit to China in 1972 caused Japan to feel uncertain and anxious about China's potential to become a world power. Tanaka Kakuei, who was Japan's Prime Minister between 1972 and 1974, played an important role in enhancing Sino-Japanese relations. He established diplomatic relations with China, visiting China in September 1972. On August 12, 1978, the "Treaty of Peace and Friendship between Japan and the People's Republic of China" further consolidated diplomatic relations between the two nations.
11 After China opened its doors, the number of foreign tourists visiting the nation increased steadily. In 1978, there were 229,600 foreign tourists. In 1980, the number rose to 529,124, and in 1984 it increased to over 1 million (Zhang, 2003, p. 16). In 1984 and 1985, Japanese tourists constituted 34 percent of the total number of foreign tourists visiting China (Sorifu, 1987, p. 63).
12 In 1971, China (the People's Republic of China) was admitted into the United Nations at the same time that Taiwan (Republic of China) was expelled. Japan's establishment of diplomatic relations with China also implied that Japan recognized the People's Republic as the legitimate government of China and Taiwan as part of China.
13 Although Japan severed diplomatic relations with Taiwan, the two were still closely connected through exchange activities in culture, sports, and science (Fan, 1999, p. 27). Japan's baseball player Oh Sadaharu (a.k.a. Wang Chen-chih) is a symbol of amicable relations between Japan and Taiwan. With a Chinese father and a Japanese mother, Oh was born and raised in Japan. Originally, he was a Japanese citizen, but his family adopted Taiwan citizenship after the Second World War and he never changed his nationality since then. He is one

of the greatest baseball players in Japan, holding a world record of hitting 868 home runs. In 1977, he received the first People's Honor Award from the Japanese government. He is not only well respected in Japan, but also in Taiwan. In 2001, Oh was appointed as Taiwan's Ambassador-at-Large responsible for Taiwan-Japan affairs and enhancing Taiwan's participation in international sporting events and exchange activities.
14. It is believed that some right-wing Japanese secretly interfere with Taiwan's political sector and support "Taiwan Independence" because they do not want Taiwan to reunite with China (Fan, 1999, p. 33).
15. In 1992, it was discovered that Tokyo Sagawa Express had contributed large sums of secret funds to Japanese politicians, including the deputy chairman of the Liberal Democratic Party, Kanemaru Shin, who received ¥500 million. It was also noted that Tokyo Sagawa Express had offered funding and guaranteed loans to a *yakuza* group called Inagawa-kai. Since many politicians were found to be receiving secret funds from the company, Japan's political sector was greatly affected by this incident.
16. Between 1989 and 2001, there were 10 prime ministers in office. These constant changes ended when Koizumi Junichiro became Prime Minister between 2001 and 2006.
17. The Sarin Gas Incident was an act of domestic terrorism perpetrated by members of the religious sect Aum Shinrikyo in 1995. The sect released sarin gas in several lines of the Tokyo subway, killing 12 people, injuring 54 and adversely affecting the vision of thousands. Asahara Shoko, the founder of Aum Shinrikyo, was sentenced to death in 2004. Members of the group consist of graduates from Japan's top universities instead of common people. Mostly aged 30 to 40, such individuals felt frustrated for losing their jobs during the recession. As economic conditions worsened, the cult became increasingly hostile towards society.
18. China has been one of the most popular destinations for foreign direct investment (FDI) since the 1990s. Between 1992 and 1997, China received US$196.8 billion in FDI. In 2002, it surpassed the United States and became the top recipient of FDI (Thun, 2006, p. 63). In 2001, China successfully entered into the World Trade Organization (WTO) and won its bid to host the 2008 Olympic Games.
19. In spite of the Asian financial crisis in 1997, South Korea remained one of Asia's few expanding economies, with a growth rate of 10 percent in 1999 (Lee, 2001, p. 102).
20. The music for *The Purity of Asia* was composed by Okuda Tamio and its lyrics were written by Inoue Yosui. All of them are popular artists in Japan.
21. Other pop idols in Japanese movies include Gloria Yip in *Hong Kong Paradise*, Andy Hui in *Swallowtail* (1996, Iwai Shunji), Anita Yuen in *Hong Kong Nightclub* (1998, Watanabe Takayoshi), and Sam Lee in *Ping Pong* (2002, Sori Fumihiko).
22. Kaneshiro Takeshi and Faye Wong introduced themselves to Japanese audiences when the movie *Chungking Express* (1994), directed by the postmodern film icon Wong Kar-wai, was released in Japan in 1995. The theme song, Faye Wong's "Meng zhong ren" (The One in My Dream), a cover version of The Cranberries' "Dreams," was the first Cantonese song that became a hit in Japan. Meanwhile, Nakatani Miki, Michele Reis and Kelly Chen appeared in commercials of Japan's top cosmetic brand Shiseido in 1997, in which they represented modern Asian beauties that could compete with Western supermodels.
23. *Swallowtail* is a fantasy of Asians hustling for yen in Japan, when the yen was the most powerful currency in the world. Foreigners call Japan "Yen Town," and "Yen Towns" are inhabited by hardworking foreigners trying to survive in Japan. Most importantly, they never give up on their dreams. Their attitudes contrast sharply with Japanese who are plagued by huge debts and willing to risk their very lives for money. In *The City of Lost Souls*, Japanese policemen as well as gangsters appear totally powerless when facing the Brazilian hero Mario. His Chinese girlfriend, Kei, also displays her

tenacity by threatening a Russian ship dealer and refusing to yield to Ko, the powerful Chinese mafia.

24 Both Iwai Shunji and Miike Takashi belong to Generation X, who were born in the 1960s. Iwai's *Swallowtail* was a pioneering film that depicted Asians from a perspective that had never been seen in previous Japanese films. Iwai once said that Asians were often portrayed as suffering people in Japanese films, but he wanted to show the vitality Asians possessed that the Japanese lacked (Schilling, 1999, p. 71). Iwai was involved in Y2K Film Partners, a project that encouraged collaboration in filmmaking between Japan and other Asian nations, for which he directed *All about Lily Chou-Chou* (2001). Other Asian directors involved in the project included Hong Kong's Stanley Kwan and Taiwan's Edward Yang, who directed *The Island Tales* (1999) and *Yi Yi* (2000), respectively, for the project. Miike's family come from Kumamoto, but he was born and raised near Osaka, where many Korean immigrants reside. His grandparents had previously lived in China and Korea and his father was born in Seoul. He, therefore, feels that he does not belong to any particular nation or culture (Mes & Sato, 2001, Question 6, para. 3). This feeling of being adrift enables him to empathize with Asian immigrants in Japan as well as Japanese living overseas. His movies tend to show, however, that Japanese encounter more difficulties adapting to foreign settings than foreigners in Japan (Mes, 2003, p. 23). Miike also collaborated with Hong Kong's Fruit Chan and Korea's Park Chan-wook in *Three…Extremes* (2004), for which he directed the segment *Box*.

25 These movies include *Swallowtail*, *Rainy Dog* (1997, Miike Takashi), *The Bird People in China* (1998, Miike Takashi), *The City of Lost Souls*, *The Guys from Paradise* (2000, Miike Takashi), *All about Lily Chou-Chou*, and *Hana and Alice* (2004, Iwai Shunji).

26 Reactions to *Calm Passionate Hearts* differed greatly in Japan and Hong Kong. Owing to the popularity of the original novels in Japan (the story was released as two novels in 1999, one written from a male perspective, the other from a female perspective), the film version was highly anticipated and warmly received by Japanese fans. It was one of the top ten films in 2001, with total box office revenues reaching Y2.7 billion. In contrast, the movie was not well-received in Hong Kong, grossing only around HK$3 million after one month in theaters.

27 In 2002, at the 31st Annual Best Dressed Award in Japan, Kelly Chen received the award in the international star category.

28 In a number of Hong Kong-Japan film co-productions, such as *The Christ of Nanjing* (1995, Tony Au) and *Kitchen* (1997, Yim Ho), Tomita Yasuko starred as a Chinese girl and the male protagonists were played by Chinese actors such as Tony Leung Ka-fai and Jordan Chan, a development unlike *tairiku eiga* in the 1930s and transnational romances in the 1960s in which male protagonists were played by Japanese actors.

29 A sequel from the Japanese film series *Perfect Education* (1999-2004), this movie is famous for its portrayal of illicit relationships between middle-aged men and young females. Part 3 was shot in Hong Kong and directed by a local director, Sam Leong. Since the 1980s, Japanese movies with Hong Kong directors have been a trend in Japanese filmmaking. Examples of this trend include *Sleepless Town* (1998, Lee Chi-ngai), *Little Cheung* (1999, Fruit Chan), and *No Problem* (1999, Alfred Cheung).

30 In *Perfect Education 3*, a Japanese high school girl named Ai (Ito Kana) comes to Hong Kong on a school trip, during which she is kidnapped by a Hong Kong taxi-driver, Bo. Owing to her parents' divorce, Ai feels neglected and unloved. Although she is abused by Bo, Ai eventually falls in love with him, as the two share the same kind of loneliness. In the end, Ai decides to remain in Hong Kong and stay with Bo. The Tokyo episode in *About Love*, directed by Shimoyama Ten, is about the encounter between Yao (Wilson Chen), a Taiwanese student, and Michiko (Ito Misaki), a Japanese painter. The story begins with the two strangers bumping into each other at an inter-

section. Yao notices Michiko in tears, as she has just broken up with her boyfriend. Yao begins to draw sketches of Michiko, leaving some behind for her everyday to cheer her up. Despite their differences in language and culture, they are able to convey their feelings through drawings. In the end Michiko draws a picture of Yao to thank him for his kindness.

31　The exact year of release is unknown, though it was likely 1922 or 1923. Some experts believe it was the first Korean feature film. It was remade in 1935 as the first Korean sound film, directed by Lee Myeong-woo.

32　The story is about an affair between Chun-hyang, the beautiful daughter of a former courtesan, and Mong-ryong, the son of a governor. Despite their class differences, the lovers secretly get married. However, when the governor is transferred to Seoul, Mong-ryong leaves with his family, promising Chun-hyang he will return. While Chun-hyang faithfully waits for her husband, the new governor, who fancies Chun-hyang's beauty, desires her for his mistress, but Chun-hyang insists on remaining loyal to Mong-ryong and rejects the governor's overtures. Her refusal leads to her imprisonment and she is tortured and sentenced to death by the governor. In the end Mong-ryong returns and rescues Chun-hyang from the evil governor.

33　Extensive footage in *Behold this, Mother* with Korean characters was cut from the film as the Japanese government was worried that it might stir up leftist sentiment. *Women Workers in the Brickyard* portrayed the relations between Japanese workers and Korean immigrant workers in city slums. Since it touched upon a sensitive issue, it was unable to pass censorship and was not released until 1946, after the war had ended.

34　Koreans refer to the Sea of Japan as the "East Sea." Both South Korea and North Korea oppose the use of the name "Sea of Japan" and have tried to influence international opinion to their point of view. Nevertheless, at the 9th United Nations Conference on the Standardization of Geographical Names held in August 2007 it was agreed that "Sea of Japan" would remain the name of the area.

35　When South Korea established the "Syng-man Rhee Line" in 1952, Japan's fishing industry was greatly affected because fishing boats that crossed the line were attacked by South Korea. The line was abolished in 1965 when both countries signed the Japan-Korea Fishery Agreement. However, Japan and South Korea still dispute the sovereignty of the Liancourt Rocks, which is surrounded by rich marine resources. The islets are now guarded by South Korea despite Japan's objections.

36　Resident Koreans, also known as *zainichi* Koreans, refers to Koreans who are permanent residents in Japan. Under Japanese colonial rule, Koreans were given Japanese nationality. When the war ended, their status became unclear. In 1947, Japan's Alien Registration Law stated that Koreans should be regarded as aliens and Koreans in Japan were to register under the nationality of *Joseon* (the old name for Korea before its separation). In 1952, the San Francisco Peace Treaty signified Korean residents' official loss of Japanese nationality. For those Koreans who stayed in Japan, their nationality status remained an unsolved problem since the nationality of *Joseon* was not recognized anymore due to the partition of Korea. In 1965, when Japan established diplomatic relations with South Korea, Koreans who applied for South Korean nationality were able to apply for permanent residency in Japan.

37　As arranged by the United Nations, Korea was divided into North and South at the 38th Parallel after the end of the Second World War in 1945, with the United States administering the southern half and the Soviet Union administering the northern half. As a result, two provisional governments were formed on each side, with Rhee Syng-man as the first president of Republic of Korea (South Korea) and Kim Il-sung as the first prime minister of the Democratic People's Republic of Korea (North Korea). Though the separation was meant to be temporary, the two governments each claimed itself as the legitimate government of Korea. This eventually led to the outbreak of the Korean War (1950-1953), when North Korean troops crossed the 38th Parallel to invade the South. The war escalated following the intervention of the US and China. After three years of war, an armistice was finally signed in 1953 to end hostilities. A three-mile buffer zone called the Demilitarized Zone (DMZ) was formed between the two states. Although both sides had signed the June 15 North-South Joint Declaration in 2000 to promote the peaceful reunification of Korea, no peace treaty concerning the Korean War was signed, so both sides are still officially at war.

38 Japanese cultural products were banned in South Korea from 1945, as South Korea wanted to eliminate the Japanese cultural influence imposed during the colonial era (Ishii, 2001, pp. 80-81). The ban was partially lifted when Japan's Prime Minister Obuchi Keizo and South Korean President Kim Dae-jung signed the "Japan-South Korea Joint Declaration of 1998." Restrictions were lifted in different stages. In the first stage, Japanese cultural products allowed included original Japanese comic books and certain movies. Later, the ban was further lifted, allowing imports of Japanese CDs, game software, movies restricted to viewers of 18 years old or above, and cable and satellite television programs.

39 When Korea was annexed by Japan, 80 percent of Koreans were farmers. When Japan reformed land ownership rights and advocated a plan to increase rice production for its own benefit, many Korean farmers lost their lands and were driven into poverty. They subsequently migrated to Japan to work as laborers. Pro-Japanese Koreans also played a role in exploiting Korean farmers (Chapman, 2008, p. 17).

40 In 1945, after the Second World War, Japan was occupied by Allied troops. During the Allied occupation, Korea was freed from Japanese colonial rule, but Korea officially became an independent state when the San Francisco Peace Treaty came into effect in 1952. Since Korea was no longer administered by Japan, Koreans were no longer entitled to Japanese nationality.

41 Those who did not apply remained stateless until 1981, when Japan revised its Immigration Control Law giving those Koreans who began residing in Japan before the Second World War the right to obtain permanent residency. In 1991, the right of permanent residency was further extended to include third generation resident Koreans.

42 The KCIA (Korea Intelligence Central Agency) was founded in 1961. It was fully utilized by the South Korean government under the leadership of Park Chung-hee (1961-1979) to suppress anti-government and pro-North Korean movements. The KCIA also monitored overseas anti-government activities. They had unlimited powers to arrest and detain any suspected dissidents, and could use extreme measures to suppress any criticisms against the South Korean government. The agency was renamed the Agency for National Security Planning in 1981. Due to public criticisms, much of the agency's power and duties have been restricted since 1999.

43 Park Chung-hee was a former military general. South Korea was in a state of political chaos under Rhee Syng-man due to corruption. In 1960, Rhee was forced to resign as a result of the April 19 Movement, which was an uprising led by students. However, the new government was unable to resolve the political crisis. Park took the opportunity to instigate a military coup in 1961 and seized power. He was elected as the President in 1963 and ruled South Korea until his assassination in 1979. Although he has been credited with implementing economic reforms that led to South Korea's rapid economic development, he has also been condemned for his authoritarian rule and anti-democratic tendencies.

44 From 1962 until the end of the 1970s, South Korea's annual GDP growth rate averaged around 9 percent. In the 1980s, the average growth rate was 8.3 percent (Matsumoto & Hattori, 2001, p. 3).

45 The June 29 Declaration in 1987 enabled South Koreans to elect their presidents, marking the beginning of democracy in the nation. Roh Tae-woo, who announced

the declaration, became the first freely elected president of South Korea in 1988.
46 In *For Kayako's Sake*, Kayako is a Japanese girl adopted by Matsumoto, a resident Korean man, and his Japanese wife Toshi. Kayako falls in love with San-jun, a resident Korean, and the young lovers run away from home and start their "dream life" together in Tokyo. However, the young couple soon realizes that reality is different from their dreams. Toshi, who regretted marrying Matsumoto because of their poverty-stricken life together, does not want Kayako to follow in her footsteps and marry a Korean man. In the end, the lovers are separated and Kayako marries a Japanese man.
47 During the late 1990s and the early 2000s, Korean high-tech industries became very competitive in the global market as they had adopted Japanese modes of operation and manufactured products at relatively low prices and acceptable quality levels. In 1994, the three Korean corporations Samsung, LG and Hyundai were among the global top ten of electronic memory suppliers (Pecht, Bernstein, Searls, & Peckerar, 1997, p. 11).
48 "386 generation" refers to people who were 30 years old in the 1990s, went to college in the 1980s and were born in the 1960s. They became an influential force in the 1990s in South Korea. Kang Je-gyu, who directed *Shiri* (1999), and Park Chan-wook, who directed *JSA: Joint Security Area* (2000), belong to the "386 generation."
49 The 2002 World Cup aroused Japanese interest in Korean culture. It was also an opportunity for people around the world to feel the energy and passion of Koreans through the South Korean soccer team's memorable performance (reaching the semi-finals) and their enthusiastic supporters known as the "Red Devils." They helped to promote a positive image of Koreans. Ahn Jung-hwan became a star after scoring the crucial goal that led to South Korea's victory over Italy and advancement into the quarter-finals. Later that year, he joined the J. League (Japan Professional Football League). Rikidozan, a professional wrestler in Japan, another legendary athlete, was revealed to be a resident Korean after his death in 1963. In 2004, a movie based on his life was made called *Rikidozan: A Hero Extraordinary* (Song Hae-sung). It was a Japan-South Korea film co-production, starring Sol Kyung-gu and Nakatani Miki.
50 *Seoul* symbolizes reconciliation between Japanese and Koreans, in that a Japanese police officer named Hayase (Nagase Tomoya) and a Korean police officer named Kim (Choi Min-su) overcome their cultural differences and successfully solve a robbery case together. During Hayase's 72-hour extended stay in Seoul, he learns to respect Korean courtesy and even tries to speak Korean to Kim. Hayase shows his eagerness to communicate with Koreans, reflecting the good intentions of Japanese to take the initiative in resolving differences with Koreans.
51 Other recent collaborations include the television drama *Rondo* (2006), produced by Japan's TBS and starring Korean actress Choi Ji-woo and Japanese actor Takenouchi Yutaka, and the movie *Virgin Snow* (2007, Han Sang-hee), starring Lee Jun-ki and Miyazaki Aoi.
52 One example is Iwai Shunji's *Love Letter*, which became a massive hit in South Korea when it was released in 1999, with some 1.2 million people seeing the movie (Park & Tsuchiya, 2002, p. 37).
53 In 1999, President Kim Dae-jung established the Basic Law for the Promotion of the Cultural Industry allocating US$148.5 million to promote exports of Korean popular culture (Sung, 2008, para. 15).
54 Korean pop singers are promoted in Japan through joint ventures involving Korean and Japanese entertainment companies. BoA, who is the most successful Korean pop artist in Japan, is managed by SM Entertainment (BoA's Korean agency) and Avex Trax (BoA's Japan record label). Se7en likewise is managed by Korea's YG Entertainment and Japan's Nextstar Records. K's case is different from the other two because he was not famous in South Korea before making inroads into the Japanese market.

His hit songs were mainly theme songs for Japanese television dramas such as *Only Human* for the drama *1 Liter of Tears*.
55 The popular reception of the television drama *Winter Sonata* gave rise to a "Korean Wave" in Japan. This led to the stardom of a number of Korean stars of which Bae Yong-joon is the most popular. In April 2004, when Bae visited Japan for the first time, 5,000 Japanese fans were waiting for him at Tokyo Haneda Airport. When he visited Japan again in November the same year, 3,500 fans gathered at Tokyo Narita Airport. Because of the stir he caused, when he visited Japan in 2005 he kept his arrival date secret.
56 An increasing number of Japanese scholars and critics study Korean and Asian films and publish essays and books on these topics. Examples include Monma Takashi's *Ajia eiga ni miru nihon* 1&2 [Japan Portrayed in Asian Films, vols. 1 and 2] (1995, 1996), Sato Tadao's *Kankoku eiga no seishin* [The Spirit of Korean Cinema] (2000), and Yomota Inuhiko's *Ajia eiga no taishuteki sozoryoku* [Mass Imagination of Asian Films] (2003).
57 Sai Yoichi (1949-) was born in Nagano, Japan. After graduating from high school in 1968, he started working in the film industry as a lighting assistant. Later he began working as an assistant director for films such as *In the Realm of Senses* (1976, Oshima Nagisa). In 1981, he began directing television movies, two years later directing his first motion picture, *Jukkai no mosquito* (Mosquito from the Tenth Floor). In 1993, he directed *All under the Moon* which won major awards at various film awards in Japan, including best picture and best director at the Japan Academy Awards. His other works include *Quill* (2004) and *Blood and Bones*. In 2007, he directed his first Korean movie, *Soo*. He is also an actor and played the role of Commander Kondo Isami in Oshima Nagisa's *Taboo* (1999).
58 *Through the Night* is also a remake of Yang's work.
59 *Break Through!* is about Kosuke, a Japanese teenage boy who falls in love with Kyun-ja, a resident Korean girl. In order to impress Kyun-ja, Kosuke studies Korean and learns to play the North Korean song "Imjin River" on guitar, hoping to play the song to her. *Summer of Chirusoku* is a love story between a Japanese teenage girl, Ikuko (Mizutani Yuri), and a Korean teenage boy, An (Jun-bei). The two first meet at a Japan-Korea sports exchange event held in Pusan. Though Ikuko returns to Japan, the two write letters and promise they will meet a year later at the next sports exchange to be held at Shimonoseki.
60 He was the director of *Hula Girls* (2006), which won five awards at the 2007 Japan Academy Awards, including Best Picture, Best Director, Best Screenplay, Best Supporting Actress and Most Popular Film. It also won Best Picture in other major Japanese film awards.
61 He was the producer of *All under the Moon, Break Through!* and *Pacchigi! Love and Peace* (2007, Izutsu Kazuyuki).
62 She has been a voice talent for many leading roles in Japanese animations such as *Fullmetal Alchemist* (2003), *Bleach* (2004) and *Nana* (2006), for which she won the best actress in the Seiyu (voice acting talent) Award in 2007.
63 Ishihara Shintaro has been the Governor of Tokyo since 1999. In 1989, he published a book called *"No" to ieru nippon* [The Japan that Can Say "No"], which encouraged Japan to stand up against the United States. He is also famous for his rightist thinking and has made several controversial remarks about Chinese and Koreans.
64 Kamikaze refers to suicide attacks by Japanese military pilots during the Second World War. It was a tactic used by the Japanese to attack Allied troops after the Japanese military had suffered several defeats.
65 After the Korean War, North Korea adopted a policy known as *Juche* (Self-reliance) and its economy industrialized in the 1960s and 1970s. However, its economy began

to decline in the 1980s due to the failure of the *Juche* policy and the North's reluctance to open its economy (Ducke, 2002, p. 150).
66 Between 1977 and 1983, a number of Japanese were abducted by North Korea. According to the Japanese government, the official number of abductees was 16, but it is believed that there were 70 to 80 Japanese kidnapped and taken to North Korea ("North Korean Defector," 2002). These Japanese abductees were sent to a North Korean spy school to teach Japanese language and culture. In 2002, the North Korean government admitted kidnapping 13 Japanese and agreed to return 5 of the captives. Japan continued to press for the return of all abductees, but North Korea claimed that aside from the captives who were sent back to Japan, the rest had all died.
67 North Korea has conducted a number of missile tests in the past decade. In 1998 and 2003, it was reported that North Korean missiles had flown over Japan and landed in the Pacific Ocean.
68 This tendency escalated after US President George W. Bush branded North Korea, Iraq and Iran an "Axis of Evil" in 2002.
69 South Korea also stated that 486 South Koreans had been abducted by North Korea.
70 Initially, the North Korean government denied the abduction, claiming that it was Shin Sang-ok's own will to go to North Korea. However, when Shin and his wife (who was also abducted) managed to escape during a business trip in Vienna in 1987, they revealed that they had been abducted.
71 Instead of demonizing North Korea, movies directed by South Korean directors of the 386 generation, such as *Shiri* and *JSA: Joint Security Area*, show a different attitude in that they depict the "human" side of North Korean people and convey a message of brotherhood and mutual victimization by other nations.
72 In the last scene of *Swallowtail*, the "Yen Towns" burn all the yen available; in *Seoul*, on the other hand, when the robbery case is solved the robbery vehicle explodes and the stolen yen are blown away by the wind.
73 The Japanese history textbook issue has been a diplomatic problem between Japan and other Asian countries. In 1982, China and South Korea objected that the textbooks glorified Japanese aggression during the Second World War. In 2000, the publication of the *New History Textbook* prompted another outcry from China and Korea, as the new textbook downplayed Japan's wartime atrocities such as the Nanjing Massacre and sexual exploitation of comfort women.
74 The Yasukuni Shrine is a Shinto shrine dedicated to those who fought for Imperial Japan during the Second World War, including Class A war criminals. Therefore, to countries who suffered under Japanese aggression during the war, such as China and Korea, the shrine is a symbol of Japan's imperial aggression. Chinese and Koreans have constantly protested against Japanese officials paying visits to the shrine. Former Prime Minister Koizumi Junichiro's visits to the shrine greatly strained relations between Japan and China and South Korea.
75 It is estimated that there were 100,000 to 200,000 women of different nationalities who were forced to become prostitutes or sex slaves for the Japanese military during the Second World War. Since the early 1990s, various lawsuits have been filed against the Japanese government by former "comfort women," demanding a formal apology and compensation. Although the Japanese government has apologized on many occasions, no compensation was given to the comfort women. The latest controversy was aroused by former Prime Minister Abe Shinzo in 2007, when he claimed that the Japanese military had not forced women to become "comfort women."
76 The movie was planned as a three-part series. The first part premiered on January 25, 2008 at Yomiuri Hall in Tokyo. It is about Class A criminals, depicting the last day of the seven people who were condemned to death at the Tokyo Trial in 1948. The movie is scheduled for showings in different parts of Japan; however, it will mainly be

shown in community centers and city halls and not be released in movie theaters.
77 *Yasukuni* is a documentary directed by Chinese director Li Ying. The documentary displays different voices (both supporters' and objectors' opinions) toward the Yasukuni Shrine. Japanese Diet lawmakers regarded the documentary as anti-Japanese after previewing the film in March 2008. The documentary was originally scheduled to screen in five theaters in Tokyo and Osaka in April 2008. However, the theaters were pressured by right-wing groups into cancelling the showings.
78 The poison dumpling crisis in early 2008 also harmed relations between Japan and China. When it was discovered that 10 Japanese suffered from food poisoning after eating frozen dumplings made in China, the safety of food imports from China was questioned. Although investigations by both authorities were carried out, this crisis greatly affected people's confidence in Chinese food products.

References

Chapman, D. (2008). *Zainichi Korean identity and ethnicity*. London and New York: Routledge.
Fan, Y. J. (1999). Shixi yingxiang riben duihua zhengce de "Taiwan qingjie" [Analyzing the "Taiwan complex" that affects Japan's policy towards China]. *Japanese Studies*, 2, 24-35.
Hirano, K. (1997). *Teresa Ten ga mita yume* [The dreams of Teresa Teng]. (Z. W. Zhang & Q. Z. Gao, Trans.). Taipei: Shangdeng.
Ishihara, S. (1989). *"No" to ieru nippon* [The Japan that can say "no"]. Tokyo: Kobunsha.
Ishii, K. (2001). *Higashi Ajia no nihon taishu bunka* [Japanese popular culture in East Asia]. Tokyo: Sososha.
Iwabuchi, K. (2000). Political correctness, postcoloniality, and self-representation of "Koreanness" in Japan. In S. Ryang (Ed.), *Koreans in Japan: Critical voices from the margin* (pp. 55-73). London and New York: Routledge.
Iwabuchi, K. (2000). *Recentering globalization – Popular culture and Japanese transnationalism*. Durham: Duke University Press.
Kim, K. H. (2002). Korean cinema and Im Kwon-Taek: An overview. In D. James & K. H. Kim (Eds.), *Im Kwon-Taek: The making of a Korean national cinema* (pp. 19-46). Detroit: Wayne State University Press.
Komota, N., Shimada, Y., Yazawa, T., & Yokozawa, C. (Eds.). (1980). *Nihon ryukoka shi (sengo hen)* [The history of Japanese pop (The postwar series)]. Tokyo: Shakai Shisosha.
Lee, J. (2001). Korea financial crisis: The crisis of a development model? In T. S. Yu & D. Xu (Eds.), *From crisis to recovery: East Asia rising again?* (pp. 101-140). Singapore: World Scientific Publishing Co. Pte. Ltd..
Matsumoto, K., & Hattori, T. (Eds.). (2001). *Kankoku keizai no kaibo* [Analysis of Korean economy]. Tokyo: Bunshindo.
McCormack, G. (1996). *The emptiness of Japanese affluence*. New York: M. E. Sharpe, Inc.
Mes, T. (2003). *Agitator: The cinema of Takashi Miike*. United Kingdom: FAB Press.
Mes, T. & Sato, K. (2001, January 5). Interview with Takashi Miike. *Midnight eye: The latest and best in Japanese cinema*. Retrieved January 31, 2008, from: http://www.midnighteye.com/interviews/takashi_miike.shtml
Min, E., Joo, J., & Kwak, H. J. (2003). *Korean film: History, resistance, and democratic imagination*. Westport, Connecticut: Praeger Publisher.
Monma, T. (1995, 1996) *Ajia eiga ni miru nihon* 1&2 [Japan portrayed in Asian films, vols. 1 and 2]. Tokyo: Shakai Hyoronsha.
Monma, T. (1994). Nihon eiga no naka no zainichi zo [The image of Zainichi Koreans in Japanese films]. In B. Lee (Ed.), *"Tsuki wa dotchi ni deteiru" wo meguru 2, 3 no hanashi* [The second and third discussion on the movie *All under the Moor*] (pp. 213-230). Tokyo: Shakai Hyoronsha.

N. Korean defector says 70-80 Japanese abducted by North. (2002, November 25). *Asian political news* (Kyodo).

Okada, A. (2003, April). Representation of popular Asian images in women's magazines: Triple aspects of "Orientalism" in Japan (S. W. Chiou, Trans.). *Envisage: A journal book of Chinese media studies, 2,* 124-139.

Park, S. A., & Tsuchiya, R. (Eds.). (2002). *Nihon taishu bunka to nikkan kankei* [Japanese popular culture and Japan-Korea relations]. Tokyo: Sangensha.

Pecht, M., Bernstein, J. B., Searls, D., & Peckerar, M. (1997). *The Korean electronics industry.* Boca Raton: CRC Press LLC.

Ryang, S. (2000). Introduction: Resident Koreans in Japan. In S. Ryang (Ed.), *Koreans in Japan: Critical voices from the margin* (pp. 1-12). London and New York: Routledge.

Said, E. W. (1978). *Orientalism.* New York: Vintage Books.

Sato, T. (2000). *Kankoku eiga no seishin* [The spirit of Korean cinema]. Tokyo: Iwanami Shoten.

Schilling, M. (1999). *Contemporary Japanese film.* Trumbull: Weatherhill.

Sorifu (Cabinet Office). (1976) *Kanko hakusho* [White papers for tourism] (Showa 51). Tokyo: Ookurasho Insatsukyoku.

Sorifu (Cabinet Office). (1987) *Kanko hakusho* [White papers for tourism] (Showa 62). Tokyo: Ookurasho Insatsukyoku.

Sung, S. Y. (2008, February 4). *The high tide of the Korean Wave III: Why do Asian fans prefer Korean pop culture?* Retrieved February 20, 2008 from http://www.asiamedia.ucla.edu/article.asp?parentid=86640

Thun, E. (2006). *Changing lanes in China: Foreign direct investment, local governments and auto sector development.* New York: Cambridge University Press.

Tipton, E. K. (2002). *Modern Japan: A social and political history.* London: Routledge.

Wade, J. (1983). The cinema in Korea: A robust invalid. In The Korean National Commission for UNESCO (Ed.), *Korean dance, theatre and cinema* (pp. 175-194). Seoul/Oregon: Si-sa-yong-o-sa Publishers/Pace International Research.

Wang, Z. (2004). *Houxiandai zhuyi cidian* [The lexicon of postmodernism]. Beijing: Central Compilation and Translation Press.

Yomota, I. (2003) *Ajia eiga no taishuteki sozoryoku* [Mass imagination of Asian films]. Tokyo: Seidosha.

Zhang, G.R. (2003). China's tourism since 1978: Policies, experiences and lessons learned. In A. A. Lew, L. Yu & Z. Guanqrui (Eds.), *Tourism in China* (pp. 13-34). New York: Haworth Hospitality Press.

• CHAPTER SEVEN •

Developing Extremists: *Madrasah* Education in Pakistan

Riaz Ahmed Shaikh
Institute of Business and Technology

The post 9/11 War against Terror led by the United States has drawn attention to the educational setting of political Islam in Pakistan, with critics suggesting that *madrasah* schools[1] are fostering militant attitudes among their students (International Crisis Group [ICG], 2004). Over the last two and a half decades, these Islamic schools have expanded throughout the country, increasing more than tenfold, from 1,000 to around 13,000 schools (Blanchard, 2008, p. 5). Some allege that ties exist between *madrasahs* and terrorist organizations such as Al-Qaeda. Thus, since the terrorist attacks on the Twin Towers and Pentagon in 2001, the Islamic mode of education at *madrasah*s has been of increasing interest to those involved in formulating US foreign policy towards the Middle East, Central Asia and South East Asia (Blanchard, 2008, p. 1).

A common problem in discussions on *madrasahs*, however, is an absence of historical context. It is assumed that *madrasahs* have always been widespread and radical in orientation and that the institution of the *madrasah* itself is a cause of terrorism. This chapter, examining the history of *madrasah* education and its changing role in Pakistani society, presents a different picture. As will be shown, many factors, both inside and outside Pakistan, have encouraged the growth and radicalization of the *madrasah* system. Attempts by *ulema* (Muslim clerics and scholars) to counter their declining authority under British colonial rule and assert their influence following the creation of Pakistan were important developments. More crucial yet were the Islamization policies of Zia-ul-Haq and official education policies during the Soviet-Afghan War (1979-1989), when the state and its Western and regional supporters promoted *jihadist* ideas in *madrasah* schools as a means to supply recruits among Afghan refugees and others for the anti-Soviet war effort.

As the growth and impact of *madrasahs* have been tremendous, they are now portrayed as breeding grounds for militancy. From being established centers of learning during the Middle Ages, *madrasahs* have changed into something that is seen as threatening regional and even global stability. How this transformation has come about is the central question this chapter aims to answer in detail.

TRADITIONAL EDUCATION IN MUSLIM SOCIETY

Madrasahs did not exist when Islam was first establishing itself as a religion in the seventh century AD. Most *madrasahs* developed during the late Umayyad (661-750 AD) and early Abbasid periods (750-1258 AD) as Sunni places of learning, as the Sunnis comprised the majority of Muslims. The Islamic social system was built upon the collected works of Mohammed, the original founder of Islam, with the initial stages of Islam's growth associated with the collection, organization and dissemination of special reports known as *hadiths*. These *hadiths* along with the Qur'an emerged during the years 720 to 770 AD as authoritative texts for Islamic religious practices, playing a crucial role in the development of Sharia (Islam-derived laws) and Sunnah (basic principles of Islam) (Black, 2006, p. 32).

The diffusion of religious texts and beliefs was the work of *ulema* who moved from city to city conveying the knowledge of Sunnah. The work of these individuals gave rise to a new type of religious leadership, a meritocracy based upon expertise in memorizing and expounding *hadiths* at first circulated by word of mouth and then written down, collected and interpreted by the *ulema* (Black, 2006, p. 33).

The *ulema*, who developed as a class from the eighth to the tenth century AD, occupied important religious positions in Islamic society on the basis of their knowledge of traditions and commandments, acquiring a special type of authority as the acknowledged moral and religious leaders of the majority of Muslims. As the *ulema* began its rise as a class, the University of Al-Karaouine, established by Fatimah bint Muhammad al-Fihri in 859 in Fez, Morocco, and now considered the world's oldest Islamic university, began to teach religious disciplines in addition to natural sciences (T. Hussain, 2007, para. 2).

However, the first true *madrasah* in the Islamic world, the Nizamiyyah *madrasah*, was founded in Baghdad in 1067 by the Seljuk vizier named Nizam ul-Mulk. This *madrasah*, like others founded by him, was dedicated to the study of Islamic law. The Nizamiyyah *madrasah* attracted many accomplished thinkers, including the Persian scholar Abu Hamid al-Ghazali (a.k.a. al-Ghazali) (d. 1111 AD) (Lumbard, 2005, p. 55), who established both *madrasahs* and *khanqahs* (Sufi religious schools). AbuSad al Kharkushi (d. 1013 or 1016 AD) and Abu Ali al-Daqqaq (d. 1015 AD), a well-known Sufi master, also founded a *madrasah* in the city of Nasa. Ali al-Daqqaq and his son-in-law Abul Qasim al-Qushayri (d. 1072 AD) taught at the Qushayriyya *madrasah* (Bulliet, 1972, p. 151). Abu Ali al-Farmadi (d. 1084 AD), known as the Shaykh of Shaykhs (Sufi teacher of Sufi teachers) in Nisharpur, is said to have professed such admiration for his Shaykh that he was inspired to move from his *madrasa* to a *khanqa* (Shirazi, 1958, p. 158). Al-Farmadi was a teacher of both Abu Hamid al-Ghazali and his brother Ahmed al-Ghazali, who both traveled freely between *madrasahs* and *khanqahs* and were revered for having reached the highest levels in both schools. Abu Hamid, the more famous and influential of the two, was appointed Chairman of Shafi Law at the Nizamiyya *madrasah*. After leaving his teaching position for over ten years, he returned to his hometown of Khurassan, where he spent his last days teaching at both a *khanqah* and *madrasah* (Hodgson, 1990, p. 213).

The numerous *madrasahs* established by Nizam ul-Mulk during the Seljuk Dynasty (1055-1194 AD), in addition to providing Islamic knowledge, imparted secular education in the fields of science, philosophy, public administration and government. Although most *madrasahs* remained centers of Islamic learning, several of them also produced scholars and philosophers who contributed greatly to secular knowledge (Oliver, 1994, p. 73). The syllabus employed at the Nizamiyyah *madrasah*, which served as a model for *madrasahs* elsewhere, represented a blend of *naqli 'ulum* (revealed sciences), including the Qur'an, the *hadith*, and *fiqh* (Islamic jurisprudence), and *tafsir* (Qur'anic commentary), on the one hand, and the *aqli ulum* (rational sciences), including the Arabic language, grammar, logic, rhetoric, philosophy, astronomy, medicine, physics and mathematics, on the other (S. H. Nasr, 2001, p. 195).

Muslim rule in Spain (756-1492 AD) is considered a golden era in Islamic history, with the same period also witnessing a blossoming of *madrasahs* in the region. Muslims ruled Spain for 800 years and showed great progress in science, philosophy and other natural sciences. Muslim Spain produced one of the greatest Aristotelian philosophers of all times and one of the most original political minds in Islam, Averroes (Ibn Rushd) (Butterworth, 1975). It was Islamic scholars from Andalusia in Spain who were responsible for preserving and furthering knowledge of Greek science and mathematics, which were on the verge of being lost during the Dark Ages in Europe (Harvey, 1990, p. 107).

Under Mameluke rule in Egypt (1250-1517 AD), *madrasahs* were established through religious endowments from *waqf*.[2] *Madrasahs* were a powerful symbol of status and an effective means of transmitting wealth to descendants who, though they retained their parents' status, were unable to inherit wealth directly. In fact, through *waqf* wealth a high status was guaranteed for contiguous generations of Mameluke rulers within the *madrasah* system, (Haeri, 2006, p. 134).

In medieval times, the *madrasahs* served as the only available centers of formal education for Muslims. Their graduates went on to assume a variety of occupations such as administrators, military officers, teachers, and prayer leaders in mosques (Holt, 1977, p. 45).

THE *MADRASAH* SYSTEM ON THE SUB-CONTINENT

Muslims entered South Asia in 712 AD, but this initial entry did not affect the heart of India, i.e. Central and Northern India. Muslim civilization began influencing Hindu India when Muslims occupied northern India in the eleventh century, after Sultan Muhammad Ghori conquered Rajasthan in 1190 (Qureshi, 1942, p. 286). The earliest available evidence of *madrasahs* here dates back to this period, in the wake of Muhammad Ghori's conquest of Amjar in 1191, shortly after which a *madrasah* was established in the town. With the expansion of Turkish rule in other parts of India, Muslim rulers established *madrasahs* in their own domains, with the provision of extensive land grants (*jagirs, madad-i-maash*) for their expenses and scholarships for their students (Rizvi, 1965, p. 207). Muslim nobles and scholars followed this tradition set by the state by establishing large educational centers in their areas. New centers of Islamic knowledge emerged in various parts of India, and *madrasahs* of Gujarat, Ucch, Multan, Delhi, Pandua and Gaur, Bidar, Gulbarga and Aurangabad were among the most renowned in the entire Muslim world in their day (Kulke & Dietmar, 1998, p. 361). Generally, despite the Qur'anic insistence on the equality of all believers and the Prophet's special plea to this effect during his last Hajj Sermon, students and faculty of these *madrasahs* normally belonged to a privileged Islamic class called *ashraf* (nobility) (R. Ahmed, 1981, p. 124). This class was comprised of migrants from Central Asia, Iran and Arabia, and their descendants. They usually accompanied the conquerors, and after their arrival they were granted lands and given revenue collection rights. Several scholars, including thirteenth century court historian Ziauddin Barani, supported this class stratification in education and opined that higher education should remain a closely guarded preserve of the *ashraf*. It was their opinion that Muslims of indigenous origin (*ajlaf*) should not be exposed to higher education but remain content with just a basic knowledge of the Islamic faith and its rituals (Faruqi, 1992, p. 81).

The syllabus of these Indian *madrasahs* went through a slow and gradual transformation over the centuries. These alternations and changes were linked to the needs and requirements of the state (Nadwi, 1971, p. 173). In the initial years, *madrasahs* essentially focused on *fiqh*. During the

Mughal period, however, the Mughal Emperor Akbar instituted changes in *madrasahs* by adding new subjects to the curriculum including philosophy and logic and other "rational disciplines" (Rizvi, 1975, p. 261). These educational reforms reduced the portion of pure religious education in the institutes. It was Shah Waliullah of Delhi who would again emphasize the teachings of pure religious education, especially through *hadiths* (M. S. Khan, 1999, p. 103), with his legacy today still apparent at most contemporary South Asian Muslim schools of *ulema* in India and Pakistan (Aziz, 1963, p. 121). After receiving an education in Arabia, he returned and joined his father's *madrasah*, Madrasah-i-Rahimiya in Delhi, where he proposed some significant alterations to the liberal curriculum introduced during the Akbar period and returned to the teaching of the canonical collections of *hadith*. He insisted that religion form the core of the *madrasah* syllabus; he was not in favor of a curriculum based on the rational sciences, particularly Greek philosophy and logic (Salim, 1988, p. 30).

His efforts toward revising the *madrasah* syllabus achieved little success, as the center for Islamic education shifted from Delhi to Lucknow (Siddiqui, 1998, pp. 268-293). In the mid-eighteenth century, Mulla Nizamuddin, scion of a family of learned Mughal *ulema*, established himself at the Firangi Mahal religious school in Lucknow. Here he set about preparing a reformed *madrasah* syllabus named after him as the Dars-i-Nizami. The syllabus of this new school of learning included new books on *hadith* and Qur'anic commentary but the main focus remained on the rational sciences. It was planned that graduates of the *madrasahs* were to be trained not only for strictly religious posts but also as general administrators and functionaries in the state bureaucracies (Robinson, 2001, p. 162).

The existence and identity of *madrasahs* were both threatened with the establishment of British rule. In the 1830s, the East India Company replaced Persian with English as the language of official correspondence in the territories under its control. State-employed *qazis* (individuals who tried both civil and criminal cases) were replaced by judges trained in British law to provide justice to Indians belonging to different religions (Aziz, 1966, p. 149). As Muslims were in the minority, the new system of education introduced by the British government had no place for Islam, though in some cases *madrasahs* were supported by the East India Company. Increasingly bereft of royal patronage and finding their avenues of employment greatly restricted, graduates of the *madrasah* system and the *ulema* as a class now had to contend with a major challenge to their survival (Ali, 2003, p. 384).

The participation of Indian *ulemas* in the Indian Mutiny of 1857, therefore, was an attempt to safeguard growing threats to their existing privileges. Once the revolt failed, several *ulemas* established a chain of *madrasahs* from the mid-1860s to the 1920s (Keddie, 1972, p. 117). Islamic social and political leaders in India identified education as the key to creating a new Muslim, but it was felt that under alien rule Islam was threatened and it was only by preserving and promoting Islamic knowledge that the younger generation of Muslims could be saved from sliding into apostasy and prevented from falling prey to the blandishments of the Christian missionaries. Because they saw Islam as under attack by the Christian British, the *ulema* adopted a deeply hostile attitude towards Western knowledge. They launched an "educational *jihad*" to preserve traditional Islamic learning as a physical *jihad* had failed and they worked to train a class of *ulema* who would exact revenge on the British for having overthrown the Mughals (G. Khan, 1998, p. 419).

Thus, the *madrasahs* set up by these *ulemas* in reaction to British policies closed their doors to modern knowledge, which was seen as "un-Islamic." This was the beginning of the great divide between what was now seen as "religious" (*dini*) knowledge, on the one hand, and modern "wordly" (*dunyawi*) learning, on the other hand. Because of the way in which this hierarchy of knowledge was constructed, the curriculum of the *madrasahs* came to be seen as almost entirely infallible, although in the past it had been subject to considerable change over time (Mayer, 1981, pp. 481-502).

Most of the well-known *madrasahs* were situated in United Province (UP). Before India's partition in 1947, a large percentage of the Muslim elite thus resided in UP. They took the lead in establishing these institutions as a part of their social and religious obligations to the community and simultaneously to create and enlarge their social and political base (May, 1970, p. 62).

THE CREATION OF PAKISTAN

The state of Pakistan was born on August 14, 1947 and India gained its independence the very next day. Pakistan was carved out of five provinces of British India, including several princely states (Cohen, 2005, p. 39). For those who were behind the independence movement of Pakistan, Islam would be the common platform and guiding force in their future. The Pakistan Movement highlighted the idea of Muslims as victims, subjected to discrimination by a Hindu majority, while the Muslim League promised a state that based on Islam, though their ideas were couched in vague and general terms with no specific blueprint for the future.

In many ways, Pakistan resembled Israel upon its creation (Kumaraswamy, 1997). Like Israel, Pakistan was faced with an assimilation problem, in this case a million migrants from India. In both countries, relations between secular and orthodox religious groups were strained. Islamist groups played an important role in helping Pakistan recover from the devastation of partition, and this gave them additional organizational skills, helping them establish a link to many new Pakistanis, especially migrants from India. The same pattern was to be repeated forty years later, when Islamic groups worked with millions of Afghan refugees who poured into Pakistan from 1980 onward (Cohen, 2005, p. 115).

The *Madrasah* System in Pakistan

At its time of independence, Pakistan had inherited various institutions from British colonial rule, the education system being one important legacy. British rulers, soon after their arrival in India, marginalized the traditional and indigenous educational system and substituted a new system tailored to British needs. Recognizing the importance of education in the creation of subordinates in implementing the policies of colonial rule, the formal educational system was heavily promoted by the government, while the religious schools received little official support. *Madrasahs* thus eked out a precarious existence by financing themselves through private donations. Unlike the colonial education system, the *madrasah* system was representative of traditional society, socially coherent, hierarchical and stable (Robinson, 2001, p. 217).

In the late 1940s, the total number of *madrasahs* imparting religious education in Pakistan was around 137, but this number surged to around 13,000 by 2002 (Samad, 2007, pp. 164-182). Pakistan's *madrasah* system of Islamic education has come under intense scrutiny in the wake of attacks in the United States on September 11, 2001. The debate evokes images of *jihad*, warfare training, terrorism and an archaic system of learning. Most of these perceptions are simplistic characterizations of a complex phenomenon. *Madrasahs* do indeed play a role in violence and conflict but they also occupy a key place in Pakistan's religious and social life (I. H. Malik, 2005, p. 29).

Types of *Madrasahs* in Pakistan

While Pakistan inherited four types of *madrasahs* at the time of its creation, there are five distinct types of *madrasahs* in the country today, and they are divided along sectarian and political lines. Two main branches of Sunni Islam in South Asia – Deobandis and Barelwis – dominate this network. Ahl-e-Hadith and Salafi Muslims also have their own schools. Another Sunni *madrasah* system, moreover, is run under the auspices of a prominent religious political party, Jamaat-e-Islami (JI), whereas Shia Muslims have organized their own educational system. The religious and doctrinal differences of these schools are irreconcilable (ICG, 2007, p. 9).

The Deobandi madrasah system. The setting up of the Darul-ulum *madrasah* in Deobandi in 1865, today the largest traditional *madrasah* in the world, marked a turning point in the history of *madrasah* education in India and Pakistan (Qasmi, 1994, p. 8). In contrast to earlier arrangements, the *madrasah* eschewed all patronage from the state and relied on public donations. The founders of Deobandi *madrasahs* made efforts to establish close links with ordinary Muslims in small towns and villages (Farquhar, 1967, p. 146). Graduates of the Darul-ulum Deoband eventually established their own small *madrasahs* in various parts of India and Pakistan, spreading the Deobandi teachings of Islamic reforms. Consequently, the social composition of the *madrasah* student body began undergoing a noticeable change, as many young men from lower class *ajlaf* families began to dominate Deoband and the network of Islamic schools that it helped spawn. For these people, access to resources associated with the Islamic scriptural tradition allowed for upward social mobility in a society deeply stratified by caste. Further, the free education, board and lodging provided by the *madrasahs* often attracted poor Muslims who could not afford to study in schools that charged fees. The hope of gaining employment as *muezzins* (persons who lead the call to Friday service and daily prayers), *imams* (Islamic leaders, often of a mosque) and teachers also attracted poor Muslims with no other reasonable job prospects. On the other hand, middleclass Muslims increasingly began to send their sons to English-medium schools, as these provided avenues for occupations in the new economy. Especially after 1947, however, wealthy Muslims only rarely sent their children to such westernized schools. As for the syllabus, hostility towards British rule meant that modern knowledge was viewed with suspicion. It was felt that "worldly" knowledge might tempt students away from their pursuit of religion, and hence was approached with extreme caution. Although some of the leading founders of Deoband are said to have legitimized the acquisition of such knowledge for the sake of the "advancement of Islam," it was not incorporated into school syllabuses. Deoband followed the basic structure of the Dars-i-Nizami[3] but reduced the liberal components of the curriculum and readings relating to *hadith, fiqh* and *tafseer*. Efforts to introduce modern disciplines met with no success. Two years after the founding of the *madrasah*, in 1859, a committee of the leading *ulama* of Deoband suggested reducing the length of the course of study from ten to six years, which the *madrasah* agreed to. The rationale given was that students would be able to study in modern schools after they graduated. At one point, the introduction of English was considered, but the proposal was rejected outright by the *ulema* (Qamaruddin, 1996, p. 119).

As a reaction to Deoband's perceived hostility towards modern subjects, the Nadwatul-Ulema was founded in Lucknow in 1892 to train *ulema* in both the traditional Islamic as well as modern disciplines (Smith, 1963, pp. 317-342). Its rector, Shibli Numani, sought to introduce the teaching of English along with modern social and natural sciences in the syllabus, arguing that early Muslims had not desisted from taking advantage of the learning of the Greeks and the Iranians. He also suggested that Islam, being an eternal religion, had always been open to new developments in the realism of the *aqli ulum*. Due to the stiff opposition of conservative *ulemas*, however, he was declared an infidel. As a result, Nadwatul-Ulema failed to develop a new class of *ulema*. The *ulemas* of Deoband today hold to the same conservative traditions in Pakistan as their nineteenth century predecessors (Giustozzi, 2007, p. 11).

Deoband and Jamaat-Ulema Hind, the political wing of the Muslim clergy, were against the partition of India and creation of Pakistan (Friedman, 1971, pp. 157-183), and after 1947 they protested against the adoption of Islamic laws in the country. Nonetheless, out of 13,000 *madrasahs* today more than 70 percent belong to the Deoband School (Evans, 2006, pp. 9-16).

Ahl-e-Hadiths. The Ahl-e-Hadith Movement was one of the most visible of the Muslim intellectual trends of the late nineteenth century because of its avowedly sectarian character and because of its membership from among the educated and wealthy. It was, like the Deobandi, a movement of people sensitive to the widespread political and social changes of the day, but its intensity and extremism were far greater and the range of its influence less (M. A. Ahmad, 1985, p. 336).

Its leadership came from the elite. In the biographical dictionary of the Ahl-e-Hadiths for Delhi and the United Provinces, a full one-fifth of the group was noted as *Sayyid* (male descendants of Muhammad) with a strikingly high percentage being descendants of the Mughals, Oudh *nawabs* (governors or viceroys of Mughal provinces), and wealthy *zamindars* (landholders with considerable powers in their territories). About one-fourth of these leaders were employed in government or princely services, all in very high positions. The Ahl-e-Hadiths justified their focus on *hadiths* by denying the legitimacy of the classical work of the four major law schools, whose commentaries and compilations of *fatwa* (religious edict) based on them had been the standard source of legal guidance for the Sunni community since the ninth century (A. Ahmad, 1964, p. 108). One clear exposition of this orientation was written by Sayyid Mahdi Ali Khan, or Mohsin al-Mulk, best known as the administrative successor to Sayyid Ahmed Khan at Aligarh College (A. M. Khan, 1969, p. 219).

The Ahl-e-Hadiths, like the *imams* of the law schools, based their legal thought on the four sources of law sanctioned in the Qur'an, *hadiths*, *qias* (analogy), and *ijma* (consensus). The Ahl-e-Hadiths felt they had special access to the Prophet because of their familiarity with *hadiths*. Like Deobandis, the Ahl-e-Hadiths opposed the Sufism of the shrines and the customs of the Shias (Sanyal, 1996, p. 276).

The Ahl-e-Hadiths experienced significant growth as a movement in Bengal in the 1830s, and their influence later spread to other parts of South Asia in the second half of the nineteenth century. Members of the movement, inspired by the lifestyles of the Prophet and his companion, called for the revival of earlier Islamic traditions such as the wearing of white robes and green turbans, the growing of beards, and other practices (De, 1974, p. 129).

Barelwi. Founded in India by Shah Ahmed Raza Khan (1856-1921), Barelwi was another Sunni movement. The core group of Barelwi *ulema* were Pathans from the major cities of Bareilly and Budaun in Rohilkhand. Their support base was primarily found in the small towns and rural areas of the United Provinces and the Punjab (Sanyal, 1996, p. 34).

The intellectual orientation of the Barelwis was foreshadowed in mid-nineteenth debates between Muhammad Ismail Shahid and Maulana Fazl-i-Rasul Badauni on the nature of God (Metcalf, 2007, p. 297). In 1872, Ahmed Raza's father founded a *madrasah* in Bareilly, the Misbahul't-Tahzib, but its name was soon changed to the Misbah-ulum. In 1894, another school was founded, Isha'at ul-ulum. These schools later fell into the hands of Deobandies, which prompted Ahmed Raza in 1915 to use a large *waqf* yielding 16,000 rupees a year for another school, the Madrasah-i-Shamsul-Hadi. He urged that great care be taken so that that school and its finances were also not by taken over by Deobandi. Like Deobandies and Ahl-e-Hadiths, he wrote extensively against the Shias. However, his work was also motivated by his opposition to the Deobandies and the Ahl-e-Hadiths. To undermine his detractors he issued *fatwa*, published letters, engaged in debates, and sent his students and associates to also participate in debates (M. A. Khan, 1964, pp. 68-75).

Barelwis founded a number of schools of their own. A major *madrasah*, Jamaat-i-Manazir-i-Islam at Bareilly, and another in Pilibhit, Darul-ulum Namuniyyah, were founded in 1887. After Ahmed Raza's death, Darul-ulum Hizbat-Ahnaf, the largest *madrasah*, was founded in 1920 (May, 1970, p. 319).

The three main groups of Sunni *ulema*, as discussed above, thought of themselves as rivals. Each represented a particular stance within the faith, emphasizing different branches of learning and jurisprudential positions, and striking different balances between their roles as mediators and educators in religious matters. The Deobandies and Ahl-e-Hadiths, who rejected customary practices and parochial cults, appealed to the more urban and educated, whereas Barelwi support was largely among the rural and less well-educated (Lapidus, 1979, p. 11).

Jamaat-e-Islami. Another voice of modernity in Islam came from Abul Ala al-Mawdudi (1903-1979), who was influenced by the thoughts of Jamaluddin Al-Afghani and Hasan al-Banna. Paying close attention to the activities of the Muslim Brethren (Jam'iyyat al-Ikhwan al-Muslimin), he developed a new type of political organization, the Jamaat-e-Islami (Islamic Association), in 1941. But it was quite different from the Brethren's. It was not a mass organization but a forum for a moral and intellectual elite, with its members dedicated to waging *jihad* against unbelief and immorality in every field of life (Mitchell, 1969, p. 264).

A still questionable issue is whether Mawdudi was somehow influenced by the European examples of Fascism and Leninism while organizing his Islamic Association. One school of thought suggests his organization closely resembled Opus Dei, a contemporary movement in the Catholic Church dedicated to the reform of public and private life through political involvement and also dominated by its founder (Choueiri, 1997, p. 84).

Mawdudi was in favor of a separate state for India's Muslims, but not along the lines of the European nation state (Kaura, 1977, p. 379). In his view, the basis of a new Muslim state would best be religious – not ethnic or national – in nature. Not an Islamic scholar in the classical sense, Mawdudi tried to elaborate a theory of Islam as a social ideology, in so doing adopting most of the values recognized as universal in the Western world. However, an important aspect within his Islamic ideology was the unconditional acceptance of *jihad*, a position which contrasted with that of the Deobandies and Barelwis, who adhered to *taqlid*.[4] Jamaat did not follow any particular school of law. However, in matters of daily life, it was influenced by the Hanafi school. The revitalization of the fundamentals of Islam put the Jamaat-e-Islami in opposition to the Barelwis and Shias (Rauf, 1965, p. 162).

Shias. The present doctrines of Twelver Imami Shiism developed during the late tenth and early eleventh centuries. This group is a minority within the Sunni school. Imami Shiite communities flourished in Iraq and Iran. The Imamis developed their own *fiqh* from the mid-ninth to the mid-eleventh centuries. They also had their own *hadiths* based on the writings of their own *imams* (Chittick, 1980, p. 68).

Shia political thought entered its modern phase during the Iranian constitutional revolution of 1905-11, when Shias were divided between the forces of constitutionalism, modernism, reason and secularism, on the one hand, and more traditional matters of faith, religious law, and clerical influence, on the other. The clerical establishment ultimately joined with secular revolutionaries in opposing European colonization. By the 1940s and 1950s, Shia political thought was addressing issues such as communism and nationalism, offering Shiism as an alternative (Petrushevsky, 1988, p. 194).

THE ROOTS OF RELIGIOUS EDUCATION IN PAKISTAN

As religious clergy did not support the concept of partition and opposed the creation of Pakistan, their influence on politics in the country was limited (Qureshi, 1972, p. 78). In the formative phase, the *madrasah* system also was weak and the number of schools did not increase to 137 until 1949. In fact, only 244 *madrasahs* existed in the entire country by 1956. From that time onward, the number doubled after every decade, though this growth was not a major issue, given that population growth averaged over 3 percent per year. The four *madrasah* unions ran 893 *madrasahs* by 1971 (Jamaat-e-Islami had no *madrasahs* until then), with the number increasing to 1,745 by 1979 and 3,000 by 1988 (Fair, 2006, p. 153).

After independence, a wide spectrum of groups and religious clergy began to press the Muslim League government to turn Pakistan into an Islamic state. The Islamists were not content with an in-gathering of Indian Muslims; they wanted to eliminate all vestiges of British-derived civil and criminal laws and create a state based upon Shariat. Most liberal Pakistanis rejected the imposition of Shariat law, but the demand was pressed incessantly by all the Islamist parties. They all demanded that Islamic provisions be included into a not yet adopted constitution. Rigid and conservative, they hampered efforts at reaching a constitutional consensus. The involvement of the *ulema* in the constitution-making process and the seeking of assistance from leading scholars like Sayyid Suleman Nadwi and Prof. Hamidullah ultimately resulted in the Objectives Resolution of 1949,[5] which would later determine the direction of future constitutions in the country (Gaborieau, 2002, pp. 43-55).

Ayub Khan initially regarded the Islamist parties as a dangerous nuisance. He banned Jamaat-e-Islami and imprisoned its leader Abul Ala al-Mawdudi. Feeling persecuted for their beliefs, Islamist leaders portrayed themselves as heroes and martyrs, invoking the memory of the great martyrs of the past. Disputes between state and religious forces increased during the Ayub period, which resulted in the establishment of the Council for Islamic Ideology (CII) and Islamic Research Institute (IRI). The government also attempted to modernize traditional Islamic activities by nationalizing the *awqaf* (landed property) system and attaching the *madrasahs* to the formal educational system so as to serve the national interest. The government accepted as literate only those who passed through its education system; other *madrasah* students were considered illiterate (Rehman, 2005a).

To further bring the clergy under its control and curb *madrasah* influence, the state attempted to monitor *madrasah* through governmental departments and reform their curricula. *Madrasahs*, in turn, developed various umbrella organizations. Deobandies founded their organization under Wafaq ul-Madaris al-Arabya in Multan in 1959. Barelwis established the Tanzim al-Madaris al-Arabya in Dera Ghazi Khan in the same year. The Ahl-e-Hadiths established the Markazi-Jamaat Ahl-e-Hadith in Faisalabad in 1955. Jamaat-e-Islami established the Tanzim Rabita al-Madaris. The few Shia organizations established their *madrasahs* under Majlis-e-Nazarat-e-Shiah Madaris-e-Arabiyyah (I. H. Malik, 1999, p. 261).

The major objectives of these umbrella organizations were to manage *madrasahs* by reforming the curriculum and enriching them with modern subjects, as well as standardize the examination system, but most of them failed to achieve their goals (Allen, 2006, p. 289).

The government convened a committee in 1961 for the revision of the curricula of the *madrasahs*. The clergy was given representation in the said committee, but their influence was less than the government's. The committee's report covered 700 *madrasahs*. Reforms suggested by the committee were justified on the grounds that the current needs of the nation and the "challenges of the time" had to be brought into equilibrium. The committee emphasized the role of the clergy in achieving these reforms. The committee further planned to widen the outlook of Darul-ulum students to better prepare then for future careers, an aim only possible if new disciplines were introduced. The committee suggested that the entire primary education plan already approved by the Education Ministry be adopted by the students of these *madrasahs*. In order to supervise the *madrasahs*, a Directorate of Religious Education was proposed within the *Auqaf* Department. The basic responsibility of this directorate was to monitor and evaluate the standards among students and faculty. The teachers of these *madrasahs* would also now be required to attend a six month reorientation at a teacher training center to adequately learn the new subjects (I. H. Malik, 1999, p. 126).

The proposals submitted by the committee for the reforming of *madrasah* were not fully implemented. With the failure of Ayub Khan and his successor General Yahya Khan, the pragmatic approach of the army towards Islamic issues also changed, with the idea of an Islamic Pakistan seized upon by Zulfiqar Ali Bhutto. Aware of a growing Islamist movement, he advanced the idea of Islamic socialism. He used the state machinery to carry out a series of measures favoring Islamic precepts, such as banning alcohol and gambling and making Friday a non-working day. The constitution adopted in 1973 also made several concessions to Islam. In 1974, he supported a move to declare members of the Ahmediyya sect non-Muslims and instructed the army chief General Zia-ul-Haq to Islamize the Pakistani military (I. H. Malik, 2001, pp. 357-377). He also applied Islamic rhetoric to Pakistan's foreign and strategic policy, hosting a major organization of the Islamic Conference meeting in Lahore in 1974. He supported various extremist groups in opposition to the Afghan government, who later played a crucial role in the war against the Soviet Union. Pakistan's nuclear program was promoted by him as an "Islamic bomb." Another development of this period was that Pakistan started developing its relations with Muslim nations of the Middle East for aid, ideological support, and strategic cooperation. As these relations further developed, several extremist elements, including Osama bin Ladin and his followers, made Pakistan and Afghanistan their second home (Mir, 2005, p. 113).

Nonetheless, supporters of Bhutto claim his main desire was to modernize the country. Under his policies, society experienced increased centralization, from which the clergy also suffered. It has been further maintained that Bhutto rejected the clergy and did little to translate Islamic principles into reality. There was a drive to strengthen the formal educational system under Bhutto, reflected in curricular reform and the introduction of religious subjects. The CII also prepared a comprehensive and detailed report on the future of the Islamic educational system. Towards the end of his tenure in government, Bhutto attempted to improve the economic and social status of *madrasah* students and faculty. The diplomas and degrees issued by these *madrasahs* were accepted by the government through the Universities Grant Commission (UGC), the nation's highest education regulatory body. Certificates issued by the Wafaq ul-Madaris al-Arabya were equated with master's degrees in *Islamiyat* (Islamic studies), subject to the qualification of students taking their Bachelor of Arts examinations in English directives (Waseem, 2004, pp. 17-33).

ZIA-UL-HAQ AND RELIGIOUS ACTIVISM IN PAKISTAN

General Zia-ul-Haq's Islamization program covered three areas: Punitive measures, reconstruction of the economic system, and the general Islamization of morals, education and science (Saeed, 2002, pp. 131-148).

We shall discuss here General Zia's educational reforms, which ultimately not only drastically increased the number of *madrasahs* in the country, but also changed the character of education from secular to fundamentalist.

Zia left an enduring mark on Pakistan's schools and institutions of higher learning. He introduced a core curriculum inculcating a particular interpretation of Pakistan, South Asia and the world. He made a new subject "Pakistan Studies" compulsory for all degree students, including those at engineering and medical colleges. This subject's purpose was to focus on Pakistan as an ideological miracle and not a geographical area;

thus, the indoctrination strategy was primarily ideological and only secondarily geopolitical (M. Ahmed, 1998, p. 116).

The Islamization of science had its parallel in the realm of social sciences, with such new subjects created as Islamic economics and Islamic anthropology. Zia encouraged researchers to develop an Islamic theory of knowledge. This approach, which served as the basis of all social sciences, saw man essentially as an ethical being who must differentiate between good and evil. In explaining the Islamic concept of equality, advocates of the theory claimed that Islam stands for social justice not in terms of equality or collective good, but on an ethical and moral basis (M. Ahmed, 1998, pp. 101, 121).

Under Zia's leadership, not only was the syllabus of formal educational institutions Islamized, but also *madrasah* activities increased in their effectiveness, reflecting the importance of religious schools in society. One year after Zia seized power, a delegation of clergy met him in Sargodha and demanded greater autonomy for *madrasahs*. Hoping to use Islamization to enhance his credibility, Zia was bound to give into the demands of *ulema* at least partially. Under his direction, the Ministry of Religious Affairs submitted a report, known as the *Sargodha Report*, about these religious schools, which included details of the syllabus, their sources of financial support, and job opportunities for graduates. The report also highlighted differences of opinion among the sects that undermined *ulema* plans to manage all schools of thought under a unified umbrella organization (Oliver, 1998, p. 78).

The Zia revolution led to the establishment of the National Committee for Dini Madaris (NCDM) on January 17, 1979. A. W. J. Halepota was appointed as the chairman of this committee, having previously held the same position in 1961 during Ayub's tenure. The committee found during their visits that these *madrasahs* not only offered poorer quality education than the formal educational system, but also that the *madrasah* curriculum did not meet the needs of the nation. Vital changes at these institutions were deemed necessary. However, the recommendations of the report stood in sharp contrast to the views of the traditional clergy maintaining the *madrasahs* (I. H. Malik, 1999, p. 162).

The committee was comprised of 27 members, with 15 *ulemas* and remaining members university officials and representatives of the Ministry of Religious Affairs and Education. *The Halepota Report* analyzed *madrasah* education in detail, noting several shortcomings such as a lack of uniformity among curricula and examination systems. It was stressed, however, that these *madrasahs* transmitted the cultural heritage of the nation and students had higher motivations for learning not known within the formal system, where corruption was endemic. The committee recommended that these *madrasahs* receive aid through governmental institutions as they had no regular source of earnings save for donations gathered at Muslim festivals or other small sources of income (N. Malik, 1995, p. 162).

To reduce the gap between the formal and informal educational systems, the committee suggested integrating various modern subjects into the prevailing Dars-i-Nizami. It proposed the establishment of an autonomous National Institute of Dini Madaris for managing examinations in *madrasahs*. For ensuring the financial sustainability of the *madrasahs* and welfare of students and faculty, the government was to provide *madrasahs* with landed property (*awqaf*). All amenities including gas, electricity and water were to be arranged by the state and housing would also be earmarked for such institutions. *Madrasah* libraries were to be supported by the National Book Foundation. *Madrasahs* were also to be exempted from any sort of taxation. Funding for institutions was to be provided from *zakat*⁶ funds. Discrimination against *madrasah* faculty and students in public employment was to be reduced. It was proposed that *madrasahs* should be restructured along such lines so that students from formal institutions of education could also study there (I. H. Malik, 1999, p. 126).

The Halepota Committee submitted its report on December 17, 1979, urging bold reforms at *madrasahs*. The religious clergy initially had joined the committee with the hope that their autonomous status would be guaranteed by financial support from the state, but the recommendations did not meet their expectations and they ultimately boycotted and rejected the report. Moulana Muhammad Yousuf Ludhianwi, a representative of the Deobandies, was critical of various steps taken by the state against *madrasahs* in the name of moderation. Rejecting the proposals of the committee in their entirety, he argued that changing the curriculum of the *madrasahs* would destroy their character and purpose (I. H. Malik, 1999, p. 133).

Increasing resistance on the part of the *madrasahs* forced Zia-ul-Haq to postpone the reforms proposed by *The Halepota Report*. Instead, he decided to constitute a National Institute for Dini Madaris Pakistan (NIDMP) with two chambers. The body was to be dominated by the *ulema*. The Chairman of NIDMP was to be only accountable to the President of Pakistan. The government continued its reforms in this fashion, organizing several *ulema* and *mashaikh* conventions between 1980 and 1984. Through these conventions, the government conveyed the message that the clergy were important for bringing about Islamization and the national political system of Pakistan could not function without their cooperation. The government ultimately surrendered to these *madrasahs* in 1982, deciding to allow certificates to bear the title of "Shahdah-ul-Alamiya min uloom il Islamia" (International sources from the corpus of Islamic bodies of knowledge), which represented the equivalent of 16 years of formal education (I. H. Malik, 1999, p. 141).

Besides having their graduates formally recognized, the *madrasahs* achieved another milestone in gaining approval for financial grants from the state through *zakat* funds. Although according to the Sharia this was not permissible and the *zakat* and the regulation of June 1980 also did not have any provision for the distribution of *zakat* funds to *madrasahs*, Section 8 of the *zakat* regulations made it possible for government to declare students of those *madrasahs* eligible to receive *zakat*. The CII also supported the receipt of *zakat* by *madrasah* students. The authority in charge of each *madrasah*, the *muhtamim*, was allowed to act as an agent of the *zakat* recipients. It is remarkable that Shia *madrasahs* were also given such support, even though its members were exempted from compulsory *zakat* collection (I. H. Malik, 1999, p. 143).

This distribution of *zakat* funding provided the government with a lever to impose certain conditions on the *madrasahs*. Although it was decided that the proper monitoring of these funds would be carried out and funds could not be used for any purpose except the day to day needs of the poor and orphaned students, in fact funds were passed on to the *madrasahs*, to *mohtamims*, and to students. Students did not receive cash payments, but *zakat* funds were left to *mohtamims* to dispense with at their discretion, with many such funds spent on costly construction activities. As a *madrasah* usually belongs to a family and as such is inheritable, certain families profited considerably from this policy.

MADRASAHS: NURSERIES FOR *JIHAD*

Pakistani *madrasahs* were once considered centers for basic religious learning and were mostly attached to local mosques. The Islamic Revolution in Iran in 1979 opened up the first wave of foreign funding for *madrasahs* in Pakistan. Fearful of growing Iranian influence and the spread of revolution to other Middle Eastern countries, Kuwait, Saudi Arabia, Iraq and many other oil-rich Muslim nations started diverting funds into hard-line Pakistani Sunni religious organizations willing to counter the perceived Shia threat. Huge sums of money were poured into the establishment of *madrasahs* across Pakistan, particularly in Baluchistan province. The process of Islamization, started by Zia-ul-Haq in 1979, also contributed to rapid growth of *madrasahs*. For the first time, the state began providing funding for religious education from *zakat* and *usher* funds (Wirsing, 1991, p. 54).

The rise of *jihad* culture after the 1980s gave *madrasahs* a new sense of purpose. As their numbers multiplied, the clergy emerged as a powerful political and social force. According to the government's own estimates, 10 to 15 percent of the *madrasahs* had links with sectarian militant groups or international terrorism. Hence, a trail of international terror often lead to *madrasahs* and mosques (R. Ahmed, 2002, p. 138).

Madrasahs were basically conservative institutions before they were radicalized during the 1980s with the Afghan *jihad*. A growing army of extremists fought the anti-Soviet Afghan *jihad* alongside Arabs and Afghans. They later served the cause of *jihad* in places ranging from Kashmir, to Chechnya, Bosnia, Egypt and Yemen. During the peak years of the Afghan *jihad* from 1982 to 1988, more than 1,000 new *madrasahs* were opened in Pakistan (R. Ahmed, 2002, p. 164). Most of these *madrasahs* were established along the border with Afghanistan in Baluchistan and NWFP (North-West Frontier Province). The majority belonged to the Deobandies of Jamiat-ul-Ulema-i-Islam (JUI),[7] though a few Jamaat-e-Islami *madrasahs* also started functioning. These *madrasahs* further flourished due to close cultural, linguistic and sectarian affinities with Afghan Pathans (ICG, 2006, p. 11).

The *madrasahs* did not usually provide military training or provide arms to students, but encouraged them to join the "holy war." The purpose was to ensure a regular supply of recruits for the Afghan resistance. The message was simple: all Muslims must perform *jihad* in whatever capacity possible. Additionally, the US and Pakistan directly or indirectly promoted militancy through supporting the clergy in the war against communism, giving rise to a culture of *jihad* (Mir, 2005, p. 162).

Since *madrasahs* in Baluchistan and NWFP bordering Afghanistan were mostly dominated by the Pashtun people, special textbooks, often funded by USAID, were designed in Dari, Pashto and other local languages. The sole purpose was to promote *jihadist* values and militant training. These books, millions in number, were distributed at Afghan refugee camps and Pakistani *madrasahs*, where students learned basic mathematics by counting dead Russians and Kalashnikov rifles. The same textbooks were later used by the Taliban in their *madrasahs* (K. Ahmed, 2001, p. 219).

During the Soviet-Afghan War years, Pakistani *madrasahs* became a transit point for foreign militants aspiring to join Al-Qaeda and to Taliban forces in Afghanistan. The *madrasahs* not only attracted local Afghani and Pakistani Pashtuns but Muslims from Central Asian States, Europe and the US eager to join the *jihad*. John Walker Lindh, a young man from an upper-middleclass family in California, converted to Islam and joined the *jihad* in Afghanistan as Suleyman al-Faris, after studying in a primitive fundamentalist *madrasah* in NWFP. He was not the only American and not the only Westerner to join Al-Qaeda and the Taliban. Many Afro-Americans were also recruited by the Tablighi Jamaat (a Muslim missionary and revival movement) and its related organizations and sent to Afghanistan after receiving basic religious training in Pakistani *madrasahs* and guerilla training at camps run by militant groups closely affiliated with religious institutions. Some of the *madrasahs* also had developed links to international Islamist Organizations such as Egypt's Akhwan-ul-Muslimeen (Muslim Brotherhood), Indonesia's Jemmah Islamiyah, Algeria's Islamic Salvation (FIS), and the Philippine's Abu Sayyaf group (Z. Hussain, 2007, p. 83).

The *madrasahs* initially established in Baluchistan and NWFP later expanded their network to other parts of the country, including Karachi. According to some estimates, around 200,000 students were enrolled in around 1,000 *madrasahs* in the city. Many of these students had close ties to militant Islamic groups. Various religious groups dispute these figures for *madrasahs*. According to the Deobandies, they alone have around 1,500 *madrasahs* in the city. The Barelwis estimate they have about 300 *madrasahs*, while Shias and the Ahl-e-Hadiths each claim 36, bringing the total number of *madrasahs* to around 1,800 in Karachi alone. When Pakistani security forces raided a Deobandi *madrasah* known as Jamia Abu Bakr in Gulshan-e-Iqbal in September, 2003, they arrested a soft-spoken Indonesian student Ahmed Hadi, who later proved to be Gun Gun Rusman Gunawan, a leading member of Indonesia's leading *jihadist* group, Al-Ghuraba, and the brother of Hambali, the mastermind of the 2002 bombing of a Bali tourist resort in which more than 200 people died (ICG, 2007, p. 9). Similarly, Shahzad Tanweer, one of the suicide bombers involved in the July, 2005 terror attacks in London, spent several months at a *madrasah* known as Manzoor-ul-Islamia in Lahore, which was connected to a radical militant Islamic organization (Wilson, 2007, p. 101).

These and other incidents demonstrated a close link between terrorism and radical *madrasahs* in Pakistan. A report by the ICG revealed that Pakistani *madrasahs* and religious centers through the 1980s and 90s had received more than 90 billion rupees (US$1.5 billion) annually through charitable donations from the Middle East, Europe and the United States. Ninety four percent of the charitable donations made by Pakistanis, including individuals and business corporations, went to religious institutions through which *madrasahs* received financial and moral support (ICG, 2005, p. 12).

MADRASAHS AND SECTARIANISM

Religious sectarianism, the principal sources of terrorist activity in Pakistan, presented the most serious threat to the country's internal security. Following the Islamization process initiated by General Zia-ul-Haq, this sectarian conflict in Pakistan took on an organized militant form in the 1980s (Saeed, 2002, pp. 131-148).

Jhang, an important city in the Southern Punjab, is considered by many to be the birth place of organized sectarian militancy in Pakistan. Sipah-e-Sahaba, Pakistan's first anti-Shia militant group, was formed here. One viewpoint suggests the area's sectarian divisions arose after merchants supported Sunni militant groups to counter the Shia feudal aristocracy that had traditionally dominated local politics (Samad, 2007, pp. 164-182). Another opinion is that sectarian militancy first appeared in educational institutions when the Islami Jamaat Talaba (IJT) student wing of Jamaat-e-Islami used violence against its opponents at campuses across Pakistan (Waseem, 2004, p. 31).

Zia's promotion of Deobandi orthodoxy alienated Shias and Barelwis, while the spread of *jihadi* literature from Afghan training camps to Pakistani *madrasahs* fostered radical ideas among impressionable poverty-stricken youth. The Islamization of education and student politics created a sectarian consciousness far beyond the confines of the *madrasah*. Conflict between the two most important Sunni sects, Barelwis and Deobandies, grew over a number of issues, including control over Sunni mosques. The appointment of *khateebs* (mosque orators) and *imams* at the *Auqaf* Department mosques became a source of friction. The *Auqaf* Department under Zia preferred the graduated of Deobandi schools, which ultimately resulted in the fall of several Barelwi mosques into the hands of Deobandies. Distribution of *zakat* funds was equally lopsided in favor of Deobandi and Ahl-e-Hadith *madrasahs*. Zia's support wavered, however, as he sometime later supported the Barelwis as Jamiat-ul-Ulema-i-Islam (JUI), the main faction of the Deobandies, supported the anti-Zia political movement in 1983 (Rehman, 2005b, p. 137).

State patronage and the use of Islam political militancy for geostrategic purposes fuelled intense sectarian conflicts. During the Afghan civil war, Pakistan's Islamic parties, especially Jamaat-e-Islami and Jamiat-ul-Ulema-i-Islam, accumulated significant financial resources along with weapons and trained fighters (Waseem, 2004, pp. 17-33).

Deobandi and Ahl-e-Hadith *mullas* spread anti-Shia sentiments amongst the populace, with some Sunni leaders funded by Iraq. Pakistani and Iranian intelligence agencies had been actively involved in the proxy war being fought in Pakistani streets since the 1980s. Shia-Sunni conflicts pre-dated the emergence of Sipah-e-Sahaba Pakistan (SSP).[8] An important clash between the rival groups took place in June 1963 in the village of Tehri, in Khairpur district, when over 100 Shias were killed by rival Sunnis. However, a major escalation in sectarian violence followed the anti-Shia riots in Lahore in 1986. In 1987, Allama Ehsan Elahi Zaheer, a Saudi-backed Sunni cleric, was killed in a bomb blast in Lahore. The following year, a prominent Shia leader, Arif Hussaini, was murdered in Peshawar by an army officer named Majid Raza Gillani. This violence worsened with the murder of SSP founder Haq Nawaz Jhangvi in 1990. Believing he was murdered by Shia militants, Sunnis gunned down Sadiq Ganji, Iran's Consul General in Lahore, as they considered Iran a supporter of the Shia militants (Institute of Policy Studies, 2002, p. 74).

Until the 1979 Iranian Revolution, Pakistani Shias were a politically moderate community and their association had limited aims, such as the publishing of separate textbooks for education. Their first political party, Tehrik Nifaz-e-Fiqh Jafaria (TNFJ), was founded in 1979. In a majority Sunni state, the party's title reflected the TNFJ's desire to impose their *fiqh* on Sunnis and a revolutionary idealism which for the Zia government and Sunnis represented an Iranian conspiracy to export its revolution to Pakistan (K. Ahmed, 2003, pp. 35-40).

The Iranian Government has and still does extend political support to Shia minorities in Pakistan. During the Zia period, this was inevitable given Zia's aggressive Sunni Deobandi Islamization policies and alliance with the US. Iran and Saudi Arabia's proxy war in Pakistan was further fuelled by the US-supported anti-Soviet Afghan *jihad*, in which Pakistan's military government was an active player. Aside from competing for control over Afghan groups, Iran and Saudi Arabia supported their respective Pakistan religious allies. It is believed that Saudi Arabia alone gave US$3.5 billion to Pakistan for the Afghan *jihad*, most of which was spent in strengthening and arming Sunni groups on either side of the border. *Madrasahs* mushroomed not only in the NWFP and Baluchistan, but also in major cities, including Karachi, Lahore, Islamabad, Rawalpindi and Faisalabad. A parallel non-governmental sector of Islamic charities supported the *jihad*, with the exact volume of direct donations from Saudi individuals and charities difficult to determine. Kuwait and Libya also contributed. Iraq, under Saddam, actively sponsored anti-Iranian Pakistani *madrasahs* and parties (Gaborieau, 2002, p. 44).

Sectarian violence has broken out in recent years in several tribal areas of NWFP, Parachinar being one of the more volatile regions. This area had no history of organized violence until Pakistan's interventionist policies in Afghanistan resulted in an influx of Afghan Islamist extremists and a flourishing trade in drugs and arms. The violence first occurred in 1986, when Afghan fighters were brought into the area to attack Turi Shia pockets on the weapon supply route from Pakistan to Afghanistan (S. V. R. Nasr, 2002, pp. 78-102).

The northern areas of Pakistan, which constitutionally are not part of the country, are mainly populated by Shias. In 1988, the last year of Zia's rule, the entire area was embroiled in bloody anti-Shia riots, resulting in the death of more than 700 Shias. Baluchistan, which had previously never experienced religious discord, witnessed the worst forms of sectarian violence in the province after a rapid increase in the strength of *madrasahs*. Though only seven *madrasahs* existed in the province in 1950, 1,045 were in evidence by 2003. More than seventy percent were managed by Deobandies of JUI and were established in areas bordering Afghanistan. Sectarian violence in Baluchistan is also a by-product of proxy wars between Iran and Arabs, represented respectively by Shia Hazara refugees settled in the provincial capital Quetta and the pro-Taliban Afghan refugee population in Pakistan (ICG, 2005, p. 20).

CONCLUSION

The recent emergence and acceleration in religious extremism in Muslim societies is now seriously discussed worldwide. In these discussions, the institution of the *madrasah* is often viewed as a root cause of fundamentalism and even terror. Many agree that there is an urgent need to reform the educational system of these religious seminaries to discourage extremist trends. Thus, efforts have been directed towards introducing moderate reforms in the system in order to produce more liberal-minded students (Blanchard, 2008, p. 6).

As seen above, however, the assumption that *madrasahs* are fully responsible for fanaticism and violence in the region is misleading. In earlier eras, this indigenous educational system produced renowned philosophers, thinkers and liberal *ulemas* in Muslim societies. Therefore, the rise of religious orthodoxy in recent years must be traced to additional factors.

The most potent and important institution which patronizes religious orthodoxy is the state of Pakistan. Right from the birth of Pakistan as a nation, the ruling elite has hesitated to adopt liberal and secular policies. Owing to *ulema* pressure, religious clauses were included in the Objectives Resolution, giving it a religious character. A perception exists that this action subsequently determined the direction of the future constitution of the country. It is again a fact that from the very beginning the state adopted a hostile attitude towards progressive individuals and groups. During the entire Cold War, the state allied itself with the capitalist West and supported religious extremism to counter the threat of communism. Progressive writers and intellectuals were discredited as agents of foreign countries (M. Ahmed, 1993, pp. 1-24). Since that time, the Pakistani state itself has been playing an active role in the propagation of religious extremism.

Through state patronage and guidance, educational institutions Islamized their curricula so every subject could be taught from a religious perspective. Islamization of the legal system and the establishment of the Sharia court undermined the judicial system. The official media propagated *jihad* and glorified martyrdom. Thus it was the state, especially during the Zia-ul-Haq period, that emerged as the main vehicle of spreading religious fanaticism in society by crushing all liberal and progressive thought. Western nations and their military and ruling class allies in Pakistan even supported the Taliban in its early days, maintaining that peace and central government could be imposed in Afghanistan through them while ignoring real political forces. The result was all too clear – the acceleration of extremist trends in Pakistani society.

It is unfortunate that instead of looking at the issues from a historical perspective and maintaining a sense of objectivity, a blame game has commenced with intellectuals – including Paul Johnson, Francis Fukuyama, Pat Robertson, Patrick J. Buchanan, Franklin Graham, and many others – developing a view of Islam as "a very evil and wicked religion" (Kristof, 2002). A few such individuals have openly declared Islam to be "a religion of the Dark Ages," claiming "mainstream Islam is essentially akin to the most extreme form of Biblical fundamentalism" and "the history of Islam has been a history of conquest and re-conquest" (Johnson, 2001, p. 20). In a similar sprit, Francis Fukuyama claimed that "Islam, by contrast, is the only cultural system that seems regularly to produce people like Osama bin Laden or the Taliban who reject modernity lock, stock and barrel" (Fukuyama, 2002). As during the Cold War era the capitalist world supported religious fundamentalism in Muslim societies to counter a perceived communist threat, the recent expansion of religious extremism in the country must also be seen in this context. The US and its allies provided financial support for *madrasahs* and the promotion of religious theology, with the *madrasah* not having represented any serious threat or challenge in the past.

In addressing the important issue of *madrasahs*, therefore, it is essential to view developments from a broader perspective and to appropriately analyze the social contradictions prevailing in the region; merely targeting the *madrasah* in isolation from its actual context will only obscure rather than clarify the sources of extremism in Pakistan and impede the formulation of much-needed solutions.

Notes

1 The Arabic word *madrasah* is derived from *dars* or "learning" (Esposito, 1995, p. 207), with *madrasah* literally meaning a place where learning and teaching is done. The *Oxford Dictionary of Islam* describes the *madrasah* as "an establishment of learning where the Islamic Sciences are taught; a college for higher studies" (Esposito, 2005, p. 184).
2 *Waqf* (plural *auqaf*) is an Islamic institution whereby the founder relinquishes his ownership of real property, which then belongs henceforth to Allah, and dedicates the income or use of the property in perpetuity to some pious or charitable purpose, which may include settlements or payments in favor of the founder's own family.
3 A study curriculum used in a large portion of *madrasahs* in South Asia. It was standardized (and named after) Mullah Nizamuddin Sehalvi (d. 1748) at Farangi Mahall, a famous seminary of a family of Islamic scholars in Lucknow, India.
4 A doctrine in Islamic theology referring to the acceptance of a religious ruling in matters of worship and personal affairs from someone regarded as a higher religious authority without necessarily asking for technical proof. Most often, this refers to the adherence to one of the four classical Sunni schools of *fiqh*, or jurisprudence.
5 The Objectives Resolution was adopted on March 12, 1949 by the Constitution Assembly of Pakistan. Through this resolution it was announced that Sovereignty be-

longs to Allah (God) alone but He has delegated it to the State of Pakistan through its people to exercise within the limits prescribed by Him as a sacred trust. This resolution was in fact a first step towards the amalgamation of religion and politics in Pakistan, which contravened Pakistan's founder Muhammad Ali Jinnah's view of religion and the state as two separate domains (Hasan, 1986, p. 215).

6 The Islamic concept of tithing and alms. Muslims are obligated to pay 2.5 percent of their net worth that they have had for a full lunar year (approximately 2.5 percent of the calendar year). Exempt from *zakat* are a man's house, his wife's jewelry and transportation (car). *Zakat* is one of the Five Pillars of Islam.

7 Jamiat-ul-Ulema-i-Islam (Society of Muslim Ulema) (JUI) of Pakistan's origin lies in the Deoband movement in pre-partition India and with the Jamaat-Ulema Hind. Originally opposed to British imperialism, it supported the aims and policies of the Indian National Congress and opposed the Muslim League's struggle for an independent Pakistan (Esposito, 2006, p. 158).

8 *Sipah*, *Jaish* and *Lashkar* are prefixes meaning "army" that are used by various *jihadi* and sectarian groups. The anti-Shia Sipah-e-Sahaba means the "Army of the Companions of the Prophet."

References

Ahmad, A. (1964). *Studies in Islamic culture in Indian environment.* New Delhi: Manohar.

Ahmad, M. A. (1985). *Traditional education among Muslims: A study of some aspects in modern India.* New Delhi: Saga.

Ahmed, K. (2003, October-December). Islamic extremism in Pakistan. *South Asian Journal,* 2. Retrieved July 24, 2008, from http://www.southasianmedia.net/Magazine/Journal/ islamicextremism_pakistan.htm

Ahmed, K. (2001). *Pakistan: The state in crisis.* Lahore: Vanguard Books.

Ahmed, M. (1993). *Pakistan: At the crossroads.* Karachi: Royal Book Company.

Ahmed, M. (1998). Revivalism, Islamization, sectarianism and violence in Pakistan. In C. Baxter & C. H. Kennedy (Eds.), *Pakistan 1997* (pp. 101-121). New Delhi: HarperCollins.

Ahmed, R. (1981). *The Bengal Muslims 1871-1906: A quest for identity.* Delhi: Oxford University Press.

Ahmed, R. (2002). *Taliban: Islam, oil and the great new game in Central Asia.* London: I.B. Tauris.

Ali, T. (2003). *The clash of fundamentalisms.* London: Verso.

Allen, C. (2006). *God's terrorists.* New York: Da Capo Press.

Aziz, K. K. (1963). *Britain and Muslim India: A Study of British public opinion vis-à-vis the development of Muslim nationalism in India, 1857-1947.* London: Heinemann.

Aziz, K. K. (1966). *Some problems of research in modern history.* Karachi: Oxford University Press.

Black, A. (2006). *The history of Islamic political thought.* Karachi: Oxford University Press.

Blanchard, C. M. (2008). *Islamic religious schools, madrasahs: Background.* Congressional Research Service, Library of Congress. (CRS report RS21654). Retrieved July 24, 2008, from http://www.fas.org/sgp/crs/misc/RS21654.pdf

Bulliet, R. (1972). *The patricians of Nishapur: A study of medieval Islamic social history.* Cambridge, MA: Harvard University Press.

Butterworth, E. C. (1975). New light on the political philosophy of Averroes. In G. F. Hourani (Ed.), *Essays on Islamic philosophy and science* (pp. 118-127). Albany, NY: University of New York Press.

Chittick, W. C. (1980). *A Shiite anthology.* London, Muhammadi Trust.

Cohen, S. P. (2005). *The idea of Pakistan.* Lahore: Vanguard Books.

Choueiri, Y. M. (1997). *Islamic fundamentalism.* London: Pinter Publishers.

De, A. (1974). *Roots of separatism in nineteenth century Bengal.* Calcutta: Ratna Prakashan.
Esposito, J. L. (Ed.). (2005). *The Oxford dictionary of Islam.* Karachi: Oxford University Press.
Esposito, J. L. (Ed.). (1995). *The Oxford encyclopedia of the modern Islamic world.* New York: Oxford University Press.
Evans, A. (2006). Understanding madrasahs. *Foreign Affairs, 85*(1), 9-16.
Fair, C. C. (2006). *Islamic education in Pakistan.* Washington, DC: Institute of Peace.
Farquhar, J. N. (1967). *Modern religious movements in India.* Delhi: Munshirim Manoharlal.
Faruqi, Z. H. (1992). *Musalmano ka talimi nizam* [The educational system of the Muslims]. Delhi: Maktaba Jamia.
Friedmann, Y. (1971). The attitude of the Jamiyyat-i-Ulama-i-Hind to the Indian National Movement and the establishment of Pakistan. In G. Baer (Ed.), *The ulema in modern history* (pp. 157-183). Jerusalem: African and Asian Studies, Israeli Oriental Society, VII.
Fukuyama, F. (2002, October 11). The West has won. *The Guardian.*
Gaborieau, M. (2002). Religion in the Pakistani polity. In S. Mumtaz, J.-L. Racine, & I. A. Ali (Eds.), *Pakistan: The contours of state and society* (pp. 43-55). Karachi: Oxford University Press.
Giustozzi, A. (2007). *Koran, Kalashnikov and laptop.* London, Hurst & Company.
Haeri, S. F. (2006). *The thoughtful guide to Islam.* Delhi: Bhavana Books and Printers.
Hasan, S. (1986). *The battle of ideas in Pakistan.* Karachi: Pakistan Publishing House.
Harvey, L. P. (1990). *Islamic Spain, 1250 to 1500.* Chicago: University of Chicago Press.
Hodgson, M. G. (1990). *The venture of Islam,* vol. 1. Chicago: University of Chicago Press.
Holt, P. M. (1977). The structure of government in the Mamluk Sultanate. In P. M. Holt (Ed.), *The Eastern Mediterranean lands in the period of the Crusades* (pp. 44-61). Warminster: Aris & Phillips.
Hussain, T. (2007, July). Madrasa education in a modern society. *Forum, 2*(6). Retrieved July 24, 2008, from http://www.thedailystar.net/forum/2007/july/madrasa.htm
Hussain, Z. (2007). *Frontline Pakistan.* Lahore: Vanguard Books.
ICG. (2004). *Unfulfilled promises: Pakistan's failure to tackle extremism.* (Report No. 73). Retrieved July 24, 2008, from http://www.crisisgroup.org/home/index.cfm?id=2472&l=1
ICG. (2005). *The state of sectarianism in Pakistan.* (Report no. 95). Retrieved July 24, 2008, from http://www.crisisgroup.org/home/index.cfm?id=3374&l=1
ICG. (2006). *Pakistan's tribal areas: Appeasing the militants.* (Report no. 125). Retrieved July 24, 2008, from http://www.crisisgroup.org/home/index.cfm?id=4568
ICG. (2007). *Pakistan: Karachi's madrasas and violent extremism.* (Report no. 130). Retrieved July 24, 2008, from http://www.crisisgroup.org/home/index.cfm?id=4742&l=1
Institute of Policy Studies. (2002). *Deeni Madaris: Problems and prospects.* Islamabad: Institute of Policy Studies.
Johnson, P. (2001, October 15). Relentlessly and thoroughly: The only way to respond. *National Review,* p. 8.
Kaura, U. (1977). *Muslims and Indian nationalism.* New Delhi: Manohar.
Keddie, N. R. (Ed.). (1972). *Scholars, saints and Sufis: Muslim religious institutions since 1500.* Berkeley and Los Angeles: University of California Press.
Khan, A. M. (1969). *Transition in Bengal.* Cambridge: Cambridge University Press.
Khan, G. (1998). *Indian Muslim perceptions of the West during the eighteenth century.* Karachi: Oxford University Press.
Khan, M. S. (1999). *Education, religion and the modern Age.* New Delhi: Asish Publishing House.
Khan, M. A. (1964). Research in the Islamic revivalism of the nineteenth century and its effect on the Muslim society of Bengal. In P. Bessaignet (Ed.), *Social research in East Pakistan* (2d ed.). (pp. 68-75). Dacca: Asiatic Society of Pakistan.
Kristof, N. D. (2002, July 9). Bigotry in Islam – And here. *New York Times.*
Kulke, H., & Dietmar, R. (1998). *A history of India* (3rd ed.). London: Routledge.

Kumaraswamy, P. R. (1997, June). The strangely parallel careers of Israel and Pakistan. *Middle East Quarterly, 4*(2), 31-39.

Lapidus, I. M. (1979, April). *The Islamic religion and the historical experiences of Muslim peoples: A challenge for contemporary scholarship.* Paper presented at the seventh Giorgio Levi Dellavida conference at the University of California, Los Angeles, California.

Lumbard, J. E. B. (2005). The decline of knowledge and the rise of ideology in the modern Islamic world. In J. E. B. Lumbard (Ed.), *Islamic fundamentalism and the betrayal of tradition* (pp. 39-78). New Delhi: Third Eye.

Malik, I. H. (1999). *Islam, nationalism and the West.* Karachi: Oxford University Press.

Malik, I. H. (2001). Military coup in Pakistan: Business as usual or democracy on hold? *The Round Table, 90*(360), 357-377.

Malik, I. H. (2005). *Jihad, Hindutva and the Taliban.* Karachi: Oxford University Press.

Malik, N. (1995, January 23). Financial squeeze to discipline madrasa. *Dawn.*

May, L. (1970). *The evolution of Indo-Muslim thought after 1857.* Lahore: Vanguard Books.

Mayer, P. B. (1981). Tombs and Dark Horses: Ideology, intellectuals, and proletarians in the study of contemporary Indian Islam. *Journal of Asian Studies, 41*(3), 481-502.

Metcalf, B. D. (2007). Islamic revival in British India: Deoband, 1860-1900. In B. D. Metcalf, R. Ahmed, & M. Asan. *India's Muslims – An Omnibus* (pp. 264-314). Karachi: Oxford University Press.

Mir, A. (2005). *The true face of Jehadis.* Lahore: Vanguard Books.

Mitchell, R. P. (1969). *The Society of Muslim Brothers.* Oxford: Oxford University Press.

Nadwi, A. H. (1971). *Hindustan ke Qadim Darsgah* [The old Islamic schools of India]. Azamgarh: Dar-ul-Musannifin.

Nasr, S. H. (2001). *Islam and the plight of modern man.* Chicago: Kazi Publications.

Nasr, S. V. R. (2002). Islam, the state and the rise of sectarian militancy in Pakistan. In C. Jaffrelot (Ed.), *Pakistan: Nationalism without a nation.* London: Zed Books.

Oliver, R. (1998). Has Islamism a future in Afghanistan? In W. Maley (Ed.), *Fundamentalism reborn?* (pp. 199-211). London: Hurst.

Oliver, R. (1994). *The failure of Political Islam.* London: Tauris.

Petrushevsky, I. P. (1988). *Islam and Iran.* London: Athlone Press.

Qamaruddin. (1996). *Hindustan ki Dini Darsgah* [The religious schools of India]. Delhi: Hamdard Education Society.

Qasmi, M. A. (1994). *Tarik-i-Dars-i-Nizami* [The history of the Dars-i-Nizami]. Bilaspur: Majma al-Bahuth al-Ilmiya.

Qureshi, I. H. (1942). *The administration of Delhi Sultanate.* Lahore: M. Ashraf & Sons.

Qureshi, I. H. (1972). *Ulema in politics: A Study relating to the political activities of the ulema on the South-Asian Subcontinent from 1556-1947.* Karachi: Ma'aret Limited.

Rauf, A. (1965). *Renaissance of Islamic culture and civilization in Pakistan.* Lahore: Vanguard Books.

Rehman, T. (2005a). Madrasahs, extremism and education. *Islamabad Policy Research Institute Journal, 1*(5), http://ipripak.org/journal/winter2005/madrassas.shtml

Rehman, T. (2005b). *Language and politics in Pakistan.* Karachi: Oxford University Press.

Rizvi, S. A. A. (1965). *Muslim revivalist movements in northern India in the sixteenth and seventeenth centuries.* Agra: Agra University Press.

Rizvi, S. A. A. (1975). *The religious and intellectual history of Muslims under Akbar's reign.* New Delhi: Munshiram Mahal.

Robinson, F. (2001). *The ulema of Firangi Mohal and Islamic culture in South Asia.* Delhi: Permanent Black.

Saeed, S. (2002). From official Islam to Islamism: The rise of Daawa-ul-Irshad and Lashkar-e-Taiba. In C. Jaffrelot (Ed.), Pakistan: Nationalism without a nation (pp. 131-148). London: Zed Books.

Salim, S. M. (1988). *Musalmano ka Nizam-i-Talim* [The educational system of Muslims]. Delhi: Markazi Maktaba-i-Islami.
Samad, Y. (2007). Islamic militancy and violence in Pakistan. In I. Talbot (Ed.), *The deadly embrace. Religion, politics and violence in India and Pakistan, 1947-2002* (pp. 164-182). Karachi: Oxford University Press.
Sanyal, U. (1996). *Devotional Islam and politics in British India: Ahmed Raza Khan Brelwi and his movement, 1870-1920*. Delhi: Alfa Publication.
Shirazi, S. D. (1958). *Al-Hikma al-Muta Alliya fi-Asfar al-Arba aal-Aqliyya* [The wisdom of four mental faculties]. Tehran: n.p.
Siddiqui, M. A. (1998). Development and trends in madrasa education. In A. W. B. Qadri, R. S. Khan, & M. A. Siddiqui (Eds.), *Education and Muslims in India since independence* (pp. 268-294). New Delhi: Institute of Objective Studies.
Smith, W. C. (1963). The ulama in Indian politics. In C. H. Philips (Ed.), *Politics and society in India* (pp. 317-342). London: Oxford University Press.
Waseem, M. (2004). Origins and growth patterns of Islamic organizations in Pakistan. In S. P. Limaye, M. Malik, & R. G. Wirsing (Eds.), *Religious radicalism and security in South Asia* (pp. 17-33). Honolulu: Asia-Pacific Center for Security Studies.
Wilson, J. (2007). *The General and Jihad*. Delhi: Pentagon Press.
Wirsing, R. G. (1991). *Pakistan's security under Zia, 1977-1988*. London: Macmillan.

Part Four:
Globalization and Development

• CHAPTER EIGHT •

Globalization and Development in Sport: Perspectives from South East Asia

CHARLES LITTLE
London Metropolitan University

JOHN NAURIGHT
George Mason University and *Aarhus University*

Since at least the 1980s, governments around the world have diverted large sums of public money into national sporting programs and sporting facilities in the hopes of competing on a global stage (Whitson & Horne, 2006, p. 73). While in Europe, North America and Australia this process has had a long genesis, in other parts of the world there has been a rush to "catch up" with the West and compete equally. In Asia, nations such as Japan, Korea, China, India and the oil rich states of the Middle East have made significant inroads into the elite circles of international sports and the hosting of major sporting events. Other Asian countries such as Malaysia, Singapore, and Thailand have also begun to show signs of being able to compete on the global stage as they have all hosted major international sporting events in recent times.

The rapid globalization of competition for major events and for sporting success were made possible by the massive investment of media corporations in sports coverage, league sponsorship and team ownership, particularly as pay television companies became global entities and media corporations sought cheap and ready-made programming. However, the global expansion of the media has privileged already well-known brands and leagues such as the Premier League in England or the National Basketball Association in the United States, making it difficult for local leagues and teams to compete with these global brands.

Sports and major sporting events have become integral components of a global political economy which has seen manufacturing shift from developed to less developed countries and an expanding focus in the developed world on the "branding," "theming" and consumption of image and lifestyle. From the restyling of individual matches as entertainment extravaganzas to specialized tournaments like the Olympic Games or the FIFA World Cup, sporting competitions have become spectacles as they compete with other leisure activities for the consumer dollar, euro, pound or yen. In addition, these large-scale events have become key factors in local, regional and national development strategies. In this process traditional sports fans, local communities and democratic practices are often ignored as growth is promoted and business and governments align in support of event-driven economies (Lenskyj, 2008). In one powerful example, Lenskyj cites the Center on Housing Rights and Evictions Report (COHRE) from Geneva that presents "indisputable evidence of negative impacts on low-income renters and homeless people in every Summer Olympic Games host city since 1988 [the Seoul Olympics], including displacement, forced evictions, escalating housing costs, reduced availability of affordable housing, and the criminalizing of homelessness" (quoted in Lenskyj, 2008, p. 2).

Increasingly, major sporting competitions and tournaments are regarded as events to be marketed and managed and terms such as "hallmark" and "mega" suggest that size really does matter. The lure of large and spectacular events is thought to be an expedient way to attract media interest in a host city or nation, which, it is hoped, will translate into an influx of capital through tourism and new investment (Black & Van der Westhuizen, 2004; Hall, 2005; Horne & Manzenreiter, 2006; Weed, 2008). In Asia this desire for capital has led many countries to bid for major events, some successfully, such as Japan and South Korea with the Olympic Games and the FIFA World Cup, among other major events; China with the Olympic Games; Malaysia and India with the Commonwealth Games; a series of countries that have hosted the Asian Games; Dubai and the many major global events now hosted there; and Doha, Qatar bidding for the 2016 and 2020 Olympic Games. Meanwhile, China, Japan, and South Korea have emerged as major sporting nations in the Summer Olympics with all three nations among the top ten medal winners at the 2008 Beijing Games.

Thus, many Asian nations and cities are becoming globally competitive in the sports arena as well as in general economic terms, though many hurdles remain. Uncertainty in the Middle East and heightened tensions between India and Pakistan concern many outsiders. Economic development remains vastly uneven in a region that shares some of the world's leading economies and some of the world's poorest. Likewise, the global sports playing field is vastly uneven as new players seek to compete with old global sporting powers in Western Europe, North

America and Australia. Nations such as China, which can mobilize a vast state apparatus to ensure successful events, or Japan with its highly developed infrastructure, can now compete on equal terms. However, Western dominance in international sports governance, sponsorships, media conglomerates, technical expertise and a global popular culture based on pop music and Hollywood means that Asian nations face an uphill battle to achieve equality of opportunity in the field of global sports. As media driven expansion of leading sports events and leagues accelerates, local sporting practices often suffer. Indeed, leading European leagues and teams in professional soccer are leveraging their position as they expand their interests and audiences globally. Phillips Electronics, parent company of the perennial Dutch League champions PSV Eindhoven, became a sponsor of the Chinese Football Association Cup in 1995 and in 2001 converted that to sponsorship of the national team (Rucai, 2004). Other sports have followed suit. The New York Yankees sponsor the Chinese Baseball Association and the Boston Red Sox Major League Baseball team have strategic marketing arrangements in Japan. In 2008, the Yankees and the Red Sox opened their seasons in China and Japan respectively (Bloom, 2007; New York Yankees, 2008).

This chapter examines the trajectory of globalization of sport's impact on cultures and societies in South East Asia and discusses the problems and prospects of playing (and spectating) on the global stage for these rapidly developing economies. To do this we use several examples of the region's engagement with the global sports system and show how that engagement has impacted on the economic development of sports within South East Asia. We examine the problems generated by the popularity of the English Premier League for the development of local leagues, the global flows of athletic talent both to and from South East Asia, attempts to establish transnational leagues, the complex relationship of the nation to the global, and finally the lure of mega-events.

THE ENGLISH PREMIER LEAGUE AND SOUTH EAST ASIA

Nowhere is this phenomenon more evident than the popularity of European football leagues, especially England's Premier League, within South East Asia. English clubs, and especially the big three of Manchester United, Liverpool and Arsenal, have a huge following within the region. In Singapore, for example, as we have observed firsthand, the front pages of newspapers are regularly devoted to news and reports from the Premiership, newsagents' shelves burst with a plethora of magazines focusing on the league and its clubs, live coverage of matches dominate the pay television industry, and broadcasts of live matches draw large and animated crowds to open-air coffee-shops in the early hours of the morning.

The international interest in Manchester United is revealed by the fact that over eighty per cent of visitors to the official club website (www.manutd.com) are from outside of the United Kingdom, with Malaysia (3rd), Indonesia (5th), and Singapore (7th) featuring among the ten leading providers of viewers (Alexa, 2008). Clubs like Manchester United have tapped into this interest by staging pre-season tours to the region, having visited Singapore, Malaysia, and Thailand in recent years (in additional to other Asian markets such as China, Hong Kong, Japan and South Korea). These tours are extremely lucrative for the clubs involved, providing a steady source of income. South East Asia is also an important market for club merchandise, with Manchester United operating branches of their club Megastore in Kuala Lumpur and on Singapore's famous shopping stretch of Orchard Road (Brick, 2001, p. 11).

The downside of the popularity of the Premier League is that local leagues struggle to match the attention given to it and other overseas leagues, and consequently face difficulties in attracting spectators and sponsors. Despite the efforts of Singapore's S-League to promote itself to local football fans, it has struggled to develop an established following since its founding in 1996. Even in its first year of existence, the league was forced to reschedule a round of matches from their regular evening kick-off time to early afternoon in order to avoid a clash with a Premier League match between Manchester United and Liverpool which was being broadcast live on local television, and it continues to be viewed as a second-rate league by local supporters (Lim, 2008).

There are also concerns that European leagues and clubs view Asia as little more than a cash cow. The global television audience certainly offers rich financial pickings for leagues and clubs, with the international television rights for the English Premiership reaching £625 million per year in a three-year deal signed in 2007 (Harris, 2007). The bulk of this revenue was generated from Asia and the Middle East, with the Singaporean rights alone selling for an estimated US$160 million, generated on the back of advertisers keen to target the 31.6 percent of the male population who watch televised football on a regular basis (Singapore Sports Council, 2005). Such figures represent a vast transfer of funds from South East Asia to Europe, with the Asian Football Confederation (AFC) claiming that 61 percent of all football revenue generated in Asia goes to the Premier League (*Asian Football Business Review* [AFBR], 2007).

These fears of economic exploitation were given further grounds when the Premier League announced plans to stage an additional round of league matches in overseas cities from 2010 onwards. Dubbed the "39th Game," the plan would have seen matches played in five cities each year (with South East Asia indentified as one of the likely locations), and was intended to capitalize on the existing audience for English football that had been developed through television coverage. The plan met with fierce criticism from almost all overseas football federations, with the AFC refusing to sanction any matches being played within any of its 46 member countries (Bond, 2008).

The relationship between the Premiership and South East Asia is not a one-way street, however, which forces us to reconsider notions of "core" and "periphery" and to question where the power lies within the relationship. Premiership clubs, once predominantly owned by local businessmen, have in recent years been subject to a number of takeovers by overseas investors. Almost half of the clubs in the competition, including heavyweights Liverpool, Manchester United and Chelsea, are owned by foreign investors, many of whom have been attracted to them by the economic opportunities offered by their global following (Nauright & Ramfjord, in-press). Among these investors is former Thai Prime Minister Thaksin Shinawatra who, after an unsuccessful bid to buy a stake in Liverpool (Phongpaichit & Baker, 2004, pp. 243-246), took ownership of Manchester City in 2007.

Companies from the region are also heavily involved in sponsorship of the Premier League. Thai brewer Chang Beer is the main sponsor of Everton; Malaysian-based low cost carrier Air Asia is the official airline partner of Manchester United (one of their aircraft is emblazed with the club's logo and players) and sponsors the uniforms of match officials; and breweries from Singapore and Vietnam regularly buy pitch-side advertising hoardings and hold official partnerships with leading clubs. While sponsorship in the Premiership is increasingly becoming the prerogative of multinational companies, what is unique in this case is that the companies mentioned here have little or no interest in selling to the English domestic market (Air Asia flies exclusively within South East Asia, while Chang Beer is only available in Thai Restaurants in the UK) and that their sponsorship is solely intended for consumption through the medium of satellite television in their domestic markets in South East Asia since that is the only other place to consume the beer (Chang Beer, 2006).

It is not only in the legitimate economy that these influences are evident. The match-fixing scandal that engulfed English football in the mid-1990s also had its roots in South East Asia. Betting on football is massively popular across in the region, where the huge sums being wagered and the illegal nature of most gambling has led to widespread corruption in football, with major match-fixing scandals having hit Malaysia, Singapore and Vietnam in recent years (Ampofo-Boateng, 2002). This spread to England when a number of leading players were implicated in a 1993 match-fixing syndicate engineered by Malaysian gamblers (House of Lords, 2002), while another Malaysian betting syndicate was behind attempts to manipulate gambling markets by sabotaging the floodlights at Premiership matches in the late 1990s (Chaudhary & Gregoriadis, 1999).

The growing influence of the global sporting market has also profoundly altered the nature of football within Britain. Giulianotti (2005) notes that the growing commercialization of the sport has already resulted in a small number of clubs becoming financially dominant and being able to use their economic advantage to maintain a leading league position. Nauright and Ramfjord (in-press) further illustrate this in discussing how few Premier League clubs have finished first or second during the entire history of the League. Only Blackburn Rovers have won the Championship since 1992 in a competition dominated by Manchester United, Arsenal and Chelsea, who have combined to win every other year through 2008. A number of commentators have expressed fears that the cash boost provided by the most recent international television deal will further exacerbate these divisions: even the lowest finishing club in the Premier League is now guaranteed £29 million in prize money, compared to just £1 million for the clubs in the lower-tier Championship (Eason, 2008). The benefits of being in the "right place at the right time" could well mean that Derby County, the recipients of that £29 million, will now have a perpetual advantage over traditional East Midlands rivals Nottingham Forrest and Leicester City, ending over a century of close rivalry and fluctuating levels of success between these clubs. With winnings dispensed in such a fashion, those at the bottom of the Premier League face catastrophic losses while those promoted stand to receive a huge windfall. The outcomes for each season are now rather predictable: Manchester United, Arsenal, and Chelsea, followed fairly closely by Liverpool, fill the top spots and are followed by a second tier of clubs with large local/regional followings including Aston Villa, Everton, Manchester City and Newcastle United. There are occasional exceptions to this rule, but since 2000 they have been exceedingly rare. It is not surprising that these rankings resemble the global following and hierarchy of English clubs as well.

Perhaps even more profoundly, the globalization of the premiership has exacerbated already existing fissures between clubs and their traditional constituencies. Williams' (2001) analysis of self-defined "traditional" Liverpool fans reveals their concerns and insecurities about the increasing global interest in *their* club, which includes scepticism towards the club's international supporters and questions about their entitlement to claim an attachment to the traditions of the club. Anecdotal evidence from fan websites of other clubs also suggests some hostility, and occasional racism, towards South East Asian supporters of the club. Many football fans in England were also just as concerned about the implications of the "39th Game" as were football federations within Asia. The

Football Supporters' Federation (FSF), a fans' advocacy organization, launched a campaign against the proposal arguing that it was "completely unfair" to the club's traditional fans (FSF, 2008).

Referring to these changes in the nature of the game, Sandvoss (2003) claims that:

> physical localities are increasingly divorced from a sense of home and *Heimat*. In other words, in the face of globalization the automatism between local and lifeworld and between place and community is eroded. Similar to the locale itself, a sense of belonging, community and *Heimat* is negotiated through the consumption of global resources. This sense of belonging is directly articulated through football fandom which is based upon the imagined bond between the fan and the object of fandom. Given the increasing geographical diffusion of fans of large-scale professional football clubs, fandom increasingly lacks territorial referentiality, it becomes "deterritorialized." (p. 171)

The issue that Sandvoss has identified is encapsulated by Liverpool's Merseyside Derby, traditionally a parochial struggle for local bragging rights between the two leading clubs of a tough English working-class city. Today, however, this match sees one of the clubs owned by American investors (and being pursued by the investment arm of the Dubai government) and the other part-owned by the American-based owner of the Planet Hollywood restaurant chain, .players wearing jerseys emblazoned with the logos of a Thai brewery and a Europe-based transnational brewing giant (Carlsberg), an officiating referee whose kit is sponsored by a Malaysian-based airline, and players who hail mainly from outside of England – all watched by a global television audience of millions.

GLOBAL PLAYER MIGRATION

As mentioned in the context of football's Merseyside Derby, one of the most visible (and often contentious) impacts of the globalization of sport has been the emergence of a global talent market for athletes. South East Asia has not been a significant exporter of athletic talent to overseas leagues, however. In football, the lack of success of regional teams on the international stage means that only a handful of players (such as Thailand's Kiatisuk Senamuang and Singapore's Fandi Ahmad) have competed in European leagues. In fact, the only significant outflow of players from the region occurred in the 1970s, when there was an exodus of Malaysian players to Hong Kong as the territory became the first country in Asia to establish a professional league (Sallihudin, 2004, p. 70).

Instead, the region has been a net importer of athletes. Again, this has been most prevalent in football, where most clubs in national leagues field at least some foreign players. When Singapore's professional league was launched in 1996 its 8 clubs featured 40 overseas players from 15 countries. The truly global dimensions of the international talent market were reflected in the continental break-down of these players, with 20 hailing from Europe, 8 from Oceania, 7 from South America, 3 from Africa, and 2 from Asia. The strong representation of players from former Yugoslavia (13) also reflected the outflow of athletic talent from the former Soviet bloc following the fall of the Iron Curtain (S-League, 1996, pp. 45-52).

The development of this global market for athletes has proved controversial. One viewpoint holds that an influx of foreign talent in any domestic league will stifle the development of local players and undermine the prospects of the host nation's national side, and this issue has been a regular source of debate among fans in many nations. Such concerns have led the Malaysian Football Association to exclude all overseas players from the Malaysian Super League, with one official claiming "with the presence of foreign players, local players have not been given the opportunity (to develop)" (Reuters, 2008).

More widespread are concerns that aspects of the global athlete migration process showcase the exploitative elements of globalization. In particular, there are concerns that athletes from the developing world are exploited by agents and foreign clubs in what some claim is a form of economic imperialism. Examples of these concerns relate to the recruitment of Latin American baseball players by Major League Baseball clubs and the treatment of young African footballers by European clubs. Darby (2001) comments on the "exploitative practices of the increasing numbers of scouts, agents and speculators who, unfettered by the types of regulatory systems operating in Europe, have recognised the trade of African talent as an opportunity for personal financial gain" (p. 226).

One such example of exploitation was the Sporting Afrique Football Club, which gained a place in Singapore's S-League in 2006. A number of existing clubs in the league were already fielding African players (as were clubs in Cambodia, Indonesia, Malaysia, Thailand and Vietnam), but Sporting Afrique aimed to field a team comprised exclusively of players from Africa. The club had been established by local investors, who aimed to turn a profit from transfer fees by showcasing players and then on-selling their contracts to other clubs. The club's players, who were recruited predominantly from Nigeria, Ghana, Kenya and Cameroon, were promised salaries of approximately US$1,000 per month. In reality, however, the players were paid only US$60 per month (far below the most basic wage in Singapore) and forced to live six to a room in club-supplied accommodation before the club folded after just one season (BBC, 2006). Further misfortune confronted one of the club's players, Ayi Nii Aryee, when, in a case of life imitating art (or at least a Tom Hanks movie), he found himself trapped in immigration limbo at a airport in the Philippines for six months after his visa to Singapore was cancelled after he quit the club (Bandini, 2006).

TRANSNATIONAL SPORTS LEAGUES

Not only are sports leagues increasingly featuring athletes drawn from across the globe, but there is also movement for leagues themselves to move from a national to transnational foundation such as the Champions League in Europe or the Super 14 rugby competition between teams from Australia, New Zealand and South Africa. Within Asia the Asian Football Confederation Champions League competition has mirrored developments in Europe by moving from a simple knockout competition to a multi-phase group tournament featuring clubs drawn from the Mediterranean to Australia (AFC, 2008).

Another manifestation of this phenomenon is the expansion of national leagues to include clubs from other nations. American leagues have a history of this with expansion including teams from Canada (such as the addition of Toronto FC into Major League Soccer), though the National Hockey League has always included teams from both the US and Canada. In Oceania, several Australian sports leagues have included teams from New Zealand (Higham & Hall, 2003, pp. 135-136). The Singapore Premier League football competition experimented with this concept in 1994 when it added teams from Perth and Darwin in Australia in an effort to boost the profile of the league. Although the teams proved to be an on-field success, with the Perth Kangaroos winning the league the experiment proved to be economically unsustainable (Duke & Crolley, 1996, pp. 64-65).

Ironically, this occurred at the same time Singapore was ending its involvement in what had become another transnational competition, albeit one that was the consequence of the earlier colonial era, the Malaysian League and Cup. Singapore had played in what had originated as the Malaya Cup since its inception in 1921, and continued to compete (alongside another independent state in Brunei-Darussalam) despite the subsequent political changes which included its independence from Malaysia in 1965. Singapore's post-independence participation in these competitions was affected on a number of occasions by the fractious political relationship between the two countries, with the team withdrawn or excluded from competitions on a number of occasions. The final split came in 1995 when Singapore withdrew following an acrimonious debate over gate receipts and match fixing (Duke & Crolley, 1996, pp. 64-65).

In the wake of Singapore's withdrawal from the Malaysian League, a new professional league, the S-League, was established in Singapore.

The league struggled to establish itself and attract spectators, with many local football supporters either lamenting the withdrawal from the Malaysian Cup or preferring the attraction of televised matches from the English Premier League. In an effort to tap new spectators (including large ex-patriot communities living in Singapore, themselves another feature of the globalized economy) and to enhance the competitiveness of the league, the Football Association of Singapore again sought to internationalize the competition. Beginning with the Chinese-backed Sinchi Football Club in 2003, the league experimented with the introduction of "foreign" teams, fielding players drawn exclusively from another country or region, although all matches were played within Singapore. Japanese, Korean and other Chinese teams have competed in subsequent years, with a number of these clubs being established as satellite teams for clubs competing in the Chinese and Japanese leagues (Dalian Shide Siwu, for instance, is an affiliate of Dalian Haichang of the Chinese Super League, who plan to use the Singaporean venture as a farm club to develop young players) (Voon, 2008).

Beyond football, Singapore also gained a franchise in Australia's National Basketball League (NBL), with the Singapore Slingers (the name being a reference to the iconic cocktail associated with Raffles Hotel) entering the league in 2006. Belying its "national" moniker the NBL already contained a franchise based in Auckland, New Zealand, and became the first Australian sporting league to field a team in Asia, which it saw as a lucrative area for future development. Despite the hopes of local basketball officials that the team would help to develop Singaporean basketball players, the side featured an almost entirely foreign player line-up. An attempt was made to counter concerns that this lack of local players would deter attendance by importing overseas players with Asian heritage (including a Malaysian-Australian, Korean-American and Filipino), but the club announced its withdrawal from the league after just two seasons (Murillo, 2008; Voon, 2007).

THE NATION-STATE RESISTANT

The failure of the Slingers, and of other transnational ventures like the World League of American Football/NFL Europe, points towards one of the greatest paradoxes of the global era – the persistence of the local (and particularly the national) in the face of global challenges. The persistence of the state as the most significant agent within global politics, and the inevitable associated phenomenon of rivalries between states, is reflected in the ongoing dispute between Thailand and Cambodia over the Preah Vihear temple complex. Ongoing political and cultural rivalries between the two states have also manifested themselves through sport, including a dispute over the origins of what is now known as *Muay Thai* (kickboxing). Cambodia claims that it is the true home of this form of kickboxing (which they refer to as *Pradal Serey*) and that that the sport has been unfairly appropriated by Thailand, going so far as to boycott *Muay Thai* events at the South East Asian Games in protest over the utilization of the Thai name for the sport (Vail, 2007, p. 122).

Despite the resurgence of the local, however, it is clear that this has occurred in a context of rapid globalization whereby leading leagues with an international presence and media coverage, largely from the US and the UK, have begun to saturate the global market at the expense of the local. As we have suggested, the prominence of the Premier League among local spectators has had serious consequences for professional soccer in the region. Michael Jordan in the 1990s and David Beckham and Tiger Woods since 2000 have clearly been more popular worldwide than local sporting heroes. Thus, the global and the national coalesce uneasily and this has led many nation-states to capitalize on support for the national in attempts to attract the global in the form of mega-events.

STATES AND MEGA-EVENTS

In South East Asia, it has been Malaysia that has most enthusiastically embraced sporting mega-events in recent years. These events were consciously cultivated as part of the Mahathir government's Vision 2020 agenda, a development plan that sought to lift the nation to Newly Industrialized Country (NIC) status by the year 2020 (Muda, 1998). Vision 2020 was an ambitious project that sought to "re-engineer the social, political and economic culture of Malaysia" (Silk, 2001, p. 283), and hosting international sporting events was seen as an important means of both developing domestic infrastructure and raising the international profile of the nation. Among the events that Malaysia has hosted since the mid-1990s are an annual Formula One motorsport Grand Prix, (1999-), the yearly Tour de Langkawi cycling race (1996-), football's FIFA World Youth Championships (1997), the World Squash Open (1997), badminton's Thomas Cup (2002) and the field hockey World Cup in (2002) (Khoo, 2005, p. 57).

The most high-profile of these events was the 1998 Commonwealth Games in Kuala Lumpur, which marked only the second occasion (after Kingston, Jamaica in 1966) that this event had been held outside the old (white dominated) Commonwealth. To fulfil the political objectives that lay behind hosting the Games, Malaysia sought not just to host a successful event but to deliver the most spectacular Commonwealth Games ever. To achieve this it spent more than US$555 million in the process, much of which went on extravagant new venues, despite the country being in the grip of a severe regional economic crisis (Van der Westhuizen, 2004, p. 1277). Silk (2002) has shown how the state-owned host broadcaster mediated the representations of the city and country to further enhance these objectives, reinforcing the vital significance of the media in the contemporary globalized sporting environment.

On the back of what was widely recognized as a successful Commonwealth Games Kuala Lumpur launched a bid to stage the 2008 Olympics, and was joined in the process by another regional city in Bangkok, which had itself successfully hosted the 1996 Asian Games. The International Olympic Committee (IOC) evaluation group, however, decided that neither city was adequately prepared to stage the event and they were not able to progress to the final candidature stage (IOC, 2000). This outcome illustrates concerns that opportunities to host the world's premier sporting events, especially the Olympic Games and the football World Cup, are increasingly becoming the preserve of only a handful of wealthy developed nations. Nauright (2005) notes that

> while there has been a modicum of expansion by major sporting events into the developing world, this process has been slow, uneven and reluctant, a process carefully managed under the guise of stability, security and willingness to conform to the dominant expectations of the industrial and post-industrial core. (p. 209)

The power politics involved in bids for mega-events are not always simply a matter of perpetuating North/South or developed/developing inequalities, however, as Malaysia discovered when it sought to stage the 2000 Asian Cup football tournament. By tradition this event has always alternated between East and West Asia and with the 1996 event having been held in the United Arab Emirates it was seen to be East Asia's turn. In the lead-up to the selection, however, it became known that Middle Eastern delegates had already decided to overturn this rotation and to support a Lebanese bid for the event, in spite of the fact that Malaysia's bid was widely regarded as far superior to that presented by the Lebanese. This decision reflected the reality that, although the AFC may have had its headquarters in Kuala Lumpur, the real power within Asian football now lay in the Middle East, and the Malaysians were forced to make a face-saving withdrawal from the contest (Sugden & Tomlinson, 1998, pp. 158-165).

While most mega-events involve competition between rival bidders and display a trend towards the gargantuan that excludes all but a few wealthy potential hosts, the region's own international games, the South East Asian (SEA) Games, operate according to a very different ethos. Cooperation is emphasized in selecting the host rather than competition, and an attempt is made to rotate the hosting of the event among all of the member nations. To allow the region's smaller states to share in this rotation, the South East Asian Games Federation reshapes the games to fit the needs of the host rather than the other way around. Thus, to enable Vientiane, the capital of Laos, to stage the 2009 edition of the Games the number of sports will be reduced from 45 to 23 to reduce costs and not overburden the small and relatively poor nation (Associated Press, 2007). Such an approach is unique among these types of sporting events and represents a conscious effort by the organizers to utilize these Games as tools for regional development.

NATIONALISM AND SPORT IN SOUTH EAST ASIA

The end of the Cold War itself brought about the break-up of the Soviet Union and Yugoslavia, while the continued expansion of the European Union has boosted the aspirations of nationalists in places such as Scotland and Catalonia who envision statehood within a federated Europe. Such emergent nationalisms are also a significant feature of contemporary South East Asia: Burma faces challenges from numerous ethnic peoples seeking greater representation, Indonesia and the Philippines have fought sustained conflicts with major separatist movements, Thailand is currently facing a renewed insurgency in its south, while Vietnam and Malaysia face their own ethnic and regional challenges (Minchan, 1996).

Within Europe, sport has proved to be an important forum for the expression of emergent nationalism. One approach was that adopted by the national Gaelic Athletic Association in Ireland, which promoted what it billed as indigenous Irish sports as part of its opposition to British rule in Ireland (Mandle, 1987). More widespread has been the practice of sporting teams, usually football clubs, acting as representatives for regional interests on a wider stage. Dynamo Zagreb was an important facet of Croatian nationalism before Croatia attained its independence from Yugoslavia, and, in the most famous example of this phenomenon, Barcelona Football Club stood as a standard-bearer for Catalan national identity within Spain, particularly during the repression of the Franco era (e.g., Foer, 2005).

Such emergent nationalisms appear to be largely absent from the South East Asian sporting scene. This is perhaps the consequence of the growing control of sport by national governments, which have infused sport with a strong ethos of nation building. Brown (2006) has shown, for instance, the way in which the founders of modern Indonesia used the Indonesian National Games to promote national unity in the face of regional, racial and religious challenges. A recent effort was made, however, by the Unrepresented Nations and People's Organization (UNPO), a 69-member global body that includes nationalist movements from within Indonesia, Burma, Cambodia and Vietnam among its membership, to use football to generate publicity for its cause through the staging of a four team UNPO Cup football competition in 2005. Teams representing West Papua and South Moluccas (both regions within the current Indonesian state) took part in the competition held in The Hague, but the event struggled to make any impact with even a sympathetic reporter commenting that "despite [its] grandiose claims, the tournament had the air of a kickabout" (Menary, 2007).

Should any of these regions ever gain independence, then it is likely that sport will be one of the first arenas in which they will seek to display their new national status. Participation in international sport and membership in sporting institutions like FIFA and the IOC brings a level of visible recognition and legitimacy to a state, with Roche (2002) concluding that

> the Olympic Movement and the United Nations have played something of a parallel role in the international sphere in the post-war and post-colonial period. New nations in particular have needed both political and cultural "international arenas" or public spheres in which to display themselves, be recognized and be legitimated. Allowing for exaggeration there is some truth in the view that, albeit in different ways and with different implications, nations could be said to have needed recognition by the Olympic Movement – particularly participation in the periodic ceremonies and sport of the Olympic Games events – almost as much as they have needed recognition by and participation in the United Nations organization. (p. 174)

This was certainly the case when East Timor (Timor Leste) sought independence in 1999. East Timor had been forcibly annexed by Indonesia after the collapse of Portuguese colonial rule in 1975 and a long independence struggle had ensued. Following the withdrawal of Indonesian rule after a referendum in late 1999, the territory had descended into chaos, but the Timorese still sought to send a team to the upcoming Sydney Olympics. Although Timor was lacking its own government or National Olympic Committee by the time of the Games, the IOC was persuaded to allow four athletes to compete in Sydney under the banner of Independent Olympic Athletes (Fowlie & Moss, 2006). The IOC's decision to alter its established protocol for admitting new states (which mandated United Nations membership, membership of International Sporting Federations, and a fully-constituted National Olympic Committee) followed lobbying from both the United Nations and Australia, who believed that Olympic participation would help legitimate the nation-building process that they were leading in Timor (BBC, 2000).

For East Timor, sporting choices also reflected the broader decisions that the new state had to make about its post-independence political orientation. Key among these were the choice of Portuguese rather than English or Indonesian as the new national language and deciding to which of its neighbors, countries in South East Asia or Australia, it should orientate itself towards. In this context, decisions such as choosing to seek membership of the Asian Football Confederation rather than Oceania and participation in the Lusophony Games (the games of the Community of Portuguese Language Countries) are symbolic markers of national ambitions (Associação dos Comités Olímpicos de Língua Oficial Portuguesa [ACOLOP], 2008).

While simply participating in international sporting events may be sufficient for newly-independent states like East Timor, established nations are increasingly seeking validation through sporting success. Links between sporting success and national prestige have existed since the very birth of international sport in the mid-nineteenth century and, despite the opposition of Olympic founder Pierre de Coubertin, nations have looked towards the medal table and victories in other international competitions as a signifier of their international standing since the birth of the modern Olympic Games (e.g., Hoberman, 2004). This accelerated even further during the Cold War era, when international sport became a highly public arena for the ideological battle between the communist and capitalist camps.

The importance of international success did not diminish with the end of the Cold War and, if anything, gaining sporting victories is viewed with even more importance by a large number of national governments. Successful athletes and teams are increasingly garnered with financial rewards by their national governments, and may also be feted with other forms of state recognition like national honors or being depicted on postage stamps. Merely recognizing success is not enough for many states, with an increasing number of governments taking the option of investing state resources into the development of elite sports systems to produce champion athletes. The establishment of the Australian Institute of Sport in 1981 was an important precedent for this trend (Cashman, 1995) that has been increasingly replicated worldwide. The success of Great Britain at the 2008 Beijing Olympic Games, where they finished 4th in the medal table (and one place ahead of Australia), was achieved on the back of substantial state funding of £265 million over the preceding four year cycle (Department of Culture, Media, and Sports [DCMS], 2008). British programs and funding closely followed the Australian model that proved so successful in the last four Summer Olympics. As a result, other nations have followed suit in order to be more competitive. Surprisingly, there appears to be little public comment about whether it is appropriate for states to utilize scarce treasury resources in this quest for sporting dominance even when it is widely known that public resources are diverted from vital infrastructure projects including those for hospitals and schools.

Singapore's government is among those that have decided to invest state funds in the quest for athletic glory. This marked another substantial policy shift for the state, as in 1973 Prime Minister Lee Kuan Yew had declared that it was "foolish and wasteful" to invest in elite sport as "there are no national benefits from gold medallists for small countries" (Horton, 2001, pp. 103-104). By 1993, however, the Singapore Sports Council launched a Sports Excellence (SPEX) program and in 2001 the government-established Committee on Sporting Singapore recommended a further increase in government funding for elite sport on the grounds that "sports excellence helps enhance our national pride and international standing" (Committee on Sporting Singapore, 2001, p. 25). As a consequence, government funding to national sporting federations reached S$31.9 million (over US$22 million) in the lead-up to the Beijing Olympics (Singapore Sports Council, 2007, p. 15).

Singapore's quest for sporting success has also fully embraced the opportunities provided by the global era. Concerned that the national population may be lacking the raw talent for athletic success, national sporting federations and the government launched the Foreign Sports Talent (FST) scheme to persuade overseas athletes to switch their allegiance to the Republic and represent its national teams. In one early example, footballers from Croatia, Nigeria and Brazil who were playing in the Singaporean League were given fast-track citizenship to allow them to turn out for the Lions (as Singapore's national football side is known). Athletes switching national allegiance is not a new phenomenon (with athletes emigrating for personal and occasionally political reasons), but recent examples suggest that some states are increasingly utilizing their economic wealth to offer incentives for athletes to switch as a short-cut to developing a sporting profile. One high-profile case was steeplechaser Saif Saaeed Shaheen, who switched nationality (from Kenya to Qatar), religion and even his name to win Qatar's first gold medal at the World Athletics Championships, although even established sporting nations like the United States are utilizing this practice to boost their Olympic chances (Wilson & Lehren, 2008).

Singapore's leading performers at the Beijing Olympics, its silver-medal winning women's table tennis team (which won the nation's second Olympic medal and the first since 1960) and swimming finalist Tao Li, had all been cultivated under the FST scheme. All were Chinese-born, and were scouted by Singaporean sporting federations while still teenagers and persuaded to switch allegiance. Li Jiawei, captain of the table tennis team, was just 14 when she decided to leave her homeland and family in return for the financial incentives and security offered by Singapore (Lian, 2005, p.

87). Although at one level a prime example of contemporary globalization, the case of these Chinese-born athletes could also be seen as completing a historical circle, as Singapore's first-ever Olympian, footballer Chua Boon Lay, had competed as part of the Chinese team at the 1936 Olympics, which drew its members from both China itself and the wider overseas Chinese diaspora (as did the Chinese team at the 1948 Games, which included a further four Singaporean-born competitors) (Aplin, 2004).

Conclusion

The examples we use illustrate several themes that are present in the relationship of Asian nations and economies to the global sports marketplace. This relationship is highly uneven in nature, has significant social and economic consequences for communities, fan cultures, players, and nation-states. These are not the only problems facing South East Asian nations related to sports. Wheeler and Nauright (2006) show that the rush to build lush golf courses to satisfy demand from local elites and to promote top end tourism have been fraught with significant environmental and social costs to nations and communities in the region. The rush to build courses, win medals, host major events all have economic development objectives but are aimed at elites in the region interfacing with other global business elites rather than local community development. Sport can and should play a role in these areas, but so far the focus has remained quite firmly fixed on competing globally. In the twenty-first century, sport has become an integral part of an increasingly linked sport-media-tourism complex that is vastly uneven in economic terms within societies and between nations. It is clear that, while resistance to the focus on global events for capital accumulation is possible at times, the international organization and presentation of sport serves the interests of global, national and local elites. Sports spectators, participants and communities are increasingly removed from the sporting product whether this is in Europe, North America or South East Asia.

References

ACOLOP. (2008). Historia. *Association of the Portuguese Speaking Olympic Committees*. Retrieved July 16, 2008, from http://www.acolop.info/page.php?page=historia

AFBR. (2007). EPL changes Asian football television programming. *Asian Football Business Review*. Retrieved June 18, 2008, from http://footballdynamicsasia.blogspot.com/2007/08/epl-changes-asian-football-television.html

AFC. (2008). *AFC Champions League: Official guide 2008*. Kuala Lumpur: Asian Football Confederation.

Alexa. (2008). Manutd.com – Traffic details. *Alexa*. Retrieved June 18, 2008, from http://www.alexa.com/data/details/traffic_details/manutd.com

Ampofo-Boateng, K. (2002). Match fixing. In A. Yaacob, K. Ampofo-Boateng, & S. Mazlina (Eds.), *Issues in sport* (pp. 60-65). Kuala Lumpur: Bina Minda Resources.

Aplin, N. (2004). Chinese affiliations and the Olympics: The paradox of Singapore. In K. Wamsley, S. Martyn, & R. Barney (Eds.), *Cultural relations old and new: The transitory Olympic ethos: Proceedings of the seventh international symposium for Olympic research*. London: International Centre for Olympic Studies. Retrieved September 4, 2008, from http://www.la84foundation.org/SportsLibrary/ISOR/ISOR2004r.pdf

Associated Press. (2007). 2009 SEA Games to reduce number of Olympic sports. *International Herald Tribune*. Retrieved August 18, 2008, from http://www.iht.com/articles/ap/2007/12/15/sports/AS-SPT-SEA-Games.php

Bandini, P. (2006). Terminal limbo. *Guardian Sportblog*. Retrieved August 18, 2008, from http://blogs.guardian.co.uk/sport/2006/09/01/terminal_limbo.html

BBC. (2000). Olympic start for East Timor. *BBC News*. Retrieved August 19, 2008, from http://news.bbc.co.uk/1/hi/world/americas/765929.stm

BBC. (2006). Hopes dashed in Singapore. *BBC Sport*. Retrieved July 16, 2008, from http://news.bbc.co.uk/sport1/hi/football/africa/5079434.stm

Black, D., & Van der Westhuizen, J. (2004). The allure of global games for "semi-peripheral" polities and spaces: A research agenda. *Third World Quarterly, 25*(7), 1195-1214.

Bloom, B. (2007). Red Sox, A's Japan bound in 2008. *MLB.com*. Retrieved August 2, 2008, from from http://mlb.mlb.com/news/article.jsp?ymd=20071114&content_id=2300048&vkey=news_mlb&fext=.jsp&c_id=mlb

Bond, D. (2008). Asian bloc to fight Premier League "colonialism." *Daily Telegraph*. Retrieved August 18, 2008, from http://www.telegraph.co.uk/sport/football/2291625/Asian-bloc-to-fight-Premier-League-colonialism.html

Brick, C. (2001). Can't live with them, can't live without them: Reflections on Manchester United. In G. Armstrong & R. Giulianotti (Eds.), *Fear and loathing in world football* (pp. 9-22). Oxford: Berg.

Brown, C. (2006). The Indonesian National Games of 1951 and 1953: Identity, ethnicity and gender. *Proceedings of the 16th biennial conference of the Asian Studies Association of Australia*. Wollongong: ASAA. Retrieved September 4, 2008, from http://coombs.anu.edu.au/SpecialProj/ASAA/biennial-conference/2006/Brown-Colin-ASAA2006.pdf

Cashman, R. (1995). *Paradise of sport*. Oxford: Oxford University Press.

Chang Beer – Everton sponsorship (2006). Retrieved September 1, 2008, from http://www.interbevgroup.com/chang-everton-sponsorship.php

Chaudhary, V., & Gregoriadis, L. (1999, August 21). Floodlights scam to beat bookies: Far Eastern betting syndicate combined region's favourite pastimes, football and gambling, in daring sting. *Guardian*.

Committee on Sporting Singapore. (2001). *Report of the Committee on Sporting Singapore*. Singapore: Ministry of Community Development and Sports.

Darby, P. (2001). The new scramble for Africa: African football labour migration to Europe. In J. Mangan (Ed.), *Europe, sport, world: Shaping global societies* (pp. 217-244). London: Frank Cass.

DCMS. (2008). Team GB best prepared British team ever. *Department of Culture, Media and Sport*. Retrieved August 19, 2008, from http://www.culture.gov.uk/reference_library/media_releases/5361.aspx

Duke, V., & Crolley, L. (1996). *Football, nationality and the state*. Harlow, UK: Longman.

Eason, K. (2008, May 15). Manchester United set for £80m payout. *The Times*. Retrieved August 19, 2008, from http://www.timesonline.co.uk/tol/sport/football/premier_league/manchester_united/article3934447.ece

Foer, F. (2005). *How soccer explains the world: An unlikely theory of globalization*. New York: Harper Perennial.

Fowlie, F., & Moss, P. (2006). *Prayer road*. Frederick, MD: PublishAmerica.

FSF. (2008). Why Premier League matches overseas are wrong. *Football Supporters' Federa-*

tion. Retrieved August 18, 2008, from http://www.fsf.org.uk/uploaded/pressreleases/updatednotogam39fabriefingpaper.pdf

Giulianotti, R. (2005). Playing an aerial game: The new political economy of soccer. In J. Nauright & K. Schimmel (Eds.), *The political economy of sport* (pp. 19-37). Basingstoke, UK: Palgrave.

Hall, C. M. (2005). Selling places: Hallmark events and the reimagining of Sydney and Toronto. In J. Nauright & K. Schimmel (Eds.), *The political economy of sport* (pp. 129-151). Basingstoke: Palgrave.

Harris, N. (2007). Premiership prize pot up to $2.7bn following new TV deal. *Independent*. Retrieved August 18, 2008, from http://www.independent.co.uk/sport/football/premier-league/premiership-prize-pot-up-to-16327bn-following-new-tv-deal-432713.html

Higham, J., & Hall, C. (2003). Sport tourism in Australia and New Zealand: Responding to a dynamic interface. *Journal of Sport Tourism*, 8(3), 131-143.

Hoberman, J. (2004). Sportive nationalism and globalization. In. J. Bale & M. K. Christiansen (Eds.), *Post-Olympism?: Questioning sport in the twenty-first century* (pp. 177-188). Oxford: Berg.

Horne, J., & Manzenreiter, W. (Eds.). (2006). *Sports mega-events: Social scientific analyses of a global phenomenon*. Oxford: Blackwell.

Horton, P. (2001). Complex creolization: The evolution of modern sport in Singapore. In J. Mangan (Ed.), *Europe, sport, world: Shaping global societies* (pp. 77-104). London: Frank Cass.

House of Lords. (2002). Judgements – Grobbelaar (Appellant) vs. News Group Newspapers Ltd. and another (respondents). *United Kingdom Parliament. Retrieved August 18, 2008, from* http://www.publications.parliament.uk/pa/ld200102/ldjudgmt/jd021024/grobb-1.htm

IOC. (2000). *Candidate acceptance procedure games of the XXIX Olympiad 2008: Report by the IOC candidature acceptance working group*. Lausanne: International Olympic Committee.

Khoo, S. (2005). *Sport for all in Malaysia: Policy and practice*. Kuala Lumpur: University of Malaya Press.

Lenskyj, H. (2008). *Olympic industry resistance: Challenging Olympic power and propaganda*. Albany: State University of New York Press.

Lian, N. (2005). Love and the city – Interview with table tennis prodigy Li Jiawei. In P. Hwa (Ed.), *In the spotlight: Stories of Singapore sports celebrities* (pp. 83-101). Singapore: Candid Creation Publishing.

Lim, L. (2008, February 17). Secondary League: S-League plays second fiddle to the EPL, which boasts world-class action. *Straits Times*.

Mandle, W. (1987). *The Gaelic Athletic Association and Irish nationalist politics, 1884-1924*. London: C. Helm.

Menary, S. (2007). *Outcasts! The lands FIFA forgot*. Studley, UK: Know the Score Books.

Minchan, J. (1996). *Nations without states: A historical dictionary of contemporary national movements*. Westport: Greenwood Press.

Muda, M. (1998). The significance of the Commonwealth Games in Malaysia's foreign policy. *Round Table*, 346, 211-226.

Murillo, M. (2008, May 6). Give and go; Pinoy import. *Businessworld*.

Nauright, J. (2005). The political economy of sport in the twenty-first century. In J. Nauright & K. Schimmel (Eds.), *The political economy of sport* (pp. 208-214). Basingstoke: Palgrave.

Nauright, J., & Ramfjord, J. (in-press). Who owns England's game? American professional sporting influences and foreign ownership in the Premier League. *Soccer and Society*.

New York Yankees (2008, January 30). *Press release: New York Yankees and Chinese Baseball Association reach landmark agreement*.

Phongpaichit, P., & Baker, C. (2004). *Thaksin: The business of politics in Thailand*. Chiang Mai: Nordic Institute of Asian Studies.

Reuters. (2008). *Malaysia shows door to foreign players.* Retrieved August 18, 2008, from http://uk.reuters.com/article/UK_WORLDFOOTBALL/idUKSP15427320080803

Roche, M. (2002). The Olympics and "global citizenship." *Citizenship Studies, 6*(2), 165-181.

Rucai, L. (2004). Phillips in China: Fishing with a long line. *China Today.* Retrieved September 1, 2008, from http://www.chinatoday.com.cn/English/e2004/e200406/p37.htm

Sandvoss, C. (2003). *A game of two halves: Football, television and globalisation.* London: Routledge.

Sallihundin, A. (2004). *Power of dreams: 50 years of the Asian Football Confederation.* Shah Alam: Times Editions – Marshall Cavendish.

Silk, M. (2001). Together we're one? The "place" of the nation in media representations of the 1998 Kuala Lumpur Commonwealth Games. *Sociology of Sport Journal, 18*(3), 227-301.

Silk, M. (2002). "Bangsa Malaysia"; global sport, the city and the mediated refurbishment of global identities. *Media, Culture & Society, 24,* 775-794.

Singapore Sports Council. (2005). *National sports participation survey 2005.* Singapore: Singapore: Singapore Sports Council.

Singapore Sports Council. (2007). *Leading the field: Singapore Sports Council annual report 2006/2007.* Singapore: Singapore Sports Council

S-League. (1996). *The S-League handbook: Season 1996.* Singapore: Singapore Professional Football League Private Limited.

Sugden, J., & Tomlinson, A. (1998). *FIFA and the contest for world football: Who rules the people's game?* Cambridge: Polity Press.

Vail, P. (2007). Thailand's Khmer as "invisible minority": Language, ethnicity and cultural politics in north-eastern Thailand. *Asian Ethnicity, 8*(2), 111-130.

Van der Westhuizen, J. (2004). Marketing Malaysia as a model modern Muslim state: The significance of the 16th Commonwealth Games. *Third World Quarterly, 25*(7), 1277-1291.

Voon, T. (2007, April 25). Slingers short on local flavour: BAS hopes that national players will play more in Australian NBL. *Straits Times.*

Voon, T. (2008, January 30). China's top club, Dalian, to join S-League. *Straits Times.*

Wheeler, K., & Nauright, J. (2006). A green game?: A global perspective on the environmental impact of golf. *Sport in Society, 9*(3), 427-443.

Whitson, D., & Horne, J. (2006). Underestimated costs and overestimated benefits? Comparing the outcomes of sports mega-events in Canada and Japan. In J. Horne & W. Manzenreiter (Eds.), *Sports mega-events: Social scientific analyses of a global phenomenon* (pp. 73-89). Oxford: Blackwell.

Williams, J. (2001). Kopites, "Scallies" and Liverpool fan cultures: Tales of triumph and disasters. In J. Williams, S. Hopkins, & K. Long (Eds.), *Passing rhythms: Liverpool FC and the transformation of football* (pp. 99-128). Oxford: Berg.

Wilson, D., & Lehren, A. (2008, June 15). Swapping passports in pursuit of Olympic medals. *New York Times.* Retrieved August 17, 2008, from http://www.nytimes.com/2008/06/15/sports/olympics/15citizen.html?_r=1&pagewanted=all&oref=slogin

• CHAPTER NINE •

Globalization, Tourism Development, and Japanese Lifestyle Migration to Australia

JUN NAGATOMO
University of Queensland

In the 1970s, Australia underwent a dramatic social transformation. Increased transnational population and financial flows as well as new political, social and cultural forces prompted the nation to reconsider its "White Australia" policy and adopt multiculturalism "as a method for dealing with the consequence of ethnically diverse immigration" (Jupp, 2002, p. 101). Australia subsequently accepted large numbers of Asian immigrants in the 1980s and 1990s (Ang & Stratton, 1996; Castle, Foster, Iredale, & Withers, 1998; Jayasuriya & Kee, 1999; Jupp, 2002; Viviani, 1984). Over the same period, Australia also increased its overseas tourist numbers and revenues, especially from Japan (Bell & Carr, 1994; Bureau of Tourism Research & David H. Jacobs Consultants [BTR & DHJC], 1992; Hadju 2005).

One clear sign of globalization in Australia has been a rise in the visible presence of Japanese in the nation. In South East Queensland, which attracted Japanese tourism investment in the late 1980s, Japanese tourists and working holidaymakers are a common sight (Bell & Carr, 1994; Dept. of Immigration, Multiculturalism & Indigenous Affairs [DIMIA], 2003; Hadju, 2005; Tourism Australia, 2005; Tourism Queensland, 2005). Moreover, the number of Japanese permanent and long-term residents has increased since the 1990s, when Japan suffered from an economic recession. According to the Ministry of Foreign Affairs (2006), there were 52,970 Japanese in Australia in 2005, including 25,315 permanent residents and 27,655 long-term residents (e.g., working holidaymakers, retirement visa holders, etc.). The 2001 Australian Census indicates that the Japanese population in Australia increased by 11 percent from 1996 to 2001 (DIMIA, 2003). While 25.7 percent of the Japanese population in Australia live in Queensland, the largest concentration of Japanese is in New South Wales, where 40.1 percent reside (DIMIA, 2003). The Japanese community in Queensland is smaller compared to that of New South Wales; however, the Queensland Japanese community is characterized by its growing population and involvement in the tourism industry (Bell & Carr, 1994; BTR & DHJC, 1992; Hadju 2005).

Moreover, a new type of migration has been increasing among Japanese in Australia since the 1990s. Research by Sato (2001) and Nagatomo (2007a, 200b) suggests that the majority of Japanese coming to Australia do so for lifestyle purposes. This form of migration, which Sato (2001) calls "lifestyle migration" (p. 66), is characterized by the following factors: 1) economic motives are less important for Japanese than other Asian migrants (Nagatomo, 2007a, p. 1); 2) the majority of Japanese do not migrate permanently, except for those married to Australian partners (Nagatomo 2007a, p. 1); 3) Japanese migrants commonly retain their citizenship, visit Japan regularly, and maintain ties with their home community in Japan (Nagatomo, 2007a, p. 13).

The above characteristics of Japanese migrants raise two important questions. First, why have Japanese found Australia such an attractive destination? Second, what is the correlation between tourism development and Japanese lifestyle migration to Queensland since the 1990s? Focusing on Japanese migrants in Queensland, this chapter examines the relationship between tourism development in Australia and the decision making of Japanese migrants in Australia by using qualitative data obtained from fieldwork conducted in South East Queensland, Australia from June 2006 to May 2007.

TOURISM DEVELOPMENT AND JAPANESE TOURISTS

Tourism development was closely associated with Australia's high unemployment levels during the 1970s and early 1980s. At that time, Australia's manufacturing sector declined, making tourism development attractive to policymakers at all levels of government (Carroll, 1991, p. 7). Supported by stakeholders in the tourism industry, the federal government took two important steps to attract tourism. First, it promoted deregulation in the airline industry to encourage competition and hence lower airfares. The domestic airline industry was deregulated in the 1970s, with the international airline industry following in the 1980s. Second, it relaxed controls on foreign investment in the late 1970s to attract foreign funds toward Australian tourism development. This policy was highly successful. From 1987 to 1988, the federal government approved a total of AU$1.8 billon in foreign investment for tourism. According to the Bureau of Tourism Research (1999), in 1996-97 the tourism industry directly contributed 5.4 per cent of GDP at factor cost and its indirect effects added a further 3.5 per cent of GDP at factor cost (p. 1).

During the investment boom, Queensland in particular attracted foreign funds owing to its geographical location and favorable policies adopted by local governments. Queensland was a popular location primarily of Japanese investors who had benefited from Japan's "bubble economy" in the 1980s and early 1990s, and the scale and speed of development by these investors resulted in protest campaigns by local residents in some areas such as Yeppoon and the Gold Coast (Hajdu, 2005; Viviani & Selby, 1980). In Queensland in the late 1980s, Japanese investors focused particularly on real estate in Cairns and the Gold Coast. In 1983-84, AU$9 million was invested in real estate by Japanese investors. Japanese investment increased from AU$85 million in 1984-85 to AU$1.005 billion in 1985-86 and AU$8.443 billion in 1988-89 (Hadju, 2005, p. 25).

As a result of Australian efforts aimed at tourism development, the number of overseas arrivals increased substantially. In 1975, about 516,000 short-term visitors came to Australia; however, this figure increased to 1.1 million in 1985 (BTR, 1989). The number continued to rise in the 1990s, and it reached 4.1 million in 1996 and 5.2 million in 2004 (Australian Bureau of Statistics [ABS], 2006).

Among these incoming visitors, an increase in Japanese was a notable trend. In 1980, Japanese visitors, including tourists, businessmen and others, totalled 48,860 (Tourism Australia, 2005, p. 2). In 1987, this rose to 215,560, and in 1989 it reached 349,540 (BTR, 1991, p. 7). The number of Japanese continued to increase until 1996, when it surged to more than 800,000 persons. Among the Japanese entering Australia a defining characteristic was a high percentage of tourists among visitors (See Table 1).

Table 1 indicates the main reasons individuals from the top five countries of origin visited Australia in the year ended March 2005. In 2004, Japanese visitors represented the second largest group after New Zealanders; however, the percentage of tourists among Japanese visitors was much higher than that of other countries. The number of Japanese who visited for holidays/leisure was 549,701, constituting 83.2 percent of Japanese visitors. This ratio was much higher than that of New Zealand (46.5 percent), the United Kingdom (52.9 percent), and the United States (44.2 percent). Furthermore, the figure for Queensland was much higher than for other states. In 2004, the number of Japanese tourists was 403,432, comprising 88.1 percent of Japanese visitors to Queensland (Tourism Queensland, 2005, p. 7). In addition, Australia has become a common tourist destination for young Japanese females. In 2000, female visitors between the ages of 20 to 29 accounted for 62.4 percent of Japanese visitors to Australia (Ministry of Land, Infrastructure and Transport [MLIT], 2001). Considering the high percentage of tourists among female visitors and low percentage of business visitors, Australia can be perceived as a major destination for Japanese tourists, particularly Japanese female tourists. In addition to being encouraged by policy changes

Table 1 *Purpose of Visits to Australia – Top 5 Sources for Year Ended March 2005*

	Holiday/Leisure		Visiting friends/relatives		Business		Other	
	Visitors	%	Visitors	%	Visitors	%	Visitors	%
New Zealand	442,358	46.5	265,517	27.9	188,146	19.8	54,620	5.7
Japan	549,701	83.2	33,688	5.1	38,253	5.8	39,207	5.9
United Kingdom	346,553	52.9	234,312	35.8	46,164	7.0	27,821	4.2
Europe (excl. UK and Germany)	225,985	55.2	89,535	21.9	47,273	11.5	46,775	11.4
United States	180,154	44.2	85,927	21.1	88,246	21.7	53,015	13.0
Total international visitors	2,665,781	54.4	1,040,462	21.2	709,020	14.5	481,604	9.8

Source: Tourism Queensland (2005).

within Australia, the increase of Japanese tourists to Australia can be linked to the expansion of the overseas tourism market in Japan. During the recession of the 1990s, FIT (Foreign Independent Travel) – in Japanese *kojin-tehai-ryoko* (individual arranged trip) – became the most common method to have overseas trips for Japanese. In contrast to the guided tour, which had been common until the beginning of the 1990s, FIT was promoted as a packaged tour product containing only transport and accommodation and characterized by its moderate price. With FIT, tourists were attracted to the idea that they could engage in private travel through a packaged tour. Another selling point was that the choice of optional tours at tourist destinations made schedules and activities more flexible for tourists. The increased popularity of FIT since the 1990s has been reflective of general leisure trends among Japanese, which have witnessed a shift from group-oriented to more personalized forms of leisure (Nagatomo, 2006).

The increase in the number of Japanese overseas tourists in the 1990s also owed a lot to young female tourists. The percentage of female tourists aged in their twenties was about twice as high as that of males throughout the 1990s. For instance, females aged 20 to 29 accounted for 39.8 percent of tourists in 1991, while males of the same generation constituted only 19.5 percent (MLIT, 2001). Likewise, the number of females in their twenties was 32 percent in 2000 while that of males was 16.1 percent (MLIT, 2001).

Numerous factors account for the high numbers of Japanese female tourists. The consumer-oriented outlook of young single females is one important factor that must be considered. The average propensity to consume (APC) of female householders in their twenties was approximately 87 percent in 2003, higher than that of males from the same generation (Statistics Bureau, 2004). Also significant was an increase of single people living with parents, with so-called "parasite singles" a social issue in the 1990s (Yamada, 1999). The percentage of single females living with their parents increased from 59.2 percent in 1986 to 71.8 percent in 2001, while that of males increased from 53.8 percent in 1986 to 64.2 percent in 2001 (Ministry of Health, Labor & Welfare, 2003). Living with parents provides young individuals with a degree of financial stability, even though they live on part-time incomes. Such young people living with their parents also have disposable income to spend on international travel. In 2002, while single men on average spent ¥1,892 for package tours per month, single women spent ¥3,340 (Statistics Bureau, 2001). A higher ratio of Japanese females engaged in part-time employment and increased leisure time among single "office ladies" (female general office employees) also contributed to the overseas tourism boom in the 1990s. The percentage of part-time employees among the female labor force aged between 24 and 34 in 1985 was about 26 percent and it increased to about 31 percent in 2003 (Statistics Bureau, 2007). Such women were more likely to take overseas trips on their holidays due to the flexibility of their schedules. Additionally, even full-time female workers other than career women in Japan find it relatively easier to enjoy holidays compared to full-time male workers given their relatively shorter working hours.

JAPANESE LIFESTYLE MIGRATION TO AUSTRALIA

Research Method and Research Area

For this project, the researcher conducted 31 in-depth interviews with both Japanese permanent residents and long-term residents who migrated after the 1970s. The interviews were conducted after one year of participant observation as well as library work. Mason (1996) refers to participant observation as "methods of generating data which involve the researcher immersing herself or himself in a research setting, and systematically observing dimensions of that setting, interactions, relationships, actions, events and so on" (p. 60). In this regard, the participant observation of the Japanese community in the research area enabled the researcher to gain an in-depth understanding of the community and also assisted the development of questions for the in-depth interviews upon which the research was based.

Burgess (1984) refers to the in-depth interview as "conversation with a purpose," with the method characterized by flexibility for both the researcher and interviewee (p. 102). The advantage of in-depth interviews is that the researcher can obtain a deeper understanding of informants' perspectives through their own words. One disadvantage of the method, on the other hand, is the possibility of a gap in ethnographic context between informants and the fieldworker (Crapanzano, 1990, p. 281). Other limitations include the "researcher effect" (Hammersley, 2003, p. 344) and interference from the presence of recording devices (Lee, 2004, p. 879; Speer & Hutchby, 2003, p. 317). However, as classic examples such as Willis (1977) reveal, building personal nexus and credibility can lead to highly detailed and informative narratives. In the present case, the researcher's status of being Japanese in Australia was beneficial in eliciting a more detailed narrative as it enabled the researcher to share a common language and cultural outlook with interviewees.

The research for this chapter was conducted in Brisbane, the Gold Coast and the Sunshine Coast, an area generally referred to as South East Queensland (Figure 1). Some use the term South East Queensland in a much broader sense, to include other inland cities such as Toowoomba or areas north of Sunshine Coast such as Bundaberg. Others use the term in a narrow sense, meaning only coastal cities from the Sunshine Coast to

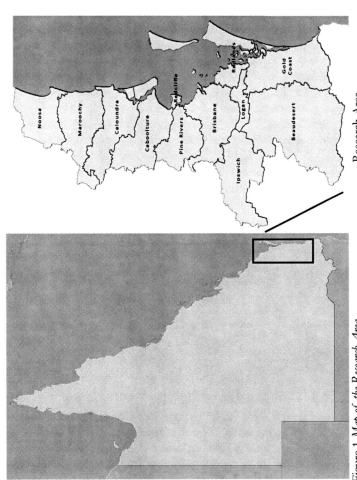

Figure 1 *Map of the Research Area*
Source: GNU Free Licensed Maps, http://commons.wikimedia.org/wiki/Image:Queesland_location_map.png

areas north of Sunshine Coast such as Bundaberg. Others use the term to mean only coastal cities from the Sunshine Coast to the Gold Coast. The present chapter adheres to the latter definition. As far as census data is concerned, most Japanese in Queensland live in the Gold Coast, Brisbane or Cairns, so this definition accurately represents the main subjects of the study. The reason for choosing South East Queensland as the specific region of study was that this area is a common destination for both Japanese tourists and migrants. Given that the relationship between tourism and migration was a key research question for this project, the area's popularity in both regards was a key factor for selecting South East Queensland as the research field.

The number of Japanese in Australia and the research area is as follows. According to the Ministry of Foreign Affairs (2006), Japanese in Australia in 2005 totalled 52,970, with 25,315 permanent residents and 27,655 long-term residents. In Queensland, there were 13,132 Japanese in 2005, including 7,221 permanent and 5,911 long-term residents. 2,460 were in Northern Queensland above Mackay including Cairns and surrounding areas, and 10,672 were in Southern Queensland, including Brisbane and the Gold Coast (see Table 2).

Table 2 *Parent Population: Japanese in the Research Area with Male to Female Ratio*

		Total	Permanent residents	Long-term residents
Research area	Male	3,988 (37.4%)	2,288 (38.2%)	1,700 (36.3%)
	Female	6,684 (62.6%)	3,706 (61.8%)	2,978 (63.7%)
	Total	10,672	5,994	4,678
Australia total	Male	19,405 (36.6%)	9,189 (36.3%)	10,216 (36.9%)
	Female	33,565 (63.4%)	16,126 (63.7%)	17,439 (33.1%)
	Total	52,970	25,315	27,655

Source: Ministry of Foreign Affairs (2006).

Imbalances in gender and age structure are prominent in this population. People in the prime working age range of 25 to 49 years comprise 49.4 percent of the population, and females account for 63.3 percent (Nagata, 2001, p. 225). The gender imbalance is largely the result of the recent migration of Japanese women married to Australian men (Nagata & Nagatomo, 2007, p. 29).

The 2001 census taken by the Australian government does not indicate that Japanese in the research area have a tendency to concentrate in particular suburbs or form ethnic enclaves. However, a concentration of population can be seen among short-term residents and some long-term residents (e.g., working holidaymakers) who were not counted in the census. Direct observation indicated that a large population of Japanese working holidaymakers frequent or live near Surfer's Paradise, although those who have retired are distributed around retirement villages and the Gold Coast suburbs. Brisbane is a common place for Japanese students; however, they are not concentrated in a specific suburb.

At the end of 2006, Japanese in the research area had one ethnic organization in the Gold Coast and two in Brisbane, in addition to several business-related organizations. One of the clubs in Brisbane, the Japanese Society of Brisbane (JSB), was mainly for workers and their families in Japanese companies; they managed a Japanese school. The other, the Japan Club of Queensland (JCQ), in which the researcher conducted participant observation, was run mainly by permanent residents. These two clubs in Brisbane agreed to unite in 2007 and work together as a single ethnic community organization.

Roughly eight types of Japanese residents were observed (see Figure 2) during the course of research. The following typology helps to grasp the current situation of the Japanese community.

Permanent residents

-Cross-cultural marriage
 -War brides
  -Contemporary marriage

-General skilled migration (e.g., Subclass 136, 138, 856)
 -Migrants in the 1980s
 -Migrants since the 1990s

Long-term residents

-Business visa holders
-Retirement visa holders
-Students visa holders
-Working holiday makers

Figure 2 *Typology of Japanese Residents in the Research Area*
Source: Nagatomo (2008a, p. 174).

Figure 2 shows the typology of Japanese residents in the research area based on participant observation. Japanese residents can be roughly divided into two categories, according to the visa status of permanent visa holders and others. The permanent visa holders belong to two sub-categories. One sub-category is the permanent visa holders through cross-cultural marriage, and the other is the general skilled migrants who have independently immigrated to Australia. There are two generational groups among Australian-Japanese couples. War brides who migrated to Australia in the 1950s belong to the first group; the majority of these women in the research area belong to the Japan Club of Queensland.

The second group consists of younger women with Australian partners, with the majority of the women in their thirties to forties.

Skilled migrants are also comprised of two groups. One consists of migrants from the late 1980s, with the majority currently in their fifties and sixties. Most of them are individuals from middleclass backgrounds who had prior job experience in Japan. The majority of the migrants from the 1980s moved to Australia to attain a semi-retired lifestyle; however, those who have stayed in Australia generally have achieved economic success based on their job skills and experience. The other group of general skilled migrants consists of those who have migrated after the 1990s. The majority of these individuals are in their thirties to forties and migrated after working for Japanese companies.

Due to the "point system" associated with Australian immigration policy, there are not so many migrants without work experience in Japan; however, some Japanese working holidaymakers receive permanent visa sponsorship from Australian companies. On the other hand, long-term residents can be divided into four categories – business visa holders, retirement visa holders, student visa holders, and working holiday visa holders. Some business visa holders work for Japanese or Australian companies, and others run businesses such as Japanese restaurants, mainly in Brisbane and the Gold Coast. In addition, the Gold Coast attracts Japanese retirees and working holidaymakers, while Brisbane attracts Japanese students (Nagatomo, 2008b, p. 190).

Profile of the Respondents

The respondents in this study were recruited through "snowball sampling" (Biernacki & Waldorf, 1981, p. 141), in this case through personal introductions and referrals from "gatekeepers" in the Japanese community, such as community leaders and members of community organizations. Any sampling method poses a risk of mismatch between the sample and general population; therefore, the verification of the sample is a necessary process. The following section describes the profile of the respondents and verifies the sample.

The total number of respondents for the in-depth interviews in this project was 31. Their age structure is shown in Table 3. Among the respondents, 14 were male (45.2 percent) and 17 were female (54.8 percent). Compared to the parent population of Japanese in the research area, the ratio of interviewed females in relation to males was about 8 percent lower. However, the gender imbalance in the parent population is largely due to the number of Japanese females married to Australian men as well as war brides who arrived in Australia in the 1950s (Coughlan, 1999; Nagata, 2001). If we consider these Japanese as what Sato (2001) calls "circumstantial migrants" (p. 22) and note that they are not the main focus of the study, the gap between the sample and statistical population is not as significant.

Table 3 *Age and Gender Distribution among Respondents*

	Twenties	Thirties	Forties	Fifties	Sixties	Total
Male	1 (7.1%)	7 (50%)	2 (14.3%)	3 (21.4%)	1 (7.1%)	14
Female	2 (11.8%)	8 (47.1%)	2 (11.8%)	3 (17.6%)	2 (11.8%)	17

Among 31 respondents, there were 26 permanent visa holders and 5 long-term visa holders. Eight of the 26 (30.8 percent) permanent visa holders have obtained permanent residency through cross-cultural marriage, and 4 of the 8 Australian-Japanese couples married after their working holiday in Australia and chose to remain in Australia.

The ratio of those obtaining Australian citizenship among the respondents was 14 percent lower than in the 2001 census data. Two of the 26 (7.7 percent) permanent residents have obtained Australian citizenship. However, this discrepancy can be attributed to the fact that the ratio of citizenship among war brides is high in the census data. As far as the researcher's participant observation is concerned, it would be safe to say that the ratio of 7.7 per cent reflects the actual state of Japanese residents in the research area.

As for the occupation of respondents before and after migration, this data is shown in Tables 4 and 5. Table 4 shows the occupation of the respondents in Australia. "Office clerk" was the most common occupation among female migrants, accounting for 22.6 percent of the total. "Professional" was also common among Japanese migrants, representing 19.4 percent of all interviewees. "Retired and semi-retired" made up 12.9 percent. The table indicates that the majority of the respondents belong to the middleclass in Australia.

On the other hand, Table 5 presents the occupation of respondents before their migration. "Office clerk" was the most common occupation, accounting for 29 percent of the total, and it was especially common among female respondents. "Professional" constituted 22.6 percent. "Manager" accounted for 19.4 percent; however, no female respondents selected this occupational title. In comparing Table 4 and Table 5, it can be said that as a general trend the respondents experienced downward social mobility. This can be seen in the decrease of the ratio of those in the category of "Manager," which was 19.4 percent in Table 5 and 9.7 percent in Table 4, as well as the increase of "Retired and Semi-retired" persons, which made up 0 percent in Table 5 and 12.9 percent in Table 4. Another characteristic of the statistics is that a high percentage of individuals identified themselves under the category "office clerk" before migration, particularly females.

Table 4 *Occupation in Australia*

	Office clerk	Manager	Business owner	Professional	Researcher/ teacher	Factory worker	House- keeping	Student	Retired/ semi-retired	Unemployed
Male	1	2	3	2	1	1	0	2	1	1
Female	6	1	0	4	2	0	1	0	3	0
Total	7	3	3	6	3	1	1	2	4	1
%	22.6%	9.7%	9.7%	19.4%	9.7%	3.2%	3.2%	6.5%	12.9%	3.2%

Table 5 *Occupation before Migration*

	Office clerk	Manager	Business owner	Professional	Researcher/ teacher	Factory worker	House- keeping	Student	Retired/ semi-retired	Other
Male	1	6	1	4	1	0	0	0	0	1
Female	8	0	1	3	2	0	1	2	0	1
Total	9	6	2	7	3	0	1	2	0	2
%	29.0%	19.4%	6.5%	22.6%	9.7%	0%	3.2%	6.5%	0%	6.5%

LIFESTYLE AS A MOTIVATION FOR MIGRATION

From the perspective of migration studies, the Asian middleclasses who are a part of the transnational population flows into Australia can be viewed as "new migrants." What characterizes the new migrants is that lifestyle choice plays a significant role in prompting them to migrate. For instance, migrants from Hong Kong in the 1990s emigrated to Australia and other Western countries mainly for political reasons or the education of the children (Wong, 1992) as well as quality of life (Ley & Kobayashi, 2005). Ip, Wu, and Inglis (1998) describe how contemporary middleclass Taiwanese immigrated to Australia not only for economic reasons but also for lifestyle factors such as educational benefits, family and personal ties, and a fondness for Australia. Sato (2001), Shiobara (2005) and Mizukami (2006) also refer to the importance of lifestyle factors for Japanese migration to Australia. In looking at lifestyle migration in the existing research, geographical studies conducted in Western nations have examined both domestic and international lifestyle-motivated migration mainly from the perspective of counter-urbanism as well as the return to an Arcadian lifestyle. For instance, research by Burnley and Murphy (2004) discusses the increase of domestic migration from Australian inner cities to surrounding areas in relation to anti-urban/pro-rural sentiment. Swaffield and Fairweather (1998) also assess lifestyle migration to rural areas of New Zealand from a similar perspective. Salva-Thomas (2002) suggests British and German migration toward Spain's Balearic Islands is motivated by a quest for a more leisurely lifestyle, and McHugh and Mings (1996) also discuss elderly seasonal migration between northern states and Phoenix, Arizona in the United States along these lines. These studies share a similar view as this study as they recognize lifestyle as a broad pull factor that entices individuals to migrate.

The interview data in this project demonstrated that lifestyle factors are especially important for Japanese migration to Australia. For instance, responses to an open-ended question, "What were the most important factors in your deciding to migrate to Australia?" were dominated by lifestyle factors. The most common response to the question was "escape from the work-oriented lifestyle of Japan." It was referred to by 14 respondents (45 percent) among the 31 respondents. In conjunction with this, "time with family" was also mentioned by 9 respondents (29 percent) as a decisive factor. "Interest in/longing for a life in a foreign/English speaking county" was referred to by 13 respondents (42 percent), and it was relatively common among young female respondents. Other than these reasons, "the mild climate in Australia," "escape from poor living standards in Japan (e.g., urban life, expensive commodity/property prices)," and "nature/beaches/open spaces in Australia" were mentioned by more than 20 percent of the respondents; "gender inequity in Japanese society" was referred to by 2 (12 percent) of the 12 female respondents. The following extracts of respondents who had experienced a hectic lifestyle in Japan are typical responses that show the importance of such factors as "escape from a work-oriented lifestyle" and "time with family." A respondent in his forties, who had a company-oriented lifestyle in Japan and currently has a semi-retired life in Australia, noted:

> I didn't want to sacrifice work, my family or my private time. In Japan the ratio seems to be 90 percent work, 8 percent family and 2 percent my own time, besides time for sleeping.... I think I have achieved what I hoped for before migration. Being able to do what is quite normal here, like eating evening meals with my family everyday, probably means that my ideals were achieved. Though I spend less time working, I do not think my productivity has changed. Recently, I have felt quite busy due to an increased workload...However, I still manage to cook the evening meal everyday and ferry our child about. This is possible because I don't have to stay at work till around 11 p.m. like in Japan.

Similarly, a respondent in his fifties, who used to have a busy lifestyle in Japan but now works part-time in Australia, stated:

> Work and leisure are balanced in my life. In the end, it depends on time and money. If one works for money, time will be scarce. I feel good now that I can have my own time. Even on a Monday, after [giving] my morning lesson [for a part-time job], I can still go to the golf driving range in the afternoon, a kind of lifestyle which seems impossible in Japan.... Apart from golf, I have also enjoyed fishing and playing with radio-controlled model airplanes.

As is shown in the responses above, "balance between work and leisure" and "time with family" were mentioned commonly. Such comments were prominent among those who had work-oriented lifestyles in Japan. For such individuals, relatively shorter working hours in Australia have improved their quality of life, providing them with more time for their families in particular. The respondents' emphasis on quality of life also means they are relatively indifferent to upward social mobility after migration, unlike many other migrants. Although the majority of Japanese, having passed the "point system" of Australian immigration, were directly incorporated into the middleclass in Australia after migration, few respondents were visibly enthusiastic or ambitious about raising their economic status in their adopted nation. Owing to their experience with a work-oriented culture in Japan, migration for such individuals has become a way to pursue their ideal of a lifestyle in which work and leisure are more balanced.

On the question of living standards in Japanese cities and the attraction of an Australian lifestyle, the following responses reflect the general sentiments of Japanese migrants from urban areas in Japan. A male respondent, in his thirties, who had a stressful life working in the TV industry noted:

> In general, there are many good things in Japanese society, but as far as our lifestyle is concerned, it seems a little uncomfortable to live in, for example, managing time, crowded trains, the education system and poor public administration. I think it would not be a fruitful life wasting time and energy for these things.

The perspective above is shared by most Japanese who critically view their own society. As the respondent noted, problems in education and government are typically associated with an "uncomfortable" life in Japan. A common characteristic of respondents critical of Japan is that they are indifferent to the notion of reforms in Japan. Rather than trying to change Japan's system, they escaped from it by means of migration. A male respondent in his fifties with a semi-retired life in Australia noted:

> Why do so many people gather in Tokyo? It is because the government does nothing to counter it.... If Tokyo is too small for its huge population, its functions as a city could be maintained for example by limiting the number of issued car licence plates, like in Singapore, or by implementing a park-and-ride system, as seen here, but no steps are taken. There are no limits or boundaries.... This can also be seen in how companies all close for the holidays at the same time and cause major holiday crowds and traffic jams.

For this respondent, who had overseas experience through his shipping company business, the paradoxical nature of Japanese society was so visible that he complained about Japan when asked about his reasons for migration. As described above, he was dissatisfied with Japanese society, and his dissatisfaction acted as push factor in his decision to migrate.

In addition to imbalances in Japanese society and the lure of an Australian lifestyle, respondents cited other practical reasons associated with lifestyle or quality of life for migrating. For instance, "education for children" was mentioned by 4 respondents (13 percent). Here, the Japanese mass examination system has become a "push factor," and at the same time a less competitive Australian education system has become a "pull factor." The following response illustrates this point. A male respondent in his fifties, who migrated to Australia after working for a major Japanese company and currently works part-time in Australia, remarked:

> Of all the developed countries in the world, only Japan still has the mass exam system. When I said this to my son, who grew up in Aus-

tralia, he said, 'Why would you have to sit for an exam to go to university? If you can go to university by passing an exam, what would you go to high school for?' In Japan there is a tendency to disregard the process and do whatever it takes to pass the university entrance exam, going to cram schools and so on. Students seem to feel there is no point in listening to the teachers at high school. Ideally, the most important criteria for entering university should be assessment by the teachers at high school, like if they say 'Good work, I'll give you an 'A'. This is normal practice here and so students listen more to what the teachers say and the value of teachers has increased.

This father's response can be seen as typical among those who have a negative impression of the Japanese education system. For such individuals, Japanese education is considered stifling and oppressive while Australian education is seen as flexible and liberal. At the same time, the importance of language education was also mentioned by some parents; however, no respondents referred to raising children in an English-speaking environment.

The quality of life in Japanese urban society is poor in terms of housing conditions and leisure facilities. Japanese cities that have experienced rapid economic growth in the post-war era have become concrete jungles where urban planning has scarcely been an issue. As a result, Japanese cities lack space for parks and other public areas, a situation that differs completely from that found in Australian cities. Furthermore, Japanese housing conditions compare unfavorably to those in Australia, due to high land prices and population pressures. These contrasting living conditions, in general, have been functioning as push and pull factors in a broad sense. As a clear example of these influences, a respondent in his thirties who once worked as an architect in Tokyo noted:

> In Australia, any camping site and park is well-developed. In South Bank, the park even has an artificial beach and we can enter the park for free. In Japan, we definitely would have to pay for that kind of facility, but here we do not have to pay much for leisure activities.

This answer shows the typical sentiment of most respondents who referred to the better living environment in Australia. Japanese cities do not have many parks and people have to pay admission fees for parks with well-developed facilities, such as pools and gardens. The high quality of leisure facilities in Australia creates a favorable impression of the Australian lifestyle among Japanese.

Parents with children in particular find this aspect of Australia appealing, as indicated by the following comment of a respondent, in his thirties, who worked for a Japanese company and currently studies at a graduate school in Brisbane:

> Besides a demanding company life, I would say that having a baby was also one of the reasons why I came here. Raising a child in Japan seemed undesirable from a financial and social standpoint. We thought that we could raise him [their child] to be an open and natural person in this environment. In Australia we have plenty of parks and nature.

For most Japanese migrants with children, raising a child in Australia after leaving Japan is thought to be meaningful as it offers an escape from the demands of urban life in Japan. The respondent used the Japanese term *nobi-nobi sodateru* ("raise freely and easily" in direct translation) to express the meaning of raising his child to be an "open and natural person," but it must be noted that this expression also contains another meaning that refers to avoiding Japan's *jyuken-senso* (exam war), or the race for students to get into prestigious universities.

Negative perceptions of the interaction of the individual with Japanese society heavily influenced most respondents in their decision to migrate. For some who had experienced Japanese corporate society, the appeal of the relatively relaxed Australian lifestyle worked as a pull factor. For those dissatisfied with the poor living conditions associated with Japanese cities, Australian living standards were attractive. But one other factor was important in influencing respondents' decision to migrate. The next section will argue how these Japanese lifestyle migrants turned into migrants based on their tourism experiences.

TOURISM EXPERIENCES AND MIGRATION

As far as the interview data in this project is concerned, tourism can be perceived as a basis for Japanese lifestyle migration. Among the 31 respondents, 71 per cent of the respondents had visited Australia as tourists or business people before their migration, and most directly or indirectly related their experiences as tourists to their migration decision. The following statements of the respondents show how Japanese tourists turn into lifestyle migrants through their impressions and recollections as tourists. A respondent who had visited Australia in his university days and currently works as a translator noted:

> I had been to Australia about five times before migrating. I suppose I never liked much about Tokyo. I like relaxed places with wide-open spaces and dislike messy, crowded places.... I came to Australia in my university days and have since fallen in love with it. The relaxed lifestyle and relaxed people left a lasting impression on me. To my eyes, the living standards seemed better than Japan.... It was a culture shock for me, that such a country and lifestyle could be achieved.... I also considered moving to some rural area in Japan if migration to Australia was not possible. However, I realized that moving to a Japanese rural town

could be done anytime, but it would not be so easy to move to Australia. If there was a chance to go, it would be best to experience this, and therefore we decided to migrate.

As his comments indicate, his tourism experience left a lasting impression on him when he saw firsthand what kind of lifestyle was possible in Australia. He strongly desired to escape Tokyo and its problems. Through his tourism experience, he found Australia to be an ideal place for his migration destination. Also interesting is that he considered domestic migration for a more relaxed lifestyle. On that point, his orientation was counter-urban, an idealistic stance commonly found among Westerners. In his case, his counter-urbanism was connected to the memory of his tourism experience as well as his subsequent migration decision.

Similarly, some respondents referred to the "atmosphere of Australia" as a pull factor in their migration decision. For instance, many respondents used the phrase when referring to the open spaces and mild climate in Australia. One respondent, who migrated for a semi-retired life in Australia in the 1980s after working long hours at a family-owned business in Japan, commented:

> One day…we were watching television and there was a program on emigration. The program introduced the lives of Japanese migrants in Australia, showing the lifestyles of business owners who had come to Australia. It was partly a documentary program and I remember saying with my husband, 'That looks nice.' We knew that TV only showed the good parts, but it really showed the nice things about Australia.… We then talked about this, and made a plan to visit Australia. My husband and I, we didn't do a round trip of Australia but we did go halfway around. We saw Sydney, Melbourne, Gold Coast and Brisbane. It was an inspection for our future immigration. Our impression of Melbourne and Sydney, because it was in the winter months, was that they were cold and wet, but when we went to the Gold Coast the weather was clear and fine. The mood was that of a tourist location, and we agreed that the Gold Coast seemed like a good place to live.

The inspiration for the middle-aged couple's migration was a TV documentary introducing the lifestyle of Japanese migrants in Australia. Having been impressed by it, they traveled to Australia to make a preliminary inspection. On their trip to Australian cities, they found that the Gold Coast matched their preferences due to its mild climate, open spaces and golf courses. As this case shows, the factors of mild climate and open spaces in Australia, when contrasted with Japanese urban areas, act as a pull factor, enticing Japanese from crowded and stress-filled urban areas.

Tourists have an opportunity to observe the living environment of the tourist destination. The following extract of a male respondent who married a British female national from Australia shows how tourism experiences make a tourist reflect on his or her own lifestyle in Japan. In referring to his impression of Australia on his visit before his marriage, the respondent stated:

> I found that Brisbane had a quiet and calm atmosphere and the people were very friendly. What surprised me were the houses in Australia. Everyone owned a car and lived in a house with a garden, even though it may not have been a gorgeous one. Living in a house in Tokyo seemed impossible for me forever. Living in such a big city, all I could see in my future was a life in a small suburban estate. Houses [in Australia] were so cheap at that time. I remember that it was about only twice or triple an annual income.... I got the impression that Australia was actually a rich country even though it was a poor country economically.

Australia for him was a rich country in terms of its living standards. For him, a work-oriented salaryman's life in Tokyo provided nothing but "a life in a small suburban estate." However, what surprised him during his trip to Australia were the high-quality housing conditions and property prices. His view on housing conditions was shared by most other respondents regarding their impressions of an Australian lifestyle, and housing can be seen as an important factor in their choice of a migration destination.

The cases presented above demonstrate a clear contrast between the push factor of a work-oriented lifestyle with relatively poor living standards in Japan and the pull factor of a well-balanced lifestyle in Australia with an attractive residential environment that appealed to Japanese tourists during their visits. The process involved in reaching decisions about migration and motivations for moving to Australia differed among individuals; however, visits as tourists were a decisive factor for Japanese who later became lifestyle migrants in Australia.

CONCLUSION

This chapter has discussed tourism development in Australia and its consequences. It first reviewed tourism development in Australia, and then examined Japanese lifestyle migration and its relationship with tourism experiences through qualitative data. In the discussion on Australian tourism development, background factors such as long-term unemployment in the 1970s and 1980s in Australia as well as policies adopted by the Australian government were highlighted. The scale of Japanese investment toward Australian tourism development was also mentioned and it was discussed how tourism development in Australia led to the popularity of Australia as a tourism destination for Japanese in the 1990s. In discussing the relationship between tourism experiences and decisions to migrate for lifestyle purposes among Japanese in Australia, lifestyle factors such as Australia's relaxed atmosphere and open spaces as well as the work-oriented lifestyle and relatively poor living environment in Japan were highlighted as the factors that enticed Japanese lifestyle migrants to venture to Australia. Japanese outbound migration to other countries remains to be studied from a comparative standpoint in order to characterize Japanese migration to Australia in its broader dimensions. Nonetheless, this study is significant in that it has demonstrated a relationship between tourism development, tourism experiences and lifestyle migration in the Australian context.

Acknowledgements

The research for this chapter was funded by a Rotary Foundation 2005-06 Ambassadorial Scholarship, University of Queensland School Research Higher Degree Support Funding, a University of Queensland International Research Travel Allowance, and funding from the Nippon Foundation Research Scheme for Students in Japan-Related Fields. The author acknowledges these programs and institutions.

References

Ang, I., & Stratton, J. (1996). Asianizing Australia: Notes toward a critical transnationalism in cultural studies. *Cultural Studies, 10*(1):10-36.

Australian Bureau of Statistics. (2006). Overseas arrivals and departures, Australia, Dec. 2005. Retrieved July 20, 2008, from http://www.abs.gov.au/AUSSTATS/abs@.nsf/DetailsPage/3401.0Dec%202005?OpenDocument

Bell, M., & Carr, R. (1994). *Japanese temporary residents in the Cairns tourism industry.* Canberra: Australia Bureau of Immigration and Population Research.

Biernacki, P., & Waldorf, D. (1981). Snowball sampling: Problem and techniques of chain referral sampling. *Sociological Methods and Research, 10*(2), 141-163.

Bureau of Tourism Research. (1989). *Tourism data book* (Catalogue no. 3401.0). Canberra: BTR.

Bureau of Tourism Research. (1991). *Japanese visitors and the Australian environment.* (BTR Occasional Paper No. 9). *A report to the Bureau of Tourism Research* (by I.R.W. Childs UQ). Canberra: BTR.

Bureau of Tourism Research. (1999). *Tourism's economic contribution,* 1996-97. Canberra: BTR.

Bureau of Tourism Research and David H. Jacobs Consultants. (1992). *Japanese tourism in Australia.* Canberra: BTR.

Burgess, R. G. (1984). *In the field: An introduction to field research.* London: Allen and Unwin.

Burnley, I., & Murphy, P. (2003). *Sea change: Movement from metropolitan to Arcadian Australia.* Sydney: University of New South Wales Press.

Carroll, P. (1991). Tourism as a focus of study: Concepts, approaches and data. In P. Carroll, K. Donohue, M. McGovern, & J. McMillen (Eds.), *Tourism Australia* (pp. 3-19). Sydney: Harcourt Brace Jovanovich Group Pty Limited.

Castle, S., Foster, W., Iredale, R., & Withers, G. (Eds.). (1998). *Immigration and Australia: Myths and realities.* St. Leonard's: Allen & Unwin in conjunction with the Housing Industry Association Ltd.

Crapanzano, V. (1990). On dialogue. In T. Maranhao (Ed.), *The interpretation of dialogue* (pp. 269-291). Chicago: The University of Chicago Press.

Department of Immigration and Multiculturalism and Indigenous Affairs. (2003). *Community information summary.* Retrieved July 20, 2008, from http://www.immi.gov.au/statistics/stat_info/comm_summ/japan.pdf

Hajdu, J. (2005). *Samurai in the surf: The arrival of the Japanese on the Gold Coast in the 1980s*. Canberra: Pandanus Books, Research School of Pacific and Asian Studies, the Australian National University.

Hammersley, M. (2003). "Analytics" are no substitute for methodology: A response to Speer and Hutchby. *Sociology, 37*(2), 339-351.

Ip, D., Wu, C. T., & Inglis, C. (1998). Settlement experiences of Taiwanese immigrants in Australia. *Asian Studies Review, 22*(1), 79-97.

Jayasuriya, L., & Kee, P. (1999). *The Asianisation of Australia? Some facts about the myths*. Melbourne: Melbourne University Press.

Jupp, J. (2002). *From white Australia to woomera: The story of Australian immigration*. Cambridge: Cambridge University Press.

Lee, R. M. (2004). Recording technologies and the interview in sociology, 1920-2000. *Sociology, 38*(5), 869-889.

Ley, D., & Kobayashi, A. (2005). Back to Hong Kong: Return migration or transnational sojourn? *Global Networks, 5*(2), 111-127.

Salva-Thomas, P.A. (2002). Foreign immigration and tourism development in Spain's Balearic Islands. In C. M. Hall & M. A. Williams (Eds.), *Tourism and migration: New relationships between production and consumption* (pp. 119-134). Dordrecht: Kluwer Academic Publishers.

Sato, M. (2001). *Farewell to Nippon*. Melbourne: TransPacific Press.

Shiobara, Y. (2005). Middle-class Asian immigrants and welfare multiculturalism: A case study of a Japanese community organisation in Sydney. *Asian Studies Review, 29*, 395-414.

Speer, S. A., & Hutchby, I. (2003). From ethics to analytics: Aspects of participants' orientations to the presence and relevance of recording devices. *Sociology, 37*(2), 315-337.

Statistics Bureau. (2001). *Syakai seikatsu kihon chosa* [General survey on social life]. Retrieved July 20, 2008, from http://www.e-stat.go.jp/SG1/estat/List.do?bid=000000150001&cycode=0

Statistics Bureau. (2004). *National survey of family income and expenditure*. Retrieved July 20, 2008, from http://www.e-stat.go.jp/SG1/estat/List.do?lid= 000000330510

Statistics Bureau. (2007). Labour force survey. Retrieved July 20, 2008, from http://www.stat.go.jp/data/roudou/report/2007/dt/index.htm

Swaffield, S., & Fairweather, J. (1998). In search of Arcadia: The persistence of the rural idyll in New Zealand rural subdivisions. *Journal of Environmental Planning and Management, 41*(1), 111-127.

Tourism Australia. (2005). *Japan visitor profile*. Retrieved July 20, 2008, from http://www.tourism.australia.com/content/japan/profiles_2005/japan_visitor_analysis_05.pdf

Tourism Queensland. (2005). *International visitor survey*. Retrieved July 20, 2008, from http://www.tq.com.au/research

Mason, J. (1996). *Qualitative researching*. London: Sage.

McHugh, K. E., & Mings, R. C. (1996). The circle of migration: Attachment to place in aging. *Annals of the Association of American Geographers, 86*(3), 530-550.

Ministry of Health, Labour and Welfare (2003). *Maitsuki kinrou tokei chosa* [Monthly statistical survey on labor]. Retrieved July 20, 2008, from http://wwwdbtk.mhlw.go.jp/toukei/kouhyo/indexkr_1_6.html

Ministry of Foreign Affairs. (2006). *Annual report of statistics on Japanese nationals overseas*. Tokyo: Ministry of Foreign Affairs.

Ministry of Land, Infrastructure and Transport. (2001). *Kanko hakusho* [White paper on tourism]. Retrieved July 20, 2008, from http://www.mlit.go.jp/hakusyo/kankou-hakusyo/ h13/006_.html

Mizukami, T. (2006). Leisurely life in a "wide brown land": Japanese views upon Australia. *Journal of Applied Sociology, 48*, 19-35.

Nagata, Y. (2001). Japanese. In M. Brändle (Ed.), *Multicultural Queensland 2001: 100 years,*

100 communities, a century of contributions (pp. 222-229). Brisbane: Multicultural Affairs Queensland, Department of the Premier and Cabinet.

Nagata, Y., & Nagatomo, J. (2007). *Japanese Queenslanders: A history*. Brisbane: Bookpal.

Nagatomo, J. (2006, November). *From tourist to migrant: Changing lifestyle and leisure values among Japanese since the 1990s*. Paper presented at Post Graduate Research Conference. Brisbane: The University of Queensland.

Nagatomo, J. (2007a). Japanese lifestyle migration to Australia: New migrants in the era of transnationalism. *Bulletin of Kyusyu Anthropological Association, 33*, 1-22.

Nagatomo, J. (2007b). 90 nendai nihonsyakai niokeru syakaihendo to Australia eno Nihonjinimin: Lifestyle kachikan no henka to ijyu no tsunagari [The social transformation of Japanese society in the 1990s and Japanese migration to Australia: The relationship between changes in lifestyle values and migration decisions]. *Otemon Journal of Australian Studies, 33*, 177-200.

Nagatomo, J. (2008a). Ijyusuru Nihonjin Kanko suru Nihonjin: Ijyu to kanko no chi toshiteno Australia [Japanese migrants and tourists: Australia as a destination for migration and tourism]. In T. Katayama (Ed.), *Asia kara miru, kangaeru: Bunkajinruigaku Nyumon* [Anthropology from Asian point of view] (pp. 169-184). Kyoto: Nakanishiya Syuppan.

Nagatomo, J. (2008b). Datsuryodoka sareta community: Australia Queensland syu nantobu niokeru Nihonjin community to network [The de-territorialized community: The Japanese community and its network in South East Queensland, Australia]. In H. Otani (Ed.), *Bunka no glocalization wo yomitoku* [Understanding cultural glocalization] (pp. 185-204). Fukuoka: Gensyobo.

Viviani, N. (1984). *The long journey: Vietnamese migration and settlement in Australia*. Carlton: Melbourne University Press.

Viviani, N., & Selby, J. (1980). *The Iwasaki tourist development at Yeppoon*. Nathan: Griffith University.

Willis, P. E. (1977). *Learning to labour: How working class kids get working class jobs*. Farnborough: Saxon House.

Wong, S. (1992). Emigration and stability in Hong Kong. *Asian Survey, 32*(10), 918-933.

Yamada, M. (1999). *Parasite single no jidai* [The age of the "parasite single"]. Tokyo: Chikuma Shobo.

• CHAPTER TEN •

Saffron-robed Monks and Digital Flash Cards: The Development and Challenges of Burmese Exile Media

RICHARD HUMPHRIES
Kansai Gaidai University

On August 15, 2007, the ruling junta of Burma (a.k.a. Myanmar[1]), the State Peace and Development Council (SPDC), without warning doubled the price of diesel, raised that of gasoline and implemented a stiff 500 percent price hike for compressed gas, largely by removing subsidies ("Fuel Price Hikes," 2007). Such increases came at a time when some 90 percent of the country's families were already living at or below a poverty line defined as US$1 per day ("UN Rights Chief Louise Arbour," 2007). As an example of what rising fuel prices mean for the average person, many residents of Rangoon, the country's largest city, pawn family possessions in order to pay for bus fares. They use public transport to search for short-term manual labor jobs, hoping to buy back their goods if they are successful and then return home via the same form of transport ("The Way of Peace," 2007). For such individuals and others like them, bus fares doubled and commodity prices, such as those of rice, beans, salt and cooking oil, also increased substantially.

Economic disaffection in Burma is longstanding, but the price increases intensified public anger, giving rise to demonstrations that began on August 19, 2007 and soon were dubbed the "Saffron Revolution," in recognition of the color of protesting monks' robes. The demonstrations quickly were politicized, in many cases being led by a prominent group of dissidents known as the 88 Generation ("Crackdown," 2007, pp. 6-7). The use of 88 in their name referred to 1988, when the regime at that time suppressed pro-democracy demonstrations triggered by similar highhandedness the year before, in the form of a demonetarization of the national currency that wiped out the savings of vast numbers of citizens (Anonymous exile-media reporter, personal communication November 27, 2007).[2]

Initially, the regime reacted harshly to the August demonstrations, though not with all out force. Junta police, as well as men from junta-created and associated organizations such as the Union Solidarity and Development Association (USDA) and the more gang-like Swan Ar-shin (a name loosely rendered as "Masters of Force"), were employed to break up demonstrating groups and seize any leaders ("The Alms Bowl," 2007). Many of the 88 Generation leaders were arrested within days and others were relentlessly hunted down ("No Return to Normal," 2007).

Monks began joining the demonstrations on August 28, 2007. A turning point was reached on September 5 at Pakkoku in Magwe State, not far from Mandalay, when security forces violently broke up a demonstration of 500 Buddhist monks, initially by firing shots over their heads. Onlookers, of whom there were reportedly thousands, were also assaulted. The monks responded by temporarily seizing several officials, to secure the release of three monks arrested during the incident, and by setting fire to several officials' cars (Mungpi, 2007). The Pakkoku monks, together with a coalition of other monk groups known as the All Burma Monks Alliance, publicly issued a series of demands to the ruling SPDC. The demands included an official apology, the release of all detained demonstrators and political prisoners, and a call for the government to ease the economic burden it had imposed on the poor. The monks set a deadline of September 17, 2007, which the government ignored. Many monks then refused to accept alms from SPDC members, or from members of SPDC related organizations, an act tantamount to the ex-communication of members of the regime ("The Alms Bowl," 2007).

The number and size of monk-led anti-government demonstrations escalated in September. On September 22, thousands of monks and civilians marched down University Avenue in Rangoon past the normally off-limits residence where National League for Democracy (NLD) leader Daw Aung San Suu Kyi is detained. Suu Kyi, who emerged briefly to pray with the monks, had been in detention since 2003, when she was imprisoned after pro-government gangs assaulted her motorcade at Depayin and massacred at least seventy people ("A Biography of Aung San Suu Kyi," 2007). Her appearance caused a media sensation and news coverage of the meeting with the monks spread worldwide.

The symbolism of her emergence represented a direct challenge to authorities, although why the meeting was allowed to happen is still not clear. There could have been a breakdown in the chain of command or the authorities may have thought her appearance would diffuse the protests (Spiller, 2007). Over the next few days, however, the demonstrations grew in size and intensity in Rangoon – involving as many as 100,000 persons – and were significant in several other urban centers. But the regime was by then issuing warnings and mobilizing frontline combat units, usually tasked with fighting ethnic insurgents, for use in the nation's urban centers ("Crackdown," 2007, pp. 99-101). It was rumored that the government intended a three-day program to end the demonstrations. On day one, September 25, there would be warnings and on the next day there would be warning shots. Finally, if necessary, the government would shoot demonstrators on the third day (Anonymous exile-media reporter, personal communication, November 27, 2007).

The crackdown began on September 26, with government soldiers and police attacking monasteries and dispersing demonstrators with tear gas, clubs, and bullets. Thousands of monks and civilians were arrested. The number of fatalities is disputed with the regime claiming ten and others such as Human Rights Watch suggesting a much higher toll ("Burma: Crackdown Bloodier than Government Admits," 2007).

The full force of the crackdown continued for several days, then slowly tapered off, though in some respects it continues as of this writing (January, 2008), with further arrests or detentions occurring and a trial underway involving fourteen Buddhist monks and nuns (Paung, 2008).

Although there were many similarities between the events of 2007 and 1988, media coverage differed considerably in both cases. In 1988, few photos and scant video footage of the demonstrations in Rangoon were available to media organizations. The most important footage was taken at considerable risk by a Burmese employee of Japan's NHK government television station, but NHK severely restricted its use claiming it would promote instability (Hadfield, 1996).

In 2007, however, the situation was quite different, with large numbers of local and foreign reporters descending upon the scene. Although some major news agencies contrived to send their regular reporters to Burma on tourist visas (Anonymous media editor, personal communication, September 5, 2007), the international community mainly acquired its information from local reporters who knew the language and had the appropriate contacts. This state of affairs lasted until the SPDC curtailed phone usage, blocked Internet communications with the outside world (Wang & Nagaraja, 2007), and targeted other sources of suspected news leakage through raids on offices and hotels (Anonymous exile-media reporter, personal communication, November 27, 2007).

Some locally-based reporters worked for major news agencies or broadcasters such as Radio Free Asia. Others were just individuals who contributed to Internet blogs. However, a large number were part of what one researcher has called the "largest shadow-state media empire in recent mainland Southeast Asian history" (Ferguson, 2006, p. 2). In contrast to NHK's suppressed video images of 1988, there was the widely available footage of Kenji Nagai, a Japanese press photographer, being murdered by a government soldier at point blank range, an event that caused the victim's government to reconsider its aid policy toward Burma (Yoshida, 2007).

This chapter examines the following. First, after a brief overview of some research on alternative media, it looks at the growth of Burmese exile or independent media groups. The career of one reporter with an ethnic media organization is analyzed toward this end. Next, the chapter returns to the dramatic events of 2007, discussing the challenges faced by exile media groups. Finally, several possible lessons are discussed so that such media organizations might be better prepared to face future challenges.

CONDITIONS FOR THE DEVELOPMENT OF A BURMESE EXILE OR INDEPENDENT MEDIA

Over the past three decades, improvements in information technologies have made media creation significantly more variegated as well as affordable. Ginsburg (1991), an anthropologist who studies Australian aboriginal communities, was one of the earliest and most influential researchers to note how technological change can expand media possibilities for members of marginalized communities. In her oft-cited article "Indigenous Media: Faustian Contract or Global Village," she describes technological advances as providing "new vehicles for internal and external communication, for self-determination, and for resistance to outside cultural dominance" (Ginsburg, 1991, pp. 91-93).

Ginsburg's notion of a Faustian bargain was that new media technologies offer access to the world as well as ways of expressing identity but may also allow the mass media a back entrance to overwhelm local cultures. Nevertheless, she suggests that the net effect of the new media is one of decentralization and democratization (Ginsburg, 1991, p. 96). In a subsequent article, she also noted an element of hybridization when trained outsiders brought production techniques to new media groups within indigenous communities. Significantly, she called for cultural analyses of media relations that understand such local contexts as well as outside ones with which local ones might interact (Ginsburg, 1994, p. 366).

With the globalization of new media technologies, alternative media have been enabled as media creators are freed from previous distribution systems, allowing for increased mobilization efforts. The use of new technology for overtly political reasons in the form of challenging a perceived oppressive governmental structure has become known as the Zapatista effect (Ronfeldt & Arquilla, 2001, chap. 6). As an example of this effect, the use of email has had a profound impact on networking possibilities for Burmese opposition groups and, combined with listservs and news compilations such as Burmanet, has created a forum for news concerning Burma as well as a later entry point for emerging exile media groups to see and spread their work online (Danitz & Strobel, 2000).

The development of Burmese exile media from the early 1990s must be understood within the context of political and economic developments in Burma in recent decades. A repressive Burmese government brutally suppressed anti-government demonstrations in 1988, causing thousands to flee to Burma's border areas or to neighboring countries. Economic mismanagement and land seizures since that time have caused even larger migrations, as has an ongoing counter-insurgency effort against armed ethnic minorities and other opponents (US Department of State, 2006).

As for press freedoms in Burma, they were broad ranging from independence in 1948 until 1962. However, since 1962, military-dominated or military-run governments have exercised firm control over the nation's media. A Press Scrutiny Board (now Press Scrutiny and Registration Division) was set up in 1962 and strengthened after 1988 (Brooten, 2003, p. 97). As a result of these measures, all editions of print publications must be submitted to this board and publishing licenses can be revoked without notice (Neuman, 2002). Censorship decisions are often arbitrary and even when stories are allowed they must be modified upon request. For example, in 2007 an employee of a Burmese government-affiliated newspaper was not allowed to publish an article mentioning suicide as a major cause of death in Burma, but when the suicides were explained as "people falling off buildings" it was allowed to go through (Anonymous government-affiliated newspaper reporter, personal communication, August 21, 2007).

A large number of publications cover sports, lifestyle and literary themes but anything of an alternative political nature is heavily censored or banned. Radio and television stations are government owned and their news programs reflect government propaganda. Censors scan literary journals and poetry compilations looking for evidence of discontent and arrest writers deemed to be threats. In January 2008, Sai Wai, a leading Burmese poet, was arrested when the authorities discovered that one of his poems, which he had published in the weekly *Love Journal*, was an acrostic in which the first letters of each line combined to form a message that criticized General Than Shwe, the junta's leader (MacKinnon, 2008). In addition to such media censorship within Burma, foreign news broadcasts are subject to jamming attempts.

In January 2008, after spending over four months in detention, several top 88 Generation leaders, including Min Ko Naing and Ko Ko Gyi, the best known opposition figure after Aung San Suu Kyi, were charged with unstated press law violations related to section 17/20 of the Printers and Publishers Registration Law (Mon & Too, 2008). This section of the 1962 law allows for individuals to be prosecuted when they distribute material that has not been vetted by an authorized censor (Amnesty International, 2008).

Advances in information technology have not escaped the SPDC's purview. In 1996, it enacted a Computer Science Development Law and in 2000 added a series of regulations to control public and private Internet usage ("Internet Filtering in Burma," 2005). The regime also monitors telephone and cellular phone conversations. Its burgeoning signals intelligence capacity, and the role of such foreign helpers such as China and Singapore, have been discussed at some length by Desmond Ball in his 1998 book *Burma's Military Secrets: Signals Intelligence (SIGINT) from the Second World War to Civil War and Cyber Warfare*, and in a subsequent article Ball wrote for *Jane's Intelligence Review* (Ball, 1998, p. 35).

As far as maintaining control of the Internet, the junta has taken several measures. Users are required to register in order to use email and, at Internet cafés, computer terminals are required to take screen shots every five minutes. The regime has also acquired the firewall filtering and blocking software package Fortiguard produced by Fortinet, an American company. Fortiguard is described by its maker as providing continuously upgraded "comprehensive Unified Threat Management (UTM) security solutions" (*FortiGuard Subscription Services*, 2007). The junta had previously been using an open source solution, DansGuardian ("Internet Filtering in Burma," 2005).

Although press freedoms were non-existent in government-controlled areas, after 1988 several critical elements converged for an independent Burmese media to develop elsewhere. First, a large borderland and diaspora population of Burmese existed, many of whom were opponents of the government. Those who were in Thailand and India, despite some restrictions on their movements and the presence of intelligence personnel, were able to organize and operate. Second, an increasingly repressive military junta was concerned not so much with Western governments' perceptions but rather with controlling the press at home. Activists soon saw it was possible for information to be smuggled out for publication, packaged and smuggled back in. Finally, rapidly improving information technologies created new possibilities for diverse alternative media enterprises. These three elements, combined with local initiative and outside support, would enhance the development of the myriad alternative Burmese media groups that exist today.

SOME DEVELOPMENTS IN BURMESE INDEPENDENT MEDIA

Brooten (2006) has identified two strands of alternative Burmese media development. One claims a pan-Burma perspective, while the other is more parochial in the sense of ethnic or other group affiliation (pp. 361-362).

The pan-Burma groups were not necessarily first upon the scene, as armed opponents of the Burmese regime had long had a media presence. The Karen National Union, the political wing of the Karen armed insurgency, ran a radio station at least into the 1980s, the Karenni National Progress Party (KNPP) had newsletters, and Shan nationalist intellectuals associated with Khun Sa's opium-financed army in Shan State were publishing a printed newspaper by the early 1980s (Ferguson, 2006, p. 3). Khuensai Jaiyen, a press secretary to Khun Sa, established the Shan Herald Agency for News (SHAN) on December 27, 1991 (Jaiyen, 2006).

Over the years SHAN has become very active, helping to train emergent media groups. When Khun Sa surrendered to the Burmese junta in 1995, Jaiyen was able to extricate himself and SHAN from reliance upon an armed group. In fact, at the time of the surrender when he told Khun Sa he did not wish to join him, he was grateful when the warlord replied, "Well, you will just have to move on and do something else in life," and let him go (K. Jaiyen, personal communication, January 19, 2001).

By late 1988 in the volatile Thai-Burma border region, as well as in insurgent controlled zones inside Burma, a mixed population was gathering in the form of refugees, displaced persons, migrants, villagers, and numerous students and other opponents of the Burmese government who had fled from the brutal crackdowns of August and September. While there were already locally-based refugee committees, as well as women and youth organizations associated with ethnic minority insurgencies, new groups formed, split, and coalesced in a highly volatile political environment. Outsiders, such as Gene Sharp and Robert Helvey, conducted training seminars and wrote materials on how to engage in non-violent resistance against the regime that were translated into local languages (Bacher, 2003, p. 10). Meanwhile, foreign donors sought to bring relief to the distressed, help opponents of the regime organize, and eventually foster the elements of a multiethnic Burmese civil society, albeit one in exile.

Relief groups, women's groups, advocacy organizations and, in particular, locally-based human rights groups, produced various reports and print publications that received mention in mainstream media outlets, but the early 1990s also saw the appearance of important Burmese-run, pan-Burma media focused organizations, one of which would be located in Norway. Three of importance are the Oslo-based radio station Democratic Voice of Burma (DVB) and Thailand-based print and Internet publications *Irrawaddy Magazine* and *New Era Journal*. These three would expand and become very active over the years and the *Irrawaddy* and the DVB would have people working for them on the ground during the Saffron Revolution of 2007.

The Democratic Voice of Burma, which first broadcast on July 19, 1992 via shortwave transmitter, was founded by exiled Burmese activists and, for its first ten years, was considered to be the voice of the National Coalition Government of the Union of Burma (NCGUB), a self-proclaimed government in exile. Since 2002, the DVB has distanced itself somewhat from the NCGUB, claiming to be more independent (Biener, 2007). The DVB now has several transmitters in addition to the one at its Oslo base, including ones in Germany, New Zealand and Madagascar (DVB, 2007).

Early on, opposition groups made use of the DVB's broadcasting capacity. In late December 1993, I visited Dawgwin, just inside Burma from the Thai side of the border, which was then the headquarters of the All Burma Students Democratic Front (ABSDF), an organized armed force of ex-students who had fled to the borderlands after the demonstrations were quashed. Their camp possessed a small recording studio with microphones and sound equipment. I was told that this was used to make short programs which were sent to Oslo for broadcasting. Their base at Dawgwin was very insecure as the frontline was only a few hours away then, and it would fall by early 1995 to Burmese government and allied forces. One member of the ABSDF did relate to me then that were the ABSDF to attempt to broadcast directly from their base they would likely face immediate censure from the Burmese Army. Hence, despite the obvious time lag in 1993 in shipping tapes to Oslo, broadcasting from a more secure location had its advantages.

The station broadcasts in Burmese and in several minority languages and has received important support from the Norwegian government and the US National Endowment for Democracy, or NED (Joseph, 2003, para. 18). The NED, it should be noted, has supported exile media over the years through direct funding as well as by supporting organizations that assist the media groups through training and other activities.

In May 2005, the station also began limited television broadcasts via satellite ("DVB via BBC monitoring," 2007). While it has usually broadcast only a few hours at a time (and in minority languages for fifteen-minute slots), at the height of the September 2007 demonstrations the station switched to almost full-time radio broadcasting via satellite. The DVB also has a permanent presence in the form of a multilingual website.

The *Irrawaddy*, an English-language monthly publication, has been based for the last eleven years in Chiang Mai, Thailand. Aung Zaw, its current editor, founded it in 1993. Aung Zaw was a one-time student activist who had fled Burma in 1993, and who was also, from 1997 to 2005, a journalist for Radio Free Asia (Zaw, 2005). The magazine also maintains a website, with English and Burmese versions, which includes articles from its print editions as well as breaking news and research links. Brooten (2006) regards this publication as "arguably the most professional independent Burmese print and online source by Western standards" (p. 363). Recently, internal disputes over staff changes, editorial policy, and the quality of writing have led to internal frictions (Anonymous former *Irrawaddy* reporter, personal communication, August 21, 2007). Nonetheless, the magazine and its website enjoy considerable popularity and Aung Zaw is often quoted in mainstream media.

The *New Era Journal* publishes a bi-monthly journal in Burmese and has articles in both Burmese and English on its website. The Burmese founders and staff of this publication based in Bangkok have, on occasion, faced arrest over immigration issues. *New Era* has received important funding from the NED, and has used an innovative method to facilitate better distribution levels for editions smuggled inside Burma. The typesetting used by *New Era*, on its front and back covers, mimics that of the government newspaper, the *New Light of Myanmar* (Latt, 2001).

Brooten (2003), who has covered the emergence of exile media for almost two decades, has criticized the media's repetitive focus on human rights discourse, which has included the stereotyping of minorities as victims and as lacking in political skills (p. 202). She also mentions intense factionalism and dependency on outside funding as problems (p. 193), as well as gender bias in which rapid moves toward professionalism tend to disadvantage women in terms of job and training opportunities with exile media groups (p. 236). Brooten also found that non-Burmans she spoke with felt marginalized in terms of support and funding from outside agencies compared to that received by Burmans (p. 237).

Donors and donor agendas have also been criticized elsewhere. Donors are varied and include governments, church groups and private individuals. In particular, some leftist and anti-globalization activists have portrayed the NED as following a sinister American program of manipulating the Burmese anti-democracy movement for its own ends (Engdahl, 2007). However, such criticisms tend to be driven by ideological agendas rather than representing accurate analyses of the context of aid recipients and their needs, plans and goals.

The sheer number and variety of small aid organizations are too numerous to mention and indicate the movement is not manipulated by Washington. Nonetheless, an occurrence on May 22, 2002 in Bangkok at the Foreign Correspondents Club suggested an inappropriate attempt at influence, when Aung Zaw from the *Irrawaddy*, Ross Dunkley, editor of the junta-affiliated *Myanmar Times*, and Priscilla Clapp, then Charge d'Affaires at the US Embassy in Rangoon, were involved in a heated discussion. After Dunkley brought up the issue of NED funding for the *Irrawaddy*, Clapp made an implied threat to such funding over the *Irrawaddy's* position on US foreign policy post-911 (Lawrence & Nance, 2002).

There is also merit to the criticism of Western media focusing excessively on Rangoon and Aung San Suu Kyi in their coverage of Burma. Ethnic minorities and their supporters have complained about this over the years and also how donor agencies initially assisted those Burman groups that were better educated, better organized, and quicker to master the intricacies of grant proposal writing. However, by the late 1990s, moves were afoot to extend help and media access to ethnic and other organizations (Anonymous NGO staffer, personal communication, April 9, 2005).

One NGO staffer deeply involved in this effort confided that developing further ethnically based information services was important in broadening the opposition and in changing community attitudes. If ethnic minority-based, Burman-based, and pan-Burma based groups could network and work together, the staffer saw this as beneficial. In addition, he noted that in many insurgent-controlled areas inside Burma, community and insurgent leaderships foster the belief that soldiering is the best career for men and nursing the most suitable one for women (Anonymous NGO staffer, personal communication, April 9, 2005).

The above source also related concerns about repeated instances of "parachute journalism" (Anonymous NGO staffer, personal communication, April 9, 2005), or how journalists of a certain type were known to fly in from Bangkok or from further away, stay for brief periods of no more than a few days, put together stories, and then leave the country. Such reportage that resulted was often one-dimensional in nature and reflective of the viewpoints and organizational biases of those outside the communities the journalists were superficially covering.

At first, several difficulties were associated with helping the newer ethnic and other media groups. Initially, news written by some of their writers tended to focus solely on politics and human rights and was lengthy, unclear and propagandistic in style. There were few if any features and little coverage of cultural and other community topics. However, as a result of training programs and networking, improvements were soon evident, with cross-group internships particularly helpful in this regard. One important measure of success was when reports by such groups began to be used by such international mass media organizations as the BBC, the Voice of America, and Radio Free Asia (Anonymous NGO staffer, personal communication, April 9, 2005). The NGO staffer considered that of the groups he had been helping, the Mizzima News Agency (MNA), an exile group headquartered in New Delhi and founded in 1998, was the largest and most influential.

Nevertheless, for all the groups the staffer was helping, his hope was that they would begin to do the following successfully: develop their own editorial strategies and financial sources; provide a forum for moderate opinion, particularly on such divisive issues as ethnic divisions; play an important role in any transition away from military rule; and, importantly, do this in local languages and so become an organic part of the larger community (Anonymous NGO staffer, personal communication, April 9, 2005).

One of the groups the staffer worked with was the Independent Mon News Agency (IMNA). A brief look at this agency sheds light on key aspects of development concerning the media opposition process. All the information in the next several paragraphs, as well as the quotations, come from a personal interview I conducted with an exile journalist on March 25, 2005 at an undisclosed location.

Chan Mon, an ethnic Mon, first came to Thailand in 1998 and worked with a Mon community relief agency. He learned computer skills, improved his English by studying with an American volunteer in Thailand, and embarked upon a distance education program. Chan Mon first became associated with journalism when he worked on audio recordings in the Mon language that were subsequently sent to Oslo for broadcast over the Democratic Voice of Burma. He related the following about his early experiences:

> First for DVB, other people, their staff, were the readers on air and all I did was typing into the machines what we wrote. Then I began to edit, to shorten the words and to make them clearer. By 1999, I was starting to use my voice. At first, I was excited because I had never worked with radio before and we didn't have radio in the Mon community that was in the Mon language.

In 2000, he attended a five-day course on journalism in Chiang Mai at the Human Rights Education Institute of Burma taught by Aung Myo Min, a Burmese human rights specialist, which covered the skills of sourcing, interviewing, writing stories, following up and double-checking for accuracy. From October 2000 to January 2001, he was an intern in Oslo with the DVB. The DVB course also emphasized writing and following-up stories but also covered packaging news items and preparing radio features. Interns were required to write stories based upon fieldwork done on the streets of Oslo.

During that period, the Independent Mon News Agency (IMNA) was founded by Nai Kasauh Mon, who was also Director of the Human Rights Foundation of Monland (HURFOM). The fledging news agency received support and funding from several organizations, including the Burmese Relief Center, *Internews*, the NED, and the George Soros founded Open Society Institute. Chan Mon would later work for IMNA and was still there as of 2005, the time of the interview.

In 2003, he attended another month-long journalism course in Chiang Mai run by *Internews*, targeted towards editors of exile and indigenous media publications. He found it very intensive and daunting as classes lasted nine hours each day. Participants received training on writing in the pyramid style of journalism, running stories, organizing meetings, running a professional publication, and in marketing and advertising.

Other members of IMNA have received varying amounts of training in Thailand and elsewhere. In 2002, a seven-day course in Chiang Mai was offered for both novices and senior journalists. Three other IMNA personnel have done lengthy courses lasting several months or more with *Internews*, who also paid for one female IMNA reporter to do a two-month internship with BBC Radio in 2004. On that course she was trained in news writing, presentation skills, and voice dynamics.

By early 2005, IMNA had nine office staffers, four senior journalists and nine stringers. Six of the stringers worked clandestinely inside Burma and some had faced arrest when caught or suspected of being journalists. Two had been jailed and threatened with lengthy imprisonments, but one was later released.

IMNA engaged in several media activities. It continued to provide DVB with radio segments, maintained its own radio station in a Mon displaced persons camp located "on the border,"[3] and published a twelve-page monthly magazine titled *Snorng Thieng* (Guiding Star) with separate Mon and Burmese stories. The magazine is sold in Thailand where there is a large Mon community and distributed in Burma, whenever possible. Chan Mon stated,

> We have trouble distributing in Burma because our paper is illegal. The government has already ordered that if they see this paper, then who is reading it they will send away for three years. We distribute secretly to reach our community and to have an impact.

The IMNA is also affiliated with Burma News International (BNI), a network of ten independent Burmese media organizations including SHAN, and has its own news aggregator website.

Initially, according to Chan Mon, IMNA tended to rely on news from already established community human rights, relief and advocacy figures, but it quickly developed its own sources. Given the volatile political climate of where the agency operates, and the stories it covers, difficulties have arisen. IMNA has encountered problems both with armed groups opposed to the Burmese government and those having a ceasefire relationship with the junta. Business interests have sometimes reacted angrily when their activities have been exposed by IMNA. The Mon journalist mentioned that,

> We often have problems with the NMSP [New Mon State Party, a Mon ceasefire group] because they are a political party and we are independent. We write that something happened in the NMSP like an

election and we write some analysis about that and their political standing in dealing with the Burmese government. Sometimes we also write about the NMSP's businesses such as logging and trading and they are not happy.

Aside from their regular work for Mon-language programs on DVB, IMNA has seen its reports, and quotes from its journalists, broadcast by the Voice of America and the BBC. Occasionally, reporters from the *Nation*, a major Bangkok English-language daily newspaper, have come to the IMNA office to do interviews. Chan Mon said that his organization has both short-term and long-term goals. In the short term, IMNA wants to increase professionalism through more training and focus more on data security issues. In the longer term, it hopes to be a much larger media organization, be based inside a democratic Burma, be self-sustaining, and appeal to a wider Mon audience.

Some journalists from media groups such as IMNA, Mizzima News Agency and the Democratic Voice of Burma have joined with various freelancers, poets and writers, and with Burmese working for VOA, BBC and other major media organizations to develop the Burma Media Association, a professional association which holds yearly conferences and aims to protect Burmese journalists. There is no doubt that protection issues are a grave concern for those working inside Burma and have become even more critical in the aftermath of the Saffron Revolution. This will be discussed in the final section.

EXILE MEDIA GROUPS AND THE SAFFRON REVOLUTION

It is not possible to provide a complete account of the Burmese exile media and its role during the Saffron Revolution. Indeed, as some participants are now incarcerated while others are in hiding, there are many details of a personal or operational nature that would be too sensitive to relate under current conditions. What this section will do instead is first discuss the state of telecommunications and the Internet infrastructure in Burma and then examine how news made its way out of the country during the demonstrations. The following synopsis relies heavily upon the observations of an anonymous eyewitness and participant in the exile media effort inside Burma at the time.

Although the Burmese government has consistently acted to control and censor its media, it has also felt the need to upgrade its telecommunications capacity and allow Internet connectivity, mostly to meet the perceived needs of its military establishment but also to facilitate commerce. The country has an urban-based landline telephony system as well as a cellular GSM system with towers in major urban centers. As of 2005, some 1000 iPSTAR satellite dishes were intended for telephony in outlying areas.

The number of subscribers for telephones remains small. Startup and subscription costs are beyond the means of many citizens, and the needs of the military and its business partners come first ("Internet Filtering in Burma," 2005).

In 2005, *Mizzima News* estimated the number of cell phone subscribers at 150,000 and at 397,000 for those with direct line accounts, this in a country with a population of close to 50 million (Thakuria, 2005). Registration for such accounts presents problems for known dissidents and for those wishing to use them for reportage. However, a black market exists for GSM SIM cards. During September 2007, such cards with cell phones cost as much as US$2,000 or more (Anonymous exile-media reporter, personal communication, November 27, 2007). Telephony has become very important for the exile media. Often, publications such as the *Irrawaddy* would simply call someone in Burma to access information or conduct an interview.

Nonetheless, it was the Internet that came to the fore in 2007 as a way for people to transmit information to and from Burma. The country has two ISP providers, the Ministry of Post and Telecommunications (MPT) and the semi-private Myanmar Teleport (a.k.a. BaganNet and formerly Bagan Cybertech), which was once owned by the son of General Khin Nyunt, the former Intelligence Chief. The first is used mostly for official purposes but the second is the one used in the country's Internet cafés, where slow dial-up connections are the rule ("Internet Filtering in Burma," 2005).

There are also people and organizations with their own Internet and communications systems. One advocacy and aid organization active inside Burma has clandestinely used a separate satellite uplink telephony product, and a number of businesses, private individuals, international agencies, and diplomatic representations have their own satellite links to the Internet.

Over the last few years the government has spent an inordinate amount of time trying to stifle activists or citizen media using the Internet. The government has been using products such as Fortiguard and DansGuard to block opposition and political and media websites. At various times it has blocked webmail sites, political web pages, blogging platforms, and Internet voice messaging services. Internet activists have countered by using encryption, proxy anonymizers, blog messaging services such as Cbox (Kirkpatrick, 2007), and web tunneling programs such as "Your-Freedom" (Crispin, 2007; "Internet Filtering in Burma," 2005). Many activists and exile media groups know these techniques well and have developed protocols for sending and receiving communications (Crispin, 2007). A group of Burmese exiles skilled in information technology and known as the Burma/Myanmar Information Technology Team (BIT) have been particularly helpful in training people about firewall circumvention (Anonymous exile-media reporter, personal communication November 27, 2007).

Many people at Internet cafés are also well-versed in how to circumvent government blocking. A popular technology in 2007 was Glite, a proxy that allowed users to access Gmail accounts relatively quickly and then upload small files or photos through firewalls (Anonymous exile-media reporter, personal communication November 27, 2007).

In August and September during the demonstrations, many of the exile news groups had full-time correspondents, visiting reporters or stringers inside Burma and especially in Rangoon and Mandalay. The Democratic Voice of Burma had as many as 100 such stringers, according to Reuters (Cropley, 2007). Some organizations were better endowed than others, possessing concealed cameras, for example; and some were better organized (Anonymous exile-media reporter, personal communication, November 27, 2007).

Additionally, there were large numbers of citizen journalists and others who dealt with various media groups or otherwise posted text and photos to blogs, both in Burma and overseas, using email and chat programs to exchange proxy server links. One of the best known and most publicized blog networks was Ko Htike's Prosaic Collection, managed from London by its Burmese owner (Holmes, 2007).

The Internet was relied on heavily by dissidents to exchange information in September 2007. After September 25, however, such Internet usage became problematic as the regime started positioning soldiers at Rangoon Internet cafés. Until September 29 it was still possible to use Glite and Google Talk for communication and for sending small files and it was even possible to use webmail directly, but sluggish upload speeds hampered efforts at communication. Until the crackdown began in earnest, those with cell phones were able to use them and those who had satellite phones accessed uplinks outside government control for transmission purposes (Anonymous exile-media reporter, personal communication November 27, 2007).

Of course, it was also possible to use slower, non-technological means of sending out reports, photos and video footage. For roughly the equivalent of US$100 per item, memory sticks and CDs could be sent abroad. Businessmen and tourists leaving the country could also be asked to relay information (Anonymous exile-media reporter, personal communication, November 27, 2007).

Major news agencies accessed information and photos from these Burmese sources. In fact, the BBC publicly requested such items ("Soldiers Break up Burma Protests," 2007). Burmese exile media groups that maintained websites faced a veritable deluge of traffic in late September. For example, the *Irrawaddy* has claimed it received 40 million hits on its website in September 2007 (Corporal, 2007) and *Mizzima News*, which had received only 248 hits during the entire month of May 2007, experienced 1,750,500 page views in September and 275,713 on September 28th alone (*Motigo webstats*, n.d). Since then, using *Mizzima News* as an example because its statistics are readily available, traffic has dropped to roughly 8,000 hits per day, but that number still is vastly in excess of the number of page views before the demonstrations started (Motigo webstats, n.d).

One could, using social network theory, consider this media work in September 2007 as a proliferation of nodes linked to a few major hosts (Diebert & Stein, 2003). As such, it would have been difficult for the regime to curtail the nodes due to their numbers and to the levels of redundancy built in with so many people covering the same events. The only way to block such a network would be to target the hosts, which is what the SPDC finally did. Suspect phone lines were disconnected as was the entire Internet system for the country. By September 29, 2007 the shutdown was completed in a process the OpenNet Initiative believes involved a gradual slowing and shutting down of routers. The Internet was offline in Burma until October 4, 2007 except for an "accidental" six-hour period on October 1 when BaganNet's service was restored after its routers became peered with a Singaporean telecom provider (Wang & Nagaraja, 2007).

The government is also believed to have used a host-targeting approach in requesting Thai authorities to clamp down on dissident media groups based in Thailand. Some of these groups considered closing their offices temporarily, but in the end no action was taken by the Thais. The Irrawaddy Publishing group has claimed, however, that its website was attacked by a "Trojan virus" on September 27, forcing it offline for a brief period (Naing, 2007).

FINAL THOUGHTS

For several reasons, the role and performance of Burmese exile media as a force for change cannot be fully assessed. This exiled sector of Burmese civil society is still evolving and still depends on outside funding for operations. Moreover, as stated before, detailed information on the activities of certain groups cannot be divulged in detail owing to security concerns. Thus, what this final section will touch upon is the following. First, it will look at what can be expected in developing media capacity to benefit a country's political transition from an authoritarian system of government to democracy. Then, it will discuss what was accomplished by the Saffron Revolution and the exile media during the revolution. Finally, it will consider the lessons learned that could be helpful for the future.

The anonymous NGO staffer mentioned earlier was hopeful that the developing exile media groups would aid a political transition from military rule. Such a transition is something Burma issue-related groups often speak of desiring and wishing to be part of (Anonymous NGO staffer, personal communication, April 9, 2005).

There is some research literature available on how well media reform works in transitions to more democratic contexts. Becker and McConnell (2002), focusing on the democratization process, define a political transition stage as a historical moment in which previous political rulers no longer hold sway, such as when militaries no longer control or supervise the primary functions of government. They suggest that media can be most supportive of democratic reform in the early euphoric stages of change before any level of cynicism or factionalism sets in. Accepting Rozumilowicz (2002)'s model of media reform, they see positive change occurring in four stages: a pre-transition stage, where constraints relax; a primary stage, where many changes occur; a secondary stage, where media networks form and training for journalists takes place; and, finally, a mature stage in which such processes and networks become institutionalized (p. 7).

Burma is not yet undergoing any discernible transition away from military rule, making some of this discussion premature. Nonetheless, the above process is worth noting, even if most building of independent media capacity occurs outside the country's borders. With that concession in mind, Rozumilowicz's model is helpful and would suggest that the Burmese exile media could be situated in stage two.

Pasek (2006) suggests that there is no clear model consistent on a global scale to prove whether media reform aids democratization, is neutral regarding that process, or works to hinder it. He believes multiple models should be employed, as should measurements of economic progress, government efficiency and growth in civil society, in which a nation's media might account for only a part of the democratization process. Nevertheless, he does believe a symbiotic relationship exists between media reform and the growth of democracy (pp. 2, 8-10).

Inevitably, many of the concerns expressed in this chapter relate to the future. However, the following question can be asked: What role did the demonstrations play in changing the political landscape and how did the exile media perform during the process?

Although it is too early to tell to what extent the Saffron Revolution has affected the political scene in Burma, a key issue at the time was whether the demonstrations, and word of what was happening, spread from urban to rural areas. Apparently, this did not happen on a significant scale (Anonymous exile media reporter, personal communication November 27, 2007), revealing that the mere existence of new information technologies and individuals reporting on events in Burma were not enough to effectively mobilize citizens. In this regard, inadequate technological infrastructure outside cities and possibly low levels of education among the populace hindered the flow of information.

Although any definite predictions cannot be made about Burma's political future, the government's arrest and persecution of monks indicates that disaffection continues, violence could erupt again at any time, and that the general public does not view the government's self-proclaimed democratic road map as a real, free or even fair form of transition from military rule. Thus, the events of 2007 may eventually prove to be pivotal for later developments. If that is the case, the exile media will have an important role to play in the democratization process.

Clearly, the regime regarded the marches and news coverage of them as serious threats and acted accordingly. Political opponents were targeted for arrest and the clandestine Burmese stringers, bloggers, and correspondents were as well. A DVB report noted that officials were seen photographing and filming not just the demonstrations but also the media covering them. An October 3, 2007 report claimed that government photographers from the Ministry of Information were doing this with help from the security forces and Swan Ar-shin (Htoo, 2007).

Government officials also are in possession of information gathered by the international and exile press and shown around the world. Evidence analyzed from such sources likely has been used to find demonstration leaders and those who filmed them. Indicative of how easily available information sources are which can be turned against those directly or indirectly involved in protests, in the market of the Thai border town of Mae Sot in December 2007 I was able to purchase a video CD that showed Burmese photographers with the 88 Generation leaders.

As far as having an immediate effect, the demonstrations and crackdown led to a flurry of diplomatic activity and attempts by the United Nations in particular to arrange a dialogue between a regime official and Aung San Suu Kyi. However, the short-term prospects for change are not encouraging. The government continues to arrest and prosecute dissidents and the army continues to attack ethnic minorities in the borderlands. Unfortunately, well-intentioned internationally fostered attempts at progress have been made before but to little avail.

As for lessons learned by the exile media, both positive and negative outcomes are apparent. Images and information did make their way out of Burma, with major media often disseminating the information that was made available. World leaders spoke about Burma and issued calls for action. In some countries, sanctions were implemented or strengthened. The Burmese media became part of the story. Some like Aung Zaw of the *Irrawaddy* saw this as a coming of age for independent Burmese journalism (Zaw, 2008).

Nonetheless, a great deal of information remained uncirculated, and intense real time demands resulted in lapses in which rumor substituted for actual news and accuracy suffered. Organizations on the ground could have better pooled their resources, and could have prepared for the shutting down of Internet and telephony services through readying alternative methods of relaying information out of the country. Only a few organizations had taken precautions in this regard, with the result that much information never reached its intended audiences (Anonymous exile-media reporter, personal communication November 27, 2007).

It must also be assumed that the regime is learning from what it perceives to be its mistakes. For example, it likely regrets not having censored the Internet before news of events in Burma began filtering out of the country. Although it has allowed the nation's Internet cafés to reopen, the regime is now much more serious about monitoring Internet usage and requiring café owners to deliver CDs of user screen shots to the Special Police on a weekly basis (Too, 2008). Another issue is that the SPDC regards the alternative press in an increasingly negative light and will do all in its power to disrupt its operations and harass those involved in gathering and spreading information on events in Burma.

To enhance their viability and maintain momentum, exile media groups should continue to request assistance from donors and supporters to improve levels of professionalism, acquire appropriate equipment, augment personal and data security, develop more secure means of communicating with contacts within Burma, and make plans for possible obstacles. What happened in 2007 will not be the end of the story.

Notes

1 The debate over whether to use Myanmar or Burma is a protracted one. Since this paper focuses on media organizations that exclusively use Burma, this paper shall do that also, unless a name or quote is used with the word Myanmar. Although use of the name Yangon is becoming as common as Rangoon and lacks the political baggage of the Burma/Myanmar debate, this paper will use Rangoon as well.
2 The use of "anonymous" for four of my sources is necessary, as to reveal their names could impact negatively upon their jobs and organizations, other people's livelihoods and quite possibly the situation of persons currently incarcerated by the SPDC or otherwise hiding from it. "Anonymous media editor" works with a major wire service news agency, "Anonymous exile-media reporter" works directly for Burmese exile media and was present in Burma during both the larger demonstrations and for part of the crackdown. The third person needing anonymity, "Anonymous government-affiliated newspaper reporter," works in Rangoon, and "Anonymous NGO staffer" has worked directly for many years with various ethnic media organizations and helped several commence operations. Finally, "Anonymous former *Irrawaddy* reporter" was just that, someone who had worked for some time at that publication.
3 This is Halockhani camp, which is really just inside Burma. Thailand says it is "on the border" so as to evade charges of *refoulement* dating back to the mid-1990s.

References

A biography of Aung San Suu Kyi. (2007, November 19). *The Burma Campaign UK*. Retrieved January 29, 2008, from http://www.burmacampaign.org.uk/aboutburma/aung_san_suu_kyi.htm

Amnesty International. (2007, November). *No return to normal.* Retrieved January 25, 2008, from http://www.amnesty.org/en/alfresco_asset/39d7db79-a2da-11dc-8d74-6f45f3998 4e5/asa160372007en.html

Amnesty International. (2008, February 20). *Document – Myanmar: Further information on health concern: Fear of torture or ill-treatment.* Retrieved May 29, 2008, from http://www.amnesty.org/en/library/asset/ASA16/003/2008/en/ASA160032008en.html

Arquilla, J., Ronfeldt, D. (2002). Emergence and influence of the Zapatista social netwar. In J. Arquilla & D. Ronfeldt (Eds.), *Networks and netwars: The future of terror, crime, and militancy* (pp. 171-199). Santa Monica: Rand Corporation. Retrieved January 8, 2008 from http://www.rand.org/pubs/monograph_reports/MR1382/MR1382.ch6.pdf

Bacher, J. (2003, April-June). Robert Helvey's expert political defiance. *PeaceMagazine*, 19, 10. Retrieved January 27, 2008, from http://archive.peacemagazine.org/ v19n2p10.htm

Ball, D. (1998). *Burma's military secrets: Signals intelligence (SIGINT) from the Second World War to civil war and cyber warfare.* Bangkok: White Lotus.

Ball, D. (1998, March 1). SIGINT strengths form a vital part of Burma's military muscle. *Jane's Intelligence Review*, 10, 35. Retrieved January 23, 2008, from http://www.burmafund.org/Pathfinders/Research_Library/Military/Signals.htm

Becker, L. B., & McConnell, P. J. (2002, July). *The role of media in democratization.* Paper presented at the International Association for Media and Communication Conference in Barcelona, Spain.

Biener, H. (2007, July 10). *Radio for peace, democracy and human rights.* Retrieved January 27, 2008, from http://www.evrel.ewf.uni-erlangen.de/pesc/peaceradio-BRM.htm

Brooten, L. (2003) *Global communications, local conceptions: Human rights and the politics of communication among the Burmese opposition-in-exile.* (Doctoral dissertation, Ohio University, Athens, 2003). Retrieved November 30, 2007 from http://www.ibiblio.org/obl/docs3/Lisa_Brooten_dissertation-ocr.pdf

Brooten, L. (2006). Political violence and journalism in a multiethnic State: A case study of Burma (Myanmar). *Journal of Communication Inquiry, 30(4), 354-373*. Retrieved January 25, 2008, from http://jci.sagepub.com/cgi/content/abstract/30/4/354

Burma: Crackdown bloodier than government admits (2007, December). *Human Rights Watch.* Retrieved January 27, 2008, from http://hrw.org/english/docs/2007/12/07/burma17494.htm

Corporal, L. (2007, November 9). Burma: Keeping the flame alive over radio. *CommonDreams.org.* Retrieved January 28, 2008, from http://www.commondreams.org/arc

Crackdown: Repression of the 2007 popular protests in Burma. (2007, December). *Human Rights Watch.* Retrieved January 27, 2008, from http://www.hrw.org/reports/2007/burma1207/index.htm

Crispin, S. (2007, September 21). Burning down Myanmar's firewall. *Asia Times Online.* Retrieved January 28, 2008, from http://www.atimes.com/atimes/Southeast_Asia/II21Ae01.html

Cropley, E. (2007, September 12). Myanmar's secret press pack gives junta a headache. *Burma Media Association.* Retrieved January 28, 2008, from http://www.bmaonline.org/BMW_2007_Jul_Sep.html

Danitz, T., & Strobel, W. (2000, December). *Networking dissent: Cyber-activists use the Internet to promote democracy in Burma.* Retrieved January 30, 2008, from http://www.usip.org/virtualdiplomacy/publications/reports/vburma/vburma_intro.html

Democratic Voice of Burma. (2007, September 29). Democratic Voice of Burma via BBC Monitoring: Oslo-based Democratic Voice of Burma to air "almost full time" from 28 September. *Burmanet News.* Retrieved January 27, 2008, from http://www.burmanet.org/news/2007/09/29/democratic-voice-of-burma-via-bbc-monitoring-oslo-based-democratic-voice-of-burma-to-air-almost-full-time-from-28-sep/

Diebert, R. J., & Stein, J. G. (2003). Social and electronic networks in the war on terror. In R. Latham (Ed.), *Bombs and bandwidth: The emerging relationship between information technology and security* (pp. 157-174). New York: The New Press.

Engdahl, F. (2007, October 17). The geopolitical stakes of "Saffron Revolution." *Asia Times Online*. Retrieved January 27, 2008, from http://www.atimes.com/atimes/Southeast_Asia/IJ17Ae01.html

Ferguson, J. M. (2006, March). *Digital media in the borderlands: National media, stateless subjects, and video production at the Thai-Burma border*. Paper presented at the 25th Bilan du Film Ethnographique, Paris, France. Retrieved January 28, 2007, from http://www.comite-film-ethno.net/colloque/pdf/borders-lines/ferguson.pdf

FortiGuard subscription services. (2008). Retrieved January 27, 2008, from http://www.fortinet.com/products/fortiguard.html

Fuel price hikes inflame Burmese people. (2007, September 14). *ALTSEAN Burma*. Retrieved January 22, 2008, from http://www.altsean.org/Reports/Fuelpricehikes.php

Ginsburg, F. (1991). Indigenous media: Faustian contract or global village? *Cultural Anthropology, 6*(1), 92-112.

Ginsburg, F. (1994). Embedded aesthetics: Creating a discursive space for indigenous media. *Cultural Anthropology, 9*(3), 365-382.

Hadfield, P. (1996, May 26). *NHK Watch – Special*. Retrieved January 27, 2008, from http://www.burmalibrary.org/reg.burma/archives/199605/msg00369.html

Holmes, S. (2007, September 26). Burma's cyber-dissidents. *BBC News*. Retrieved January 28, 2008, from http://news.bbc.co.uk/2/hi/asia-pacific/7012984.stm

Htoo, N. (2007, October 3). Burmese authorities target citizen journalists. *Democratic Voice of Burma*. Retrieved January 24, 2008, from http://english.dvb.no/news.php?id=506

Intel: Myanmar Democratic Voice of Burma. (n.d.). Retrieved January 27, 2008, from http://www.clandestineradio.com

Internet filtering in Burma in 2005: A country Study. (2005). *OpenNet Initiative*. Retrieved December 18, 2007, from www.opennetinitiative.net/studies/

Internet filtering in Burma in 2005: A country Study. (2005). *OpenNet initiative*. Retrieved January 28, 2008, from http://www.opennetinitiative.net/studies/burma

Jaiyen, K. (2006, April 28). About us. *Shan Herald Agency for News*. Retrieved January 27, 2008, from http://www.shanland.org/shan/articles/shanland/aboutus.html/

Joseph, B. (2003, June 18). Hearing on "A Review of the Development of Democracy in Burma." *National Endowment for Democracy*. Retrieved January 27, 2008, from http://www.ned.org/publications/staffDocs/bJoseph071803.html

Latt, T. (2001, September 3). A sky-full of lies: The media, censorship, and democratic resistance in Burma. *All Burma Students Democratic Organization*. Retrieved January 27, 2008, from http://members.tripod.com/~thadoe_aung/vision/skyful.html#sk11

Lawrence, N., & Nance, S. (2002, May 25). Irrawaddy, Myanmar Times Spar in Bangkok. *The Irrawaddy*. Retrieved January 27, 2008, from http://www.irrawaddy.org/article.php?art_id=3009

Lintner, B. (2007, December 1). A Charity's checkered past. *The Irrawaddy*. Retrieved January 29, 2008, from http://www.irrawaddy.org/article.php?art_id=9487

Mackinnon, I. (2008, January 25). Poet held after coded attack on Burmese leader. *Guardian Unlimited*. Retrieved January 27, 2008, from http://www.guardian.co.uk/burma/story/0,,2246667,00.html

Mon, A., & Too, M. (2008, January 28). 88 student leaders charged under press law. *Democratic Voice of Burma*. Retrieved January 29, 2008, from http://english.dvb.no/ news.php?id=894

Motigo webstats. (n.d.). Retrieved January 28, 2008, from http://webstats.motigo.com/s?tab=1&link=1&id=4149780

Mungpi. (2007). Junta, monks exchange detainees in Pakhokku. *Mizzima Monthly Journal*, 5(9), 1. Retrieved January 25, 2008, from http://www.mizzima.com/Monthly%20Journal/2007/Sept/Sept_07(English).pdf

Naing, S. (2007, September 29). The Irrawaddy's web site disabled by virus. *The Irrawaddy*. Retrieved January 28, 2008, from http://www.irrawaddy.org/article.php?artid=8810

Neuman, A. (2002, February). Burma under pressure; how Burmese journalism survives in one of the world's most repressive regimes. *Committee to Protect Journalists*. Retrieved January 27, 2008, from http://www.cpj.org/Briefings/2002/Burma_feb02/ Burma_feb02.html

Pasek, J. (2006, September 3). *Fueling or following democracy? Analysing the role of media liberalization in democratic transition.* Paper delivered at the American Political Science Association Annual Meeting Philadelphia September 3, 2006. Retrieved November 12, 2007 from http://www.stanford.edu/~jpasek/Publications_files/apsa06_proceeding_152541_1.pdf

Paung, S. (2007, January 26). Writer Win Tin admitted to hospital. *The Irrawaddy*. Retrieved January 27, 2008, from http://www.irrawaddy.org/article.php? art_id=10028

Rozumilowicz, B. (2002). Democratic change: A theoretical perspective. In M. E. Price, B. Rozumilowicz, & S. G. Verhulst (Eds.), *Media reform* (pp. 9-26). London: Routledge.

Soldiers break up Burma protests. (2007, September 28). Retrieved January 28, 2008, from http://news.bbc.co.uk/2/hi/asia-pacific/7017496.stm

Spiller, P. (2007, September 27). Burma's silent symbol of hope. *BBC News*. Retrieved January 27, 2008, from http://news.bbc.co.uk/2/hi/asia-pacific/7016360.stm

Thakuria, N. (2005, August 2). Burma: Where mobile phones are still a status symbol! *Burmanet*. Retrieved January 28, 2008, from http://www.burmanet.org/news/2005/08/02/mizzima-news-burma-where-mobile-phones-are-still-a-statussymbol%E2%80%93-nava-thakuria/

The alms bowl and the duty to defy. (2007). *Article 2 special report-Burma: Political psychosis & legal dementia*, 6(5-6). Retrieved January 24, 2007, from http://www.article2.org/mainfile.php/0605/298/

The way of peace. (2007, November 4). *ABC Radio National*. Retrieved January 27, 2008, from http://www.abc.net.au/rn/encounter/stories/2007/2069188.htm

Too, M. (2007, January 7). Increased monitoring of Internet in Rangoon. *Democratic Voice of Burma*. Retrieved January 29, 2008, from http://english.dvb.no/news.php?id

UN Rights Chief Louise Arbour urges Burma to release protesters. (2007, August 27). *Voice of America*. Retrieved January 27, 2008, from http://www.voanews.com/english/archive/2007-08/2007-08-27voa23.cfm?CFID=251566884&CFTOKEN=21876982

US Department of State. (2006). *Burma: Country reports on human rights practices*. Retrieved January 25, 2008, from http://www.state.gov/g/drl/rls/hrrpt/2006/ 78768.htm

Wang, S., & Nagaraja, S. (2007, October 22). Pulling the plug: A technical review of the Internet shutdown in Burma. *OpenNet Initiative*. Retrieved January 27, 2008, from http://opennet.net/sites/opennet.net/files/ONI_Bulletin_Burma_2007.pdf

Win, S. (2003, July 2). *Mizzima News Chief Editor Soe Myint acquitted by Brasat Court*. Retrieved January 29, 2008, from http://www.burmatoday.net/mizzima2003/mizzima/2003/07/030702_smyint_ mizzima.htm

Yoshida, R. (2007, October 17). Y552 million Myanmar aid project nixed. *The Japan Times*. Retrieved December 17, 2007, from http://search.japantimes.co.jp/cgi-bin/nn20071017a1.html

Zaw, A. (2005). Aung Zaw. *Aung Zaw's official website*. Retrieved January 27, 2008, from http://www.aungzaw.net/

Zaw, A. (2008, January 23). Seeking the truth, informing the public. *The Irrawaddy*. Retrieved January 27, 2008, from www.irrawaddy.org/article.php?art_id=10016

Index

A

Ahl-e-Hadiths, 173, 174, 175, 177, 184
All Burma Monks Alliance (ABMA), 238
Asian Games, 196, 206

B

Bank Rakyat Indonesia (BRI), 52
Barelwis, 171, 174, 175, 183
Boserup, Ester, 8
Bhutto, Zulfiqar Ali, 177, 178
BRI-units, 52, 66, 67

C

Ch'ŏnggyech'ŏn Stream, 77, 78, 81, 85, 88, 89, 93, 102, 105
civil rights, 27, 116
civil society, 2, 5, 14, 15, 25, 27, 109, 114, 115, 116, 119, 127, 128, 130, 243, 252, 253, 255
Center for Japanese Filipino Families (CJFF), 9, 108, 109, 116, 117, 118, 120, 121, 122, 125, 127, 128, 129
Cold War, 3, 186, 187, 207, 209
Commonwealth Games, 196, 205, 206, 213, 214
Community and Home Based English Teachers (CHOBET), 121, 122, 123, 125, 126, 127
Confucian ideology, 78
cooperatives, 54, 57, 63, 64, 65, 68, 69
corruption, 21, 23, 33, 35, 41, 141, 199
credit rationing, 8, 46, 60, 61, 62, 63, 67, 71
culture, 9, 10, 11, 15, 103, 105, 107, 109, 112, 118, 129, 130, 141, 148, 153, 154, 156, 159, 160, 162, 163, 181, 182, 188, 190, 197, 205, 209, 211, 212, 214, 228, 231, 240

D

Daw Aung San Suu Kyi, 238
democracy, 6, 12, 20, 23, 24, 27, 33, 34, 42, 71, 110, 188, 190, 237, 238, 244, 245, 253, 256, 257, 258
Democratic Voice of Burma (DVB), 243, 244, 247, 248, 249, 254, 257, 258
Deobandies, 174, 175, 180, 182, 183, 184, 185
deregulation, 115, 216
discourse, 4, 12, 86, 88, 89, 92, 95, 103, 108, 110, 115, 153, 245

E

East India Company, 169
European Bank for Reconstruction and Development (EBRD), 21, 33, 34, 42
economic development, 8, 9, 14, 15, 21, 22, 24, 75, 76, 78, 83, 88, 120, 129, 141, 147, 158, 196, 211, 241
economic growth, 1, 3, 15, 21, 23, 24, 28, 42, 70, 75, 80, 82, 83, 84, 135, 141, 147, 230
education, 1, 3, 5, 8, 9, 10, 19, 20, 23, 24, 25, 28, 29, 31, 32, 33, 38, 39, 40, 48, 49, 50, 51, 52, 56, 59, 60, 61, 62, 67, 77, 82, 85, 87, 88, 94, 95, 96, 97, 98, 99, 108, 109, 110, 111, 115, 121, 125, 126, 127, 128, 131, 143, 144, 146, 153, 156, 165, 166, 167, 168, 169, 170, 171, 172, 176, 177, 178, 179, 180, 181, 184, 185, 186, 188, 189, 190, 191, 227, 229, 230, 247, 254

empowerment, 28, 114, 118, 119, 120, 121, 125, 127, 128, 129, 130
entrepreneurs, 9, 75, 76, 77, 78, 80, 81, 83, 84, 85, 86, 87, 88, 89, 90, 91, 92, 93, 94, 95, 96, 99, 100, 101, 102, 103, 116

F

FIFA, 196, 205, 208, 213, 214
Freedom House, 21, 33, 34, 37, 40, 42

G

gender, 8, 15, 24, 33, 41, 48, 49, 50, 67, 75, 76, 77, 78, 79, 82, 83, 84, 85, 86, 95, 96, 97, 98, 99, 100, 101, 102, 103, 105, 112, 118, 128, 129, 130, 212, 213, 222, 224, 225, 228, 245
globalization, 1, 6, 8, 11, 12, 14, 15, 16, 23, 42, 108, 115, 130, 162, 195, 197, 200, 201, 202, 205, 210, 212, 213, 215, 240, 245
good governance, 5, 14, 15, 21, 23, 24, 25, 28, 38, 41, 42
Grameen Bank, 5, 14, 45
Grand Prix, 205

H

Halepota Report, 179, 180
Haq, Mahbub ul, 3, 25, 41, 42
Harrison, Lawrence, 9, 15
HDI (Human Development Index), 22, 28, 29, 30, 31, 32, 38, 41
HDRs (Human Development Reports), 3, 22, 23, 24, 28, 29, 41, 42
healthcare, 3, 5, 6, 20, 31, 40
human development, 3, 4, 7, 15, 16, 19, 20, 21, 22, 23, 24, 25, 26, 27, 28, 30, 31, 33, 38, 39, 40, 41, 42
human rights, 3, 5, 8, 22, 23, 24, 25, 27, 34, 37, 40, 41, 42, 130, 239, 243, 245, 246, 247, 248, 256, 258
hunger, 24, 112
Huntington, Samuel, 9, 10, 15
Hwan, Chun Doo, 79

I

identity, 11, 86, 91, 93, 94, 98, 100, 101, 107, 108, 109, 116, 121, 123, 124, 127, 142, 146, 149, 150, 162, 169, 188, 212, 240
immanent development, 2, 4, 5, 10, 13
Independent Mon News Agency (IMNA), 247, 248, 249
inequality, 3, 4, 15, 19, 21, 23, 28
intentional development, 2, 6, 7, 13
International Year of Microcredit, 44
Internet, 6, 12, 239, 242, 243, 249, 250, 251, 252, 255, 256, 257, 258
Irrawaddy Magazine, 243, 244, 245, 250, 251, 252, 254, 255, 257, 258
Islamization, 10, 165, 178, 179, 180, 181, 183, 184, 185, 186, 188

J

Jamaat-e-Islami, 171, 174, 175, 176, 177, 182, 184
Jamaat-Ulema Hind, 173, 188
Japan-Philippines Economic Partnership Agreement (JPEPA), 107
jihad, 165, 170, 171, 175, 181, 182, 183, 184, 185, 186, 188, 190, 191

K

Karen National Union (KNU), 243
Karenni National Progress Party (KNPP), 243
Kim, Dae-jung, 79, 158, 159
kinship, 48, 51, 52, 57, 59, 60, 62, 67
Korean Street-Vendors Confederation (KSVC), 84, 93, 94, 100, 102, 103
Korean War, 77, 84, 147, 157, 158, 160

L

Lee, Kuan Yew, 9, 210
life expectancy, 1, 8, 19, 20, 27, 28, 31, 32, 38, 39, 40
lifestyle migrant, 12, 231, 233, 234

M

*madrasah*s, 10, 165, 166, 167, 168, 169, 170, 171, 172, 173, 174, 176, 177, 178, 179, 180, 181, 182, 183, 184, 185, 186, 187, 188, 189, 190
Marcos, Ferdinand, 110, 112, 113, 114, 116

mega-events, 11, 197, 205, 206, 213, 214
MFIs (microfinance institutions), 8, 45, 46, 52, 54, 59, 61, 62, 63, 64, 65, 66, 67, 68, 69
microfinance, 5, 8, 44, 45, 46, 51, 60, 63, 66, 67, 68, 69, 70, 71
migrants, 81, 107, 108, 115, 116, 117, 118, 119, 120, 122, 127, 128, 129, 131, 145, 156, 168, 170, 171, 215, 216, 222, 223, 224, 225, 227, 228, 229, 231, 232, 233, 234, 235, 236, 243
migration, 6, 9, 12, 48, 79, 88, 100, 107, 108, 109, 111, 112, 113, 114, 115, 116, 118, 119, 122, 123, 127, 128, 130, 131, 158, 201, 202, 212, 215, 216, 220, 222, 223, 224, 225, 226, 227, 228, 229, 231, 232, 233, 234, 235, 236, 241
Millennium Development Goals, 4, 42, 44
Mizzima News Agency (MNA), 246, 249
modernization theory, 3, 13

N

National Basketball League (NBL), 204
National Coalition Government of the Union of Burma (NCGUB), 244
National Endowment for Democracy (NED), 244, 245, 257
nationalism, 110, 113, 130, 175, 188, 189, 190, 207, 213, 234
National League for Democracy (NLD), 238
nation-state, 6, 7, 11, 204, 205, 211
neocolonialism, 108, 109, 116, 121, 128, 130
New Era Journal, 243, 245
NGOs, 5, 7, 14, 15, 40, 68, 119

O

Olympic Games, 82, 84, 135, 147, 155, 196, 206, 208, 209, 210, 211, 213, 214

P

Park, Chung Hee, 79

Polity IV Project, 33, 34, 37, 38, 42
post-development, 1, 12, 13, 15
poverty, 3, 5, 6, 8, 19, 23, 24, 41, 42, 43, 44, 70, 102, 112, 115, 130, 138, 146, 158, 159, 184, 237
Premier League, 11, 195, 197, 198, 199, 200, 203, 204, 205, 212, 213

Q

quality of life, 3, 4, 88, 103, 227, 228, 229, 230
Qur'an, 166, 167, 168, 169, 173

R

Reagan, Ronald, 4
Rhee, Syng-man, 145, 146, 157, 158
ROSCAs (Rotating Savings and Credit Associations), 45, 51, 54, 57, 60, 61, 63, 68, 69

S

Sachs, Wolfgang, 12
Saffron Revolution, 12, 237, 243, 249, 252, 253, 257
Second World War, 2, 20, 135, 136, 145, 149, 150, 152, 154, 157, 158, 160, 161, 242, 256
Seers, Dudley, 3
Sen, Amartya, 4
Shan Herald Agency for News (SHAN), 243, 257
Shiism, 175
Singaporean League, 210
Singapore Sports Council, 198, 210, 214
S-League, 198, 202, 203, 213, 214
social capital, 8, 44, 45, 46, 51, 61, 63, 64, 65, 66, 67, 68, 69, 70, 71
social movements, 9, 116, 121, 125, 127, 128, 130, 131
Soviet-Afghan War, 10, 165, 182
State Peace and Development Council (SPDC), 237, 238, 239, 242, 252, 255

T

terrorism, 6, 7, 35, 155, 171, 181, 183
Thatcher, Margaret, 4

U

Tokyo Sagawa Express, 141, 155
Tongdaemun Market, 8, 75, 76, 77, 79, 80, 81, 83, 84, 85, 86, 89, 90, 92, 93, 97, 99, 100, 101, 102, 103, 105
tourism, 11, 82, 112, 114, 130, 163, 196, 211, 213, 215, 216, 217, 219, 222, 231, 232, 233, 234, 235, 236

U

ulema, 165, 166, 169, 170, 172, 173, 174, 176, 179, 180, 182, 184, 186, 188, 189, 190
UNDP (United Nations Development Program), 1, 3, 6, 16, 19, 20, 22, 23, 24, 25, 28, 41, 42, 43
Union Solidarity and Development Association (USDA), 238
United Nations (UN), 1, 3, 42, 46, 154, 157, 208, 254
Unrepresented Nations and People's Organization (UNPO), 208, 208
USAID, 182

W

Washington Consensus, 4
World Bank, 1, 5, 14, 16, 19, 21, 33, 35, 43, 105
World Cup, 147, 159, 196, 205, 206

Y

Yasukuni Shrine, 153, 161
Yunus, Muhammad, 45

Z

Zia-ul-Haq, 10, 165, 168, 177, 178, 179, 180, 181, 183, 184, 185, 186, 191